西方文化与礼节

THE CULTURES AND ETIQUETTES OF WESTERN COUNTRIES

王淑芳　著

哈爾濱工程大學出版社
Harbin Engineering University Press

内 容 简 介

东西方之间在文化和礼仪上迥然有别，各国人民在进行文化交流和礼尚交往时的习惯也各有千秋。本书主要介绍了西方文化的起源、发展和西方文化在绘画、雕塑和音乐方面的发展，以及在这种西方文化背景下国际间交流所需要的礼节。

本书适合作为英语学习者了解西方文化和礼节知识，拓宽文化视野，培养良好的国际礼节的必备教材，也可供相关爱好者参考。

图书在版编目(CIP)数据

西方文化与礼节/王淑芳著．—哈尔滨：哈尔滨工程大学出版社，2018.8

ISBN 978－7－5661－2073－1

Ⅰ.①西…　Ⅱ.①王…　Ⅲ.①西方文化—文化史 ②礼仪—西方国家　Ⅳ.①K500.3 ②K891.26

中国版本图书馆 CIP 数据核字(2018)第174253号

选题策划　刘凯元
责任编辑　刘凯元
封面设计　博鑫设计

出版发行　哈尔滨工程大学出版社
社　　址　哈尔滨市南岗区南通大街145号
邮政编码　150001
发行电话　0451－82519328
传　　真　0451－82519699
经　　销　新华书店
印　　刷　北京中石油彩色印刷有限责任公司
开　　本　787 mm×960 mm　1/16
印　　张　12
字　　数　320千字
版　　次　2018年8月第1版
印　　次　2018年8月第1次印刷
定　　价　52.00元
http://www.hrbeupress.com
E-mail:heupress@hrbeu.edu.cn

前　　言

随着中国社会经济的发展,东西方之间的交流、交往也越来越普遍。任何一种文化的发展都离不开对其他优秀文化的汲取,因此了解东西方文化和礼节之间的差异是很有必要的。

多年来,本书著者一直从事西方文化与礼节研究。本书理论性和实践性并重,是英语学习者了解西方文化和礼节知识,拓宽文化视野,培养良好的国际礼节的必备教材,对中西方文化交流具有一定的借鉴作用。

本书的编写得到了多位领导及同事的帮助,在此对为本书的出版辛勤付出的诸位表示衷心的感谢。同时在本书的编写过程中参考和引用了一些专家、学者的论著,在此一并表示感谢。

本书还有许多待完善之处,恳请各位专家、同人不吝赐教。

著　者

2018 年 6 月

目　　录

Chapter 1 The Beginning of Western Culture

1.1 Culture of Europe before Recorded History

Stone age is the first known period of prehistoric human culture, during which work was done with stone tools. This period began with the earliest human development, about 2 million years ago. During those millennia, two developments provided the bedrock foundation for all later history. One was the gradual transition from hominid to Homo sapiens, of the human being, the other was the transformation of the human newcomer from a food gatherer who was dependent on the bounty of nature to a food producer who became increasingly independent of nature—the master of its own destiny. It can be divided into two periods—Paleolithic Period and Neolithic Period—based on the degree of sophistication in the fashioning and use of tools.

1.2 Culture of the Aegean

Ancient Greek culture originates from Aegean culture. It is the prehistoric civilization during 3000—1000 BC on the islands in the Aegean Sea and the surrounding countries. It includes Crete, the Cyclades, the Greek mainland south from Thessaly, including the Peloponnese, and Macedonia, Thrace, and western Anatolia. The most significant are the Minoan and Mycenaean cultures.

The art is the most prominent evidence of the achievement of the Aegean culture. It is remarkable for its naturalistic pictorial style, originated in Minoan Crete; the movement and variety of Minoan art, even in its earlier abstract phases, suggest living things. From Crete, this style spread to the other Aegean islands and the Greek mainland, where it was modified by geometric tendencies. The rhythmic pulse that characterizes Aegean art suggests a deep reverence for the divinities of nature. Here we talk about its art in the following three aspects: architecture, painting and sculpture, pottery and metalwork.

The organic quality of Minoan style is seen most clearly in the palaces Crete. The four major palaces known—at Knossos, Phaestos, Mallia, and Zakros—followed the same basic plan. Rooms, on several levels, were functionally organized around a large central court. These courts must have accommodated crowds of worshipers, who gathered in front of the cult rooms to the west. The palaces also had extensive basement storage areas, artists' workshops, dining halls, and sumptuous living quarters for the noble ruling families. The structures were light and flexible, rather than monumental, and entirely unfortified. The distinctive Minoan column, with its downward taper, suggests movement rather than stability. The private habitations of Minoan Crete ranged from simple peasant dwellings to rich mansions and villas, constructed with the same features and fine techniques as the palaces. A wide variety of buildings were constructed for burials. The most distinctive were the tombs of southern Crete. Circular buildings with corbelled stone vaulting, built large enough to accommodate family burials for many centuries.

On the Greek mainland, the palaces of the rulers were completely different from those of Crete. They incorporated the characteristic megaron, a dominant central hall. The Megara of the best-known palaces—at Mycenae, Tiryns, and Pylos—were strikingly similar. Each was entered from a courtyard through a porch flanked by columns and had a large central hearth surrounded by four columns. The mainland sites tended to be fortified with huge walls of cyclopean masonry, constructed of massive, irregular blocks. Recent excavations at Mycenae indicate that, as in Crete, the palaces served as centers of worship as well as of government. For royal burials the Mycenaean Greeks first used shaft graves; later they adopted the Minoan tomb and developed it into an impressive burial structure. The tombs were covered with earth tumuli, or artificial mounds, and were entered through long passageways. In the most developed tombs, such as the so-called Treasury of Atreus at Mycenae, the large, circular spaces were dramatically valued with thick canopies of stone.

Minoan painting is found in two forms, the vivid frescoes on the pace walls and the graceful designs that decorate Minoan pottery, Surviving Minoan sculpture, with a few exceptions, is largely restricted to statuettes and figurines in various materials and to intaglio semiprecious stone seals.

In Crete, the palaces and houses were often decorated with bright murals. The Minoans made a major contribution to the art of landscape painting. Only in the Aegean were landscapes depicted for their own sake, without human figures. Minoan artists represented the terrain with undulating contours and swirling striations of color to emphasize the life of earth. The scenes were enlivened with animals, such as monkeys and birds, in sprightly movement amid swaying foliage. The Minoans had a special facility among ancient peoples for capturing motion. Figures were depicted in instantaneous moments of action and in great variety of poses. Minoan figures are usually slender, which enhances their look of mobility. It is primarily in ritual scenes, such as the bull-leaping fresco from the palace at Knossos, that human figures are depicted. Occasionally, frescoes were rendered in special shorthand method of painting known as the miniature style, whereby crowds of people were depicted in a small area with a few light sketchy strokes.

Recently excavated on Thira, in the Cyclades, well-preserved frescoes from prosperous private homes show a close relationship to the art of Crete, although the nature scenes are rendered more abstractly. Many of the Thira frescoes feature children, who are portrayed at different ages and with their heads shaved, except for specific hair locks. One especially important painting, from a site known as the West House, presents a narrative scene in an elaborate setting, the most extensive landscape known before the Hellenistic period. An entire Aegean world is depicted, with a fleet of lavishly ornamented ships sailing from town to town. Despite the remarkable achievement of the painting, the artist clearly had no notion of perspective.

The Minoan pictorial repertoire and fresco technique were later adopted on the Greek mainland, where religious scenes similar to those from Crete and Thira were depicted. Hunting and fighting scenes were also popular. Recent excavations at Tall al Daba in the western delta of Egypt have uncovered fragments of frescoes, the motifs of which include bull-jumping scenes and the like painted with Minoan, not Egyptian, colors. The relationships between Egyptian and Minoan painting must now be investigated anew.

Among the most important artifacts of the Aegean civilization are the bronze figurines associated exclusively with Minoan sites. The include male and female worshippers with their arms raised in adoration as well as images of a crawling infant, a bull with a leaping figure, and a reclining goat. The Minoan artists excelled in the carving of ivory figurines to goddesses associated with animals, a further image was found in 1987at Palaikastro, Crete, of a youthful god, the body of carved ivory covered with gold leaf and the head carved from a single piece of blue-grey serpentine.

The Minoans also excelled in the sculpting of stone vessels, many of which were enhanced with relief decoration. Stone sculpting on a largescale, however, is best represented by the Mycenaeans, who embellished their architecture with reliefs. The facade of the so-called Treasury of Atreus at Mycenae is adorned with contrasting red and green marbles in the form of columns and a frieze of spirals. The stone steles, or commemorative plaques, recovered above the royal shaft graves at Mycenae, contain both geometric and figural motifs. A typical example of this kind of decoration is the monumental stone relief above the Lion Gate at Mycenae, in which two lions stand majestically either side of a column. The Mycenaeans also excelled as carvers of circular ivory containers, statuettes, and decorative plaques.

With the building of the great Cretan places came the development of pottery as a luxury art. Employing the same three-part firing technique later used by Attic potters, Cretan artists created splendid vases of numerous shapes and a seemingly endless variety of colorful decorations. Highly regarded at the ancient world, Minoan pottery was copied throughout the Aegean and even exported to Egypt and the Near East. In the later periods, the decoration included naturalistic motifs, such as floral forms and the well-known Marine style, with octopuses, shellfish, and seaweed painted in rich overall designs. Minoan pottery was imitated on the Greek mainland, where it gradually evolved in both shape and decoration into harsher, more disciplined forms. In the final phase, the Mycenaeans introduced animals and human figures as part of the decoration.

The art of fine metalworking also developed in Minoan Crete. Among the few surviving objects, the granulated gold pendant in the form of two opposed bees, from Malia, testifies to Minoan expertise at working precious metals. The most impressive Mycenaean finds of metalwork were discovered in the shat graves and tools tombs of the mainland. They include gold masks and grave goods embossed with geometric designs. The burials also contained luxurious gold and silver vases and ornamented bronze weapons, many by Minoan artisans. Some of the vessels were decorated with elaborate figures and scenes hammered in relief. Otter vessels, as well as daggers of bronze, were inland with designs of different-colored metals a technique sometimes referred to as "painting wit metal". These intricate products were the most prized objects of the Aegean.

1.3 Culture near the Ancient East

From prehistory to the end of Antiquity in the 7th century. Embracing the diverse and exotic lands at the meeting point of three continents, the Ancient Near East occupies a vastly influential position in world archaeology and ancient history, art, culture and religion.

In these eastern monarchies, there none the less grew up habits, techniques, beliefs, and institutions that are still a part of westerners' lives today. Most conspicuously, there grew up an elaborate structure of domestic and international trade. Merchants, though not clearly at the top of the social order with priest and nobles, were, especially at times in Mesopotamia, almost at the top. In Phoenicia and in other parts of the zone of fragmentation, we find genuincly commercial societies, states in which the merchant is the leader. From such a society came the great contribution of the ancient Near East to Westerners' daily living, the alphabet.

Writing itself was in large part an achievement of priests, who needed to keep records of the wealth in their temples. It must have been a difficult invention, and neither the Nile nor the Tigris-Euphrates valleys took the final steps. The first step was ideographic writing, still in use in china. Our familiar " + " sign for a crossroad is a simple example. The next step was to use the sign for the sound of a whole syllable, regardless of its picture meaning, as if we used a simplified picture of a sheep for the sound of "you", another for signs were simplified out of all recognition as pictures by the use of little wedge-shaped imprinters in wet clay to make "cuneiform" writing.

The last important step, which of using a single letter for each sound, was apparently taken first by the Phoenicians, a Semitic trading people in the zone of fragmentation, and came to us through the Greeks. Anthropologists believe that the alphabet, which has now spread around the world, is an example of the diffusion of an invention that was made only once. All true alphabets, not only our own but also such very different ones as the Hebrew, Arabic, and Sanskrit, seem to go back to this one source.

The alphabet is not the only great invention westerns owe to the ancient Near East.

Even before the cities were established, it may well be that inventions like the wheel came from this area. The historically established list of "firsts" in this area that are still important to westerners is a very long one. Here were the first sure beginnings of science—astronomy, mathematics, and particular the calendar; and here in drainage, irrigation, and construction, technology and science first appear in some kind of relation, though we must not believe that "pure" science in our modern sense made technological advance possible. Here was the first codified set of laws, the famous *Code of Hammurabi* of the 19th century BC. Here were probably the first books, the first paper, and the first architecture that has come down to westerners as something like an understandable aesthetic whole, here, finally, were the first religions that westerners can know from something more than simple material remains, religions that westerners can begin to know as theologies and as organized churches. From here came the Christianity which, after two thousand years, is still the religion professed by the overwhelming majority of men and women in the western world. All these, it must be noted, came to westerners not directly, but filtered though and in part transformed by creeks, Romans, and Hebrews.

Chapter 2 The Boom of Western Classical Culture

2.1 Culture of Early Greek

In the late period of 13th century BC, Aegean civilization fell into decay. The city-states of Mycenae unified into an army and plundered Troy, a wealthy city in Asian Minor. This was their last feat. Although they finally captured the city, ten years' long march destroyed themselves much. In the 12th century BC, the Dorian in the northern part of Balkan Peninsula drove southward. All the tribes in Greece had to migrate and Mycenaean civilization was utterly wiped out. The destruction of Troy meant the end of Aegean World and bought with it the so-called "Dark Age" or "Homeric Age."

2.1.1 Monument of Literature-Homer's Epics

The earliest literary works were two epics: *The Iliad* and *The Odyssey*, which helped to shape the Greek spirit and Greek religion. Ancient Greeks believed that they were written by a blind poet named Homer, who probably lived around 700 BC. These two epics are not about events of Homer's own time, but about great men and wars of a remoter age, probably in the period 1200—1100 BC. In both epics, Homer conveys a sense of the heroic poems inspired almost all later classical Greek literature. Homer conveys a sense of the heroic ideals and fixed code of behavior that animated early Greek life in a warrior society. The poems inspired almost all later classical Greek literature. Homer's lasting greatness lies in character's personalities and problems make *The Iliad* and *The Odyssey* timeless reservoirs of knowledge about humankind.

The Iliad is the story of a brief event in the ninth year of the Trojan War: the great hero Achilles is offended when the leader of the Greeks, Agamemnon, takes a slave girl Achilles who has been awarded. Achilles withdraws from the battle and prays to his mother. Thetis, a goddess, to turn the tide of battle against the Greeks. The gods grant Achilles his prayer, and he does not return to battle until his best friend is killed by the great Trojan hero, Hector, Achilles throws himself into the battle, fights Hector, and kills him; in a final gesture of contempt, he drags Hector's lifeless body around the walls of toy. If there is a "theme" to the epic, it is "Achilles" choice. Achilles has been offered a choice; either he can be a great and famous hero in war and die young or he can live a long, happy life without any lasting fame whatsoever. Although Achilles initially chooses not to die young, the death of his friend forces him to make the choice that will make him famous for all time, but tragically dead at a young age.

The Odyssey is the story of the homecoming of another great Greek hero at Troy, Odysseus. Unlike Achilles, Odysseus is not famous for his great strength of bravery, but for his ability of deceive and trick. (It is Odysseus's idea to take Troy by offering the citizens a large wooden horse filled, unbeknown to the Trojans, with Greek soldiers.) He is the "man of many tricks." His homecoming has been delayed for ten years because of the anger of the gods, finally, in the tenth year, he is allowed to go home. He hasn't been misspending his time, though; for most of the ten years he has been living on an island with the goddess Calypso, who is madly in love with him. Odysseus, like Achilles, is offered a choice, he may either live on the island with Calypso, be immortal like the gods, or he may return to his wife and his country and be mortal like the rest of us. He chooses to return, and much and much of the rest of the work is a long exposition on what it means to be "mortal." If *The Odyssey* has a discernible theme, it is the nature of mortal life, why any human being would, if offered the chance to be a god, still choose to be mortal. This choice becomes particularly problematic when Odysseus, meets the ghost of Achilles in the Underworld; Odysseus remarks to Achilles how all the shades of the dead must worship and serve Achilles, but Achilles replies that he would rather be the meanest and most obscure slave of the poorest landholder than be the most famous of the dead. If being dead is so awful, what is it about being human that makes up for the infinite suffering that attends our deaths? As part of this question concerning the nature of human life, much of the book deals with the nature of human civilization and human savagery. The question also deepens in the latter half of the poem; while the first half of the epic deals with the question of the value of a mortal life, the last half of the epic introduces the question of the value of an anonymous human life.

2.1.2 Hesiod and the Theology

The writings of the epic poet Hesiod, who is believed to have lived on mainland Greece during the 8th century BC signal a new departure in Greek thought and literature. While continuing in the language of Homer, Hesiod's poetry reflected his own times and concerns as a common man in an age of oligarchy. In *Works and Days*, the poet offered practical advice to the small farmer and defended him against the justices of the noble landlords. Hesiod's writings championed a new set of values for Greek civilization. Whereas Homer had praised the aristocratic virtues of a bygone heroic age and portrayed the gods as capricious, Hesiod urged the values of moderation, social justice, righteousness, and hard work, which all people could pursue. He charged Zeus with the responsibility of upholding justice and punishing excess. Like wise, in *Theogony*, a genealogy of the gods drawn from numerous myths Hesiod stress Zeus's role in imposing a just order on humanity and the gods.

2.1.3 Lyric Poetry

Homer's epics were not the only form of poetry the Greeks had written. There were other forms, such as lyric poetry. In contrast to older epic poetry, this new form placed greater emphasis on individual feelings and experiences.

One man can in many ways stand as the symbol of the vital and robust era of colonization. Archilochus, born of the island of Paros, was himself a colonist. He was also a poet of genius, the first of the lyric poets who left an indelible mark on this age. Unlike the epic poets, who portrayed the deeds of heroes, Archilochus sang of himself. He knew the sea, the dangers of sailing, and the price that the sea often exacted. He spoke of one shipwreck in grim terms and even treated the god of the sea with irony: "Of fifty men gentle Poseidon left one, Koiranos, to be saved from shipwreck."

2.2 The Prosperity of the Classical Greek Culture

With the defeat of the Persians at Plataea in 479 BC, the Greeks entered the Hellenic Age, a period that lasted until the death of Alexander the Great of Macedon in 323 BC. During the more than 150 years of the Hellenic Age, the Greeks defeated the Persians for a second time and survived a century of destructive civil war, only to succumb ultimately to Macedonians. But throughout those turbulent times, the Greeks never wavered in their supreme confidence in the superiority of their way of life.

The Greek world consisted of several hundred poleis, located on the mainland, on the Aegean Islands and the coast of Asia Minor, and in the lands bordering the Mediterranean and Black Seas. Athens was the cultural center, but many poleis contributed both materially and intellectually to Hellenic civilization. The Hellenic Age is the first stage of Classical civilization, the highest achievement of the ancient Greeks.

Slavery was the pre-condition of the development of Classical culture. In the classical age, most slavers were foreigners, generally prisoners of war and captives of privates, so the social status of local citizens was raised. This stimulated their creative enthusiasm and as a result a large number of great works appeared.

Democracy offered important condition for the flourishing of Classical Greek culture, especially in Athens, the state was a directory democracy, in which the citizens themselves, not elected representatives, made the laws. The expanding of democracy brought the initiative of Greek people. They concerned much about the future of the state, and also played an active part in political and cultural activities.

The prosperity of economy laid a solid foundation for the brilliance of Classical Greek culture. The rising of the slave-owning economy and accumulation of wealth promoted strongly the development of culture.

The heritage of Egyptian and Near Eastern culture also provided rich sources for the flowering of Classical Greek culture. The development of a culture has never been achieved in isolation, and it is bound to acquire new contents and forms ceaselessly with the progress of the times and development of the society, and nourish and enrich itself while adapting to and absorbing other cultures.

2.3 Culture of Hellenistic Age

The years between Alexander's death in 323 BC and the suicide of Cleopatra. The last Ptolemaic ruler of Egypt, in 30 BC, constitute the Hellenistic Age. During this period, the diffusion of Greek culture throughout the Near Eastern and Mediterranean world begun by Alexander's conquests continued as the Age's most important feature.

2.3.1 The Fusion of Eastern and Western Culture in Hellenistic Age

Hellenistic society was characterized by a mingling of peoples and an interchange of cultures. Greek traditions spread to the Near East, while Mesopotamian, Egyptian, Hebrew, and Persian traditions—particularly religious beliefs—moved westward, the parochialism of the city-state was replaced by growing cosmopolitanism. Although the rulers of the Hellenistic kingdom were Macedonians and their high officials and generals were Greeks, the style of government was modeled after that of the ancient oriental kingdoms. In the Hellenic Age, the law had expressed the will of the community, but in this new age of monarchy, the kings were the law. The Macedonian rulers encouraged the oriental practice of worshiping the king as a god or as a representative of the gods. In Egypt, for example, the priests conferred on the Macedonian king the same divine powers and titles traditionally held by Egyptian pharaohs. Also, in accord with ancient tradition, states of the divine king were installed in Egyptian temples.

All phases of cultural life were permeated by cultural exchange. Sculpture showed the influence of many lands. Historians wrote world histories, not just local histories. Greek astronomers worked with data collected over the centuries by the Babylonians. The Hebrew Scriptures were translated into Greek for use by Greek-speaking Jews, and Jewish thinkers began to take note of Greek philosophy. Greeks increasingly demonstrated a fascination for oriental religious cults. Philosophers also helped to break down the barriers between peoples by asserting that all inhabit a single fatherland.

2.3.2 Hellenistic Science

During the Hellenistic Age, Greek scientific achievement reached its height. When Alexander invaded Asia Minor, the former student of Aristotle brought along surveyors, engineers, scientists, and historians, who continued with him into Asia. The vast amount of data in botany, zoology, geography, and astronomy collected by Alexander's staff stimulated an outburst of activity. To integrate so much information, scientists had to specialize in the various disciplines. Hellenistic scientists attempted a rational analysis of nature, they engaged in research, organized knowledge in logical fashion, devised procedures for mathematical proof, separated medicine from magic, grasped the theory of experiment, and applied scientific principles to mechanical devices. Hellenistic science, says historian Benjamin Farrington, stood "on the threshold of the modern world, When modern science began in the 16th century, it took up where the Greeks left off."

2.3.3 Hellenistic Philosophy

Many educated people turned to philosophy for ethical guidance and emotional support in Hellenistic Age. Plato and Aristotle had both posited that to enjoy the good life, it was necessary to be a participating citizen of the polis. When the success of Macedon made it evident that the poleis were too small and strife-torn to deal with the problems of the new age, philosophers looked elsewhere for the mainstay of human conduct and happiness. The four major schools of philosophy were Epicureanism,

Stoicism, Skepticism and Cynicism.

In their attack on inherited conventions, Cynics strove for self-sufficiency and spiritual security. Theirs were the most radical philosophical quest for meaning and peace soul during the Hellenistic Age.

2.4 Classical Culture of Rome

Roman civilization is as ancient as Greek civilization, but it reached its peak later. From its legendary founding in 753 BC, Rome grew steadily forming tiny city-state ruled by kings to a powerful republic, constantly adjusting to internal and external forces, and ultimately to a vast empire that controlled the known Western world.

2.4.1 The Rise of Rome

A new and politically important stand was added to the mixture of peoples and cultures in the eastern Mediterranean with the Roman conquest, first of Macedonia and Greece, second of Seleucid Asia, and finally of Egypt. Rome began its political was at first very strongly committed to the preservation of a simple rural Latin way of life in reaction against the corruptions of both Greek and Etruscan brands of civilization. For more than a century, Romans engaged in border wars, slowly expanding their territory, but also suffering occasional setbacks when a raiding body of Gauls sacked the city and almost captured the capitol. Rapid expansion began soon thereafter so that by 265 BC all of Italy south of the Apennines was united under Roman leadership.

Rome's success rested partly on a numerous and hardy peasantry, disciplined and led by a hard-bitten and tenacious aristocracy that long remained profoundly distrustful of the corrupting luxury and wealth they saw among their more civilized neighbors. Additionally, the native peoples of Italy were but loosely organized into tribes and districts, sometimes with and sometimes without a definite urban headquarters. No stubborn defense of local autonomy hindered the Romans in fastening their military and political leadership upon these people, especially since they were already familiar with federal arrangements within their own local political systems. Hence it proved possible to unite Italy under a single city's government without much trouble, whereas the Greeks struggled endlessly among themselves and never managed to combine local loyalties with stable attachment to any larger political whole.

Rome's rise brought on collision with the imperial city of Carthage in North Africa.

Sicily, where Greeks and Carthaginians had been fighting one another for centuries, was the first bone of contention. Before they were able to defeat the Carthaginians, the Romans had to build a fleet thus becoming a naval power for the first time. By 241 BC, the Carthaginians were driven from Sicily. The island became the first Roman province, governed by a special magistrate of governor and required to pay taxes to Rome.

A second and far more severe test of Roman strength came between 2018 and 201 BC, when Hannibal, a skillful Carthaginian general, brought an army from Spain through southern Gaul and then crossed the Alps into Italy. Roman efforts to defeat Hannibal all failed. After a particularly severe defeat at Cannae the Romans decided to avoid battle, but kept armies in the field to shadow every move Hannibal mad. The Carthaginians had expected most of the subjected cities and people of Italy to rise in revolt against the Romans. A few cities did indeed welcome Hannibal as liberator, but most of Rome's subjects and allies in Italy preferred a roman to a Carthaginian master. Consequently, after twelve years in Italy, during which time he was never defeated in the field, Hanniblal was compelled to embark for Rome, because in the mean time a Roman expeditionary force had turned the tables on him by provoking revolt among natives of North Africa against their Carthaginian masters. At Zama in North Africa the Romans with their African allies won a final battle. They force Catherin to Roman control. Thereafter the Romans remained without rival in the western Mediterranean.

That war changed Rome's political structure as well as its society and economy. Popular leaders, as it happened, met defeat at Hannibal's hands early in the war, and Rome was saved by generals form old patrician families. This discredited plebeian leadership. Plebeian politicians lost support, also, when the small farmers left the land after the war. Instead, generals took over as the most important group of political leaders. Their power depended increasingly on personal loyalty of the troops to their commander. But for while the Senate retained great authority, for it was only with Senate approval that a magistrate could be appointed general with the legal right to raise an army and make war. Political careers came to depend upon being able to cultivate favor among the soldiers, so as to compel the magistrates and Senators at home to do whatever had to be done to advance the imperator's career still further. Commanders, soldiers, and often, the Senate all had an interest in keeping the troops busy far away from home. Hence Rome began to make war often and with little provocation, more because of domestic difficulties than because of dangers abroad.

2.4.2 Roman Political Theory

City growth is a capricious process and, like the sorcerer's apprentice, quickly gets out of hand. Rome, at the end of the century of political turmoil that culminated in the defeat of Antony at Actium in 31 BC, by the future emperor Augustus, was the product of more than seven hundred years of unplanned growth.

The success of Augustus owed much to the character of Roman theorizing about the state. The Romans did not produce ambitious blueprints for the construction of ideal states, such as appealing to the Greeks. With very few exceptions, Roman theorists ignored, or rejected as valueless, intellectual exercises like Plato's *Roman Republic*, in which the relationship of the individual to the state was worked out painstakingly without reference to particular states or particular individuals. The closest the Romans came to the Greek model was Cicero's *De Re Publican*, and even here Cicero had Rome clearly in mind. Roman thought about the state was concrete, even when it involved religious and moral concepts. The first ruler of Rome, Romulus, was held to have received authority from the gods, specifically from Jupiter, the "guarantor" of Rome. All constitutional development was a method of conferring and administering the emporium. Very early it was believed that only the assembly of the fathers, the family heads who formed the original senate, possessed the religious character necessary to exercise emporium, because its primal function was to consult the gods. Being practical as well as exclusive, the senators moved on to disperse the emporium, holding that their consults would possess it on alternate months, and later extending its possession to lower officials. But the important achievement was to create the idea of continuing state authority embodied only temporarily in certain upper-class individuals and conferred only when the mass of the people concurred. The system grew with enormous complexity, as new offices and assemblies were created and almost none discarded. In Roman thinking, the individual had a role in a specific state that had developed in time in a particular political form sanctified by the gods. Total demolition of an existing state, or at least of the existing Roman state, would not be just an act of madness or impiety; it would be impossible. The whole argument of the only important books of political theory that the Romans have left us, Cicero's *De Re Publica and Laws*, was the need to preserve the continuity of a great tradition. "On the customs and men of old," Cicero wore, quoting the poet Genius, "the Roman state is founded."

2.4.3 Roman Religion

The ancient Roman religion is one of the better known pagan religions. Pagan religions believed in many gods and generally worshipped the earth, sea sun, sky and various other elements of nature. The Romans were polytheistic and much of their lives were spent in a fervent effort to please their gods. This was because ancient Romans believed that their gods had great influence over their daily lives and fates. In order to placate the gods, the Romans believed that certain rituals and rites must be performed in appreciation of the gods' works. As the religion progressed, so, too, did the rituals, which made it necessary to form priesthood's with specific rituals and traditions. In keeping with the Pagan tradition the Romans had a deep respect for the earth and her cycles.

Early Roman religion was based on spirits. The Romans did not build great mythologies like the Greeks; rather they believed everything had a spirit. These spirits were thought to influence for good or evil, daily life. The Romans therefore had to keep them happy though worship and sacrifice. If the rituals and sacrifices were performed properly, the Romans believed the gods would be happy and help them.

Romans believed each God had a specific "field" of expertise. There was a god of the sun, Apollo, a god of the sea, a god of the sky and many others. As Roman life had many different aspects there were many different gods. If a Roman wanted a good crop he would pray to Ceres, the goddess of agriculture. The most important of all the spirits was Vesta, the goddess of the hearth and home and the center of Roman family life. Each household had a small shrine dedicated to the household spirits. The Romans were great copiers. They borrowed many of their gods from the Greeks, but unlike Greek gods. Theirs did not have the same definitely conceived personality, they were more cold and formal. The Roman lived under the gods and constantly tried to please them.

The Romans have a well defined state pantheon of gods. These were the official gods led by Jupiter, the father of the gods. Others included: Mars; god of war, Ceres; Goddess of agriculture, Diana; moon goddess, Juno; goddess of women and childbirth, Minerva; goddess of wisdom and healing in war.

The roman religion was based on rituals and sacred rites. These rituals had become very complex over the years and needed special people to perform them. This is where the priests came in. The chief priesthood's were usually filled by distinguished statesmen or generals. Roman religion and politics were intermeshed. There were two types of priests: priests for the general supervision of religion and priests of particular deities.

As the Roman Empire expanded it came into contact with new and different religions. Many were absorbed into the state religion. Religious tolerance was a policy among the emperors. They introduced a policy of syncretism designed to encourage the merging of pagan religions to unite people and effect greater political stability. This cemented and united the empire. So it came to pass that Romans could worship whoever they liked as long as it didn't interfere with others.

The ancient Roman religion was worshipped not only by the Romans, but by the various communities which were absorbed into the Roman Empire. These communities added to the state religion with their own specific beliefs until it was truly diverse and all encompassing religion.

2.5 The Falling of Roman Classical Culture and the Rise of Christian Culture

The great civilization discussed so far—Mesopotamian, Egyptian, Greek and Roman—were all wealthy, powerful, and culturally dynamic, and they contributed enormously to the Western heritage. Yet an even greater contribution, one that cannot be measured in buildings or governments, came from a politically insignificant people who lived in a tiny corner of the eastern Mediterranean during ancient times—the Jews. This people created a religion that helped to shape the character of the civilizations of the Western world. Through the *Hebrew Bible*—the Old Testament to Christians-Judaic beliefs were passed on into both Christianity and Islam and spread around the world. In addition, the fruitful interaction of the Judeo-Christian heritage with the Greco-Roman Classical ideals enriched an transformed the Western humanities.

2.5.1 The Decline of Roman Classical Culture

During the second century AD, Greco-Roman civilization lost its creative energies, and the values of classical humanism were challenged by mythic-religious movement. No longer regarding reason as a satisfying guide to life, the educated elite subordinated their intellect to feelings and imagination. People no longer found the affairs of this world to have purpose, they placed their hope in life after death. The Roman world was undergoing a religious revolution and was seeking a new vision for the divine.

As Roman emperors became increasingly autocratic, opportunities for political activity decreased precipitously, and interest in public affairs waned. More than ever before, individuals felt that they had no personal control over their own lives. Their political significance lost. The psychological security provided by the city gone, individuals felt abandoned and isolated. The Roman world-state, vast, remote, and autocratic, could never provide that sense of community, that air of excitement, that feeling of belonging to something larger than oneself, which had derived from an individual's attachment to a city. Nothing replaced the old ideal of civic liberty and civic participation that had generated cultural creativity.

A spiritual malaise had descended upon the Greco-Roman world. Among the upper classes, the philosophic and scientific spirit withered, rational and secular values were retreated. The roman classical culture was declining.

2.5.2 Thc Origin of Christianity and Its Principal Developments

1. The Origin of Christianity

Among all the religious by which people seek to worship, Christianity is by far the most influential in the West. Every phase of man's life is touched by this religion, so much that it has become part of western culture. In fact, it was the Jewish tradition which gave birth to Christianity. Both originated in Palestine—the hub of migration and trade routes, which led to exchange of ideas over wide areas. The founder Jesus was called "Christ" by his disciples, and so came the name "Christianity."

Our knowledge of the life of Jesus comes almost entirely from the writings of his followers, the most important being the first four books of *The New testament* called *The Gospels*. The first, by Mark, was written about 70 AD and was used by Matthew and Luke in composing their gospels as a source to which they added a large number of the sayings of Jesus and other material. Because these three Gospels have much material in common, they are called *The Synoptic Gospels*, from the Greek word synopsis, meaning "view together". The fourth Gospel, by John, was written abut 100 AD and concentrated on the spiritual message of Jesus. Since these accounts were composed after the death of Jesus by his disciple to treat them as objective documents. It is possible, however, to establish the essential facts of the life of Jesus from them and other evidence.

Augustus had been ruling in Rome for over twenty years when, somtime between 8 and 4 BC, in a small town called Bethlehem in the obscure province of Judea, a young Jewish couple named Joseph and Mary registered their first child, Jesus, who had just been born in a stable while they were in town for the tax census. Thirty years later, the young man Jesus began his meteoric three-year career as a religious and social reformer with the first of these attacks on the scribes and Pharisees who dominated the application of the Judaic religious laws. He was a sensational speaker, with the capacity to reach the uneducated in his audience through the telling of parables and the direct simplicity and kindness of his character. People attributed miracles to him, which enhanced his fame. Above all, however, he claimed to have a unique relationship to God, to be the Son of God, and alone to be able to reveal the truth about the Father. He and his followers declared that he was the Messiah, the "Anointed One", or the Christ, meaning "Messiah", whom the Jewish people had traditionally expected to come to bring abut the salvation of Israel. Most Jews believed that the Messiah would be an earthly king from the house of David, who would be born, as the prophet Micah foretold, in the city of Bethlehem, and who would bring material prosperity. Jesus himself was careful to point out that although he had come to save them, he was far from being the kind of savior they had been expecting. How different they would later realize after he had been crucified.

In 29 AD he led his followers to Jerusalem for the celeb ration of the Passover, the feast of Jewish independence, In the superheated climate of city thronged with Jews from all over Palestine, he was tried before the Jewish ecclesiastical court and found guilty of blasphemy and deserving of the death penalty. After some hesitation, the Roman governor, Pontius Pilate, agreed to his death, and his crucifixion was carried out by the Roman occupation troops. The exact responsibility for Jesus' death has been disputed ever since. The notion that the Jews were responsible for his crucifixion was used during the Middle ages and later a rationale for anti-Semitic persecution, and for this reason was specifically rejected in the pronouncements of the Second Vatican Council of the Catholic Church in 1965.

The crucifixion flung Jesus' disciples into dejection. After three days however, they later claimed, Christ's body disappeared from the tomb, and the resurrected Christ himself appeared visibly to them on several occasions during the next forty days to tell them to go forth as his witnesses and representatives throughout the world. On the fortieth day after his resurrection from the tomb, his disciples believed that they saw him ascend to heaven. Jesus, in short, who had only three years to preach his gospel, had died a horrible and ignominious death and would probably have been quickly forgotten if a handful of people had not been convinced, by what they believed was supernatural experience after his death, that he was indeed what he claimed to be, the Son of God.

The survival and future spread of Christianity is partly explained by the fact that

Jesus was Jewish. During their disturbed history in the Fertile Crescent, the Jews had developed a unique religious tradition, and Christianity was to absorb many of its ideas. The most important was the belief in the coming of the Messiah, although there had been a good deal of debate over the kind of savior he would be. Second, the Jews believed that they were the chosen people of God exclusively marked for salvation, which could be immortality of the spirit or even resurrection of the body. The idea of immortality was connected with the idea of a kingdom of heaven, where the everlasting values of goodness were observed and the virtuous were rewarded, whereas the guilty were punished or perhaps banished forever. Third, there was monotheism, the belief that there was only one God, who was personal and who intervened directly in human history. This belief forced the Jews to reject all forms of polytheism as practiced in the Greco-Roman religions, and made it impossible for them to accommodate themselves with Roman ease to the undemanding state religious ceremonies. It also posed great problems for the Christians themselves in the future. They had to decide, for example, how Christ could be treated as a deity if there was only one God, that is, what was the relationship of Father and Son in a monotheistic system. Finally, from an organizational point of view, the Jews also left a great contribution to the early Christians: the habit of meeting privately in special buildings, called synagogues, for reading the scriptures and listening to a talk on their meanings. In such synagogues, the Christians first organized.

2. Principal Developments in the First Three Century

During these centuries Christianity became "the church" as we have come to know it in its subsequent history. In every important aspect of its being, its life and its mind, the foundations were laid for its subsequent development.

From the beginning, the belief of Christians was centered on the lordship of Jesus. In him the God of *The Old Testament*, the God of Abraham, Isaac and Jacob and of the Jewish people, had brought to completion his saving work among men. In professing loyalty to him, however, many facets of their belief remained to be defined subsequently. The lively sense of an imminent end to history with the second coming of the Lord, though liable to be revived sporadically in places down to our own day, was generally eclipsed within the first two apostolic generations. Christians came to see their group apostolic generations. Christians came to see their group as a permanence came institutional development, greater crystallization of belief and standardization in worship.

Christian communities were established in Jerusalem, and very soon, Antioch, Ephesus, Alexandria and the other cities around the eastern Mediterranean. Before the end of the first apostolic generation the movement had reached Rome, and the travels of apostolic missionaries and their successors ensured that it was to reach most of the major cities, especially where there were established Jewish communities, first around the Mediterranean, then in the whole Roman empire. The pattern of this missionary enterprise gave the Christian church a strongly urban stamp, which it retained long after it began to penetrate into the countryside. The centers of Christianity remained the Greco-Roman towns. It was around them that the organization of the Church took shape. The origins of leadership and organization in the earliest Christian communities are not easily discernible in the period after the apostolic generation; there are traces of a variety in the development. Well before the end of the third century, however, the pattern had become remarkably uniform; everywhere urban churches were governed by "bishops" who had general charge of their communities, to whom priests, deacons and minor functionaries as well as lay people were subject. The areas under their charge, their "dioceses" were, generally speaking, the territories subject to the Roman caritas. The network of bishoprics of which the Church consisted thus came to reduplicate the administrative geography of Roman municipal government with considerable fidelity.

Growing uniformity and increasing definition also characterized the development of belief during the first three centuries. By the early third century a body of early Christian literature generally accepted as "Canonical" had come into being. A variety of doctrinal, devotional and other traditions were still comprised within this canon, *The New Testament*, as it came to be distinguished from the scriptures of *The Old Testament*. But the canonization of a body of scriptures, though it enshrined a variety of early and divergent traditions, was henceforth thought to be located within the canonical scriptures. Other alleged "revelations" often claiming the authority of the Lord or of one or other of his disciples became "apocryphal" and could not be invoked to justify teaching at variance with that of the bishops. In interpreting this body of canonical material the authority of the bishops was decisive. The teaching of individual bishops was legitimated by their communion with the bishops of the apostolic sees, whose occupants could claim descent in unbroken succession from the apostles themselves. Here and there these doctrinal traditions came to be formulated in "rules of faith" and perhaps in precursors of the creeds.

Through these various means the Church came to possess a coherent and homogeneous structure and a body of more or less identifiable belief. These served to distinguish the "great" or, as it came to be called "catholic" Church from various other claimants. Among these those that posed the greatest threat to the identity of Christianity, especially in the second century, were the various religious movements generally grouped together under the label "Gnostic." In the third century, the organized, official Church of the bishops could face the challenge of prophetic religious movements, such as the Monetarists, who rejected the institutionalized structure claiming direct inspiration by the Holy Spirit.

2.5.3 Early Christian Organization and Doctrines

1. Early Christian Organization

The church in each city of Rome and Christianity organized on the basis of the cities was independent. Initially, like the synagogue, it had a fairly democratic organization under a broad of elders and deacons; often too the ecstatic side of early Christianity was reflected in the presence of local "prophets", who were filled with the divine spirit and communicated with God. As time went on, the general tendency of city government toward oligarchy and the needs of the church itself for self-defense against persecution and heresy led to a concentration of powers. In the reign of Trajan the letters of Ignatius of Antioch assert that presbyters must be turned to their bishop as the strings to a harp, and that a church must be unified under its bishop to be with God. Not all churches thus had single leaders even in the later second century, but by the third century the bishop of each city, though still elected, was the spokesman for and director of his congregation. Church history came to be organized on the chain of bishops reaching back to the apostolic foundation. The doctrine of Apostolic Succession, that is, that the powers given to the disciples by Christ before his Ascension were handed down from bishop to by the sacrament of ordination, was already explicit by the end of the first century of in the letter of Clement of Rome.

The bishop's responsibilities were many. In the first place he oversaw the regular ceremonies of worship or sacraments, which became more fixed and extensive. Baptism by triple immersion in the name of the Father, the Son, and the Holy Ghost came after study in Christian doctrine; only those so baptized could partake in the most sacred rite. This was the Eucharist, originally an evening ceremony after a community meal and then shifted to the morning as an independent ceremony; it was accompanied, after the fashion of the synagogues by prayers, hymns, and the reading of *The Bible*. At regular intervals the faithful thus commemorated the Last Supper and united in the sacrifice of Christ. Penance, which was not considered by the epistles to the *Hebrews* as possible after baptism, slowly became a regular rite as a disciplinary and corrective measure. The sacraments, which eventually numbered seven, thus emerged as formal bonds of Christian brethren and as continuing reinforcement and guarantee of their faith. Salvation was possible only within the framework of the Church.

Second, the bishop administered through the deacons the property of his church, which came to encompass a meeting place, a cemetery, and the bequests of the faithful. From the famous, but brief attempt at communal living which *Acts* records, the Christian Church had a strong sense of social responsibility to care for the sick, for widows and orphans, and for the unfortunate. This social sense stood in strong contrast to the ruthless. Atomistic quality of much of pagan life as did the firm grounding in Christian doctrine of the principle that all the children of God were equally endowed with an individual soul.

Third, the bishop kept in contact with his fellow bishops to coordinate Christian belief and policy. To a large extent this communication was by messengers and by letters, following the precedent of Paul.

Eventually councils of bishops came to meet for better debate. We know of such a council at Rome under commodus to handle the thorny question of settling the date for the increasingly popular festival of Easter. This controversy, incidentally, produced the first known effort of a bishop of Rome to excommunicate those who disagreed with him as representative of the church of Peter and Paul. From the third century such meetings became more frequent as the Church grew stronger and was vexed by problems of heresy.

Since church organization tended to follow imperial divisions, the bishop of the capital city in each province often hand pre-eminence; and, indeed, his church might well have been the original center from which Christianity spread to the countryside.

2. Early Christian Doctrines

Christ had added through his teaching, however, certain doctrines of great power. First, all individuals were important in God's eyes, the poor more than the rest. People should be kindly and forgiving toward each other. Charity, self-control, and humanity were desirable virtues. These views were preached by other great religions. To these ethical views, however, Christ added the claim that his Father, God, had sacrificed him, his only Son, to redeem the world of sin. Belief in him was necessary for this redemption. Ethics was no longer enough for personal salvation, nor indeed was a belief in God along. There had to be a commitment to Christ, a man who lived in a particular time and place and yet was the savior of all humankind, irrespective of time and place.

Christ's sayings and actions were preserved by word of mouth. Sometime around 66—77 AD, Saint Mark formulated the Christian message from this oral tradition and perhaps from some material that had been put in writing earlier. Later Saint Matthew and Saint Luke, relying heavily on Mark's account, wrote somewhat longer Gospels—*The Gospels of mark*. Matthew, and Luke are called synoptic because their approach to Jesus is very similar. *The remaining Gospel*, written by Saint John, varies significantly from *The Synoptic Gospels. The Synoptic Gospels*, *The Gospel According to Saint John*, *Acts of the Apostles*, *The twenty-one Epistles*, including those written by Saint Paul, and *Revelation* constitute the twenty-seven Books of *The Christian New Testament.*

The Christian New Testament is the principal and almost the only source the early history of Christianity in the first century. Most of the Christian doctrines were taught in *The New Testament*. Here are some fundamental points.

"The Divine life common to the Three Persons in the Unity of one and the same Nature is the mystery of the Trinity, obscurely typified of outlined in *The Old Testament.*"

The Messias promised by the Prophets has come in the person of Jesus of Nazareth, who was not only a man powerful in word and work, but the true God Himself, born of a virgin, crucified under Pontius Pilate, but risen from the dead and now exalted to the right hand of His Father.

It was by an ignominious death on the Cross, and not by power and glory, that Jesus Christ redeemed the world from sin, death, and the anger of God. He is the Redeemer of all men and He united them to Himself all without distinction.

The Mosaic Law having been given only to the Jewish people, and that for a time, must disappear, as the figure before the reality. To these practices powerless in themselves Christ substitutes rites really sanctifying, especially baptism, Eucharist, and penance. However the new economy is to such a degree a religion in spirit and truth, that absolutely speaking, man be saved, in the absence of all exterior means, by submitting himself fully to God by the faith and love of the Redeemer.

Before Christ's coming men had been treated by God as slaves or children under age are treated, but with the Gospel begins a law of love and liberty written first of all in the heart; this law does not consist merely in the letter which forbids, commands, or condemns; it is also, and chiefly, an interior grace which disposes the heart to do the will of God.

The Kingdom of god preached and established by Jesus Christ, though it exists already visibly in the Church, will not be perfected until the end of the world, when He will come Himself in power and majesty to render to each one according to his works. In the meantime, the Church assisted by the Holy Spirit, governed by the Apostles and their successors under the authority of Peter, teacher and propagates the Gospel even to the ends of the earth.

Love of our neighbor is raised to the height of the love of God, because the Gospel makes us see God and Christ in all men since they are, of ought to be, his mystical members. When necessary, this love must be carried as far as the sacrifice of self. Such is Christ's commandment.

Natural morality in the Gospel is raised to a higher sphere by the counsels of perfection, which may be summed up as the positive renouncement of the material goods of this life, in so far as they hinder our being completely given up to the service of God.

Eternal life, which shall not be fully realized until after the resurrection of the body, consists in the possession of God, seen face to face, and of Jesus Christ.

Chapter 3 Christian Culture in the Middle Ages

In European history, the thousand year period following the fall of the Western Roman Empire in the fifth century is called the Middle Ages, It is so called because it come between ancient times and modern times. This is a period in which classical, Hebrew and Gothic heritages merged. And it is this fusion and blending of different ideas and practices that paved the way of the development of what is the present day European culture.

3.1 Christian Culture in Early Middle Ages

The period from the collapse of the Roman Empire in the west down to about 1000 AD provided an outstanding example of the breakdown of a whole civilization. Historians used to call these early medieval centuries from 500 to 1000 the Dark Ages. This term suggests a unique barbarian interruption between an earlier classical flowering and a later slow recovery of renaissance. Today, however, historians often use the more neutral term, Early Middle Ages, in preference to the Dark Ages. For if much of Roman civilization was lost in these years, much, including above all Christianity, was retained; and much new institutions, such as feudalism, new techniques, such as deeper plowing and better drainage, the horse-collar, a great improvement on the old yoke, the sea-worthy Norse ships, which could face the hazards of Atlantic navigation in a way the old Mediterranean vessels never could, and much more-was created.

3.1.1 Conflicts Integration of Romanic Classical, Germanic and Christian Cultures

The civilization of medieval Europe emerges as a synthesis of three cultures; Romanic classical, Christian, and Germanic. The age of the Latin Doctors witnessed the virtual completion of the Classic-Christian synthesis, but the blending of Roman and Germanic culture was as yet far from complete. Not until the eighth century or thereabouts was a fusion of Classical-Christian culture with Germanic culture fully achieved. The intervening era provides a fascinating view of a new civilization.

While Christianity was spreading in the Greco-Roman world, that world was itself undergoing revolutionary changes. The reasons for the decline and eventually collapse of the Roman Empire were numerous, and no single explanation was adequate. Internally, the empire never solved the problem of a stable, peaceful succession of competent leaders. Emperors usually appointed their successors, but some proved incompetent, emotionally imbalanced, of evil. From the beginning, the rule of force was established as superior to the rule of law, allowing many generals to contest the succession, often successfully; the result was a series of devastating civil wars and sometimes frequent changes in leadership. The simple technology of the day placed limitations on the empire's growth; for example, a peaceful society allowed for increased trade and greater prosperity, which produce larger cities but the unsanitary conditions of the larger cities also stimulated disease, which then improved transportation systems spread empire-wide. Thus the empire suffered from several serous plagues in the first and second centuries. The western empire collapsed under the pressure of the migratory tribes. Rome was sacked in 410 and 455 and was besieged three times in the sixth century; its population, nearly a million in the first and second centuries, declined to less than fifty thousand by the end of the sixth century. By the eleventh century it was only thirty thousand. In Britain urban life was completely swept away by the tribes of Angles, Saxons, and Jutes who were entering, conquering, and settling. Latin became extinct as a spoken language in Britain, and the Celtic peoples were assimilated or driven into the hills of Wales and Cornwall. Gaul was overrun by various tribes, among them the Franks. For whom the country was renamed; urban life there collapsed as well. Spain and Portugal were overrun by the Goths.

One result of the invasions was a steady shrinkage of Christendom. In the North, Britain was completely lost. Any gains in Germany were eliminated, and even in France and Spain Christianity was imperiled. The invasion of the Bulgars and southern Savs swept away Christianity in parts of the Balkans; then the Magyars occupied Hungary, destroying Christianity there. But the worst blow to Christendom was undoubtedly the spread of Islam, which ultimately eliminated or drastically weakened Christianity in half of the former Roman Empire. It would be hundreds of years before these losses were reversed, primarily though conversion of the Germanic and Slavic peoples north of the former Roman Empire. As the roads became unsafe for commerce the towns that survived had to be concentrated along waterways. But with the rise of Islam the Byzantine navy could no longer control pirates and maritime commerce ceased. In the north, the Vikings began their raids about 900, snuffing out whatever peaceful trade that had begun to develop along the North Sea and Atlantic coast. Towns became the targets of organized looting by both Saracens and Vikings, causing urban life largely to cease. With it went the merchant and aristocratic classes, the theatres and libraries, most knowledge of reading and writing, and most familiarity with the accumulated wisdom of the ancient Mediterranean civilizations. With the virtually cessation of trade, life became purely local; all food had to be raised locally and thus land became the principal source of wealth. Even coins largely disappeared from circulation and any trade that did occur had to be conducted by barter.

It is in such a period that a new world was being born, built on Classical ruins, spurred by Germanic energies, and animated by the new Christian ethos.

3.1.2 Western European Culture from the Fifth to the Eighth Centuries

Socially and politically, the effects of the breakdown of Roman were disruptive enough; culturally, they were almost disastrous. This period was at their darkest in the realm of literature, art and architecture. The early medieval centuries stand up better if we compare their textiles, metal work and grain-growing with those of Rome than if we compare their poetry, sculpture, and thought. One explanation of the rapid artistic decline in the centuries immediately after the Roman collapse is obvious. Artistic output, although it is often achieved by men born in the lower classes of a society, depends for its audience and its patronage on a certain minimum of taste and training among the well-to-do. Perhaps the businessmen who support the community symphony orchestra in a big American city do not really enjoy and appreciate Mozart and Beethoven, let alone contemporary composers of "serious" music; but they, and especially their wives, know what they ought to like, and in the whole community there are many trained musicians who know the tradition of great music. In the world of the sixth and seventh centuries the new barbarian masters were quite incapable of judging art and culture. The old aristocrats were fading out; the new intellectual class was the Christian clergy, who to a large extent were also crude, and who had the Christian contempt for, or distrust of, the sense-world in which the artist always had to work. The audience just wasn't there; naturally the play did not go on. Or rather, an inferior play did go on. Men were building churches in the west all through the Dark Ages, often from the debris of ancient buildings. They decorated the churches with mosaics, wall paintings, and statues; they adorned themselves and their altars with jewelry; and they listened to poets and minstrels. A few of them were scholars, philosophers, and teachers from books.

In the culture of the world—literature, philosophy, law, theology, and science—the late Romans had already lost much before the great barbarian invasions. Notably, natural science and technology had degenerated. Scientific investigation was almost nonexistent, although mathematics, including geometry, as applied above all to geography, never quite died out. We can see the degeneration in the recorded language itself. Writers during this period were more interested in conserving the past than in composing original works. Consequently, literature—all of it written in Latin—was eclectic, blending Christian ideas with Classical thought and often mixing genres, such as history, biography, science, philosophy and theology.

Music became integral to the church liturgy during the early Middle Ages and kept alive the Greek heritage of music as an art form. From this religious foundation ultimately arose all of the sacred and secular music of the modern west. The name of Pope Gregory the Great is preserved in the early medieval musical form, the Gregorian chant, which became the official liturgical music of the early church, used in the Mass and other services of the yearly cycle of public worship. The chants consisted of a single melodic line sung in unison, without instrumental accompaniment, by male voices. They had an impersonal, none motional quality and served religious rather than aesthetic or emotional purposes. Notwithstanding this aim, the chants cast a spell over their listeners, evoking in them feelings of otherworldliness, peace and purity.

The overall decline of living conditions in Western Europe took its toll in architecture and art as patronage evaporated, skills fell into disuse, and artistic talents were necessarily directed to more pragmatic ends. The few artisans and builders who were still in business travelled across western Europe constructing churches and chapels in protected places.

This culture of the west in this period is a very difficult one to feel and to recognize in terms of style. It is a period of transition, in which human beings are culturally immature and uncertain of themselves.

3.1.3 Carolingian Renaissance

The Carolingian Renaissance was a period of intellectual and cultural revival occurring in the late 8th and 9th century, with the peak of the activities occurring during the reigns of the Carolingian rulers Charlemagne and Louis the Pious. During this period there was an increase of literature, the arts, architecture, jurisprudence, liturgical and scriptural studies. The period also saw the development of Medieval Latin and Carolingian minuscule, providing a common language and writing style that allowed for communication across most of Europe. Instead of being a rebirth of new cultural movements, the period was typified more as an attempt to recreate the previous culture of the Roman Empire.

The Carolingian rulers, from the Mayor of the Palace, Charles Martel through the Emperor Louis the Pious, expanded Freakish authority throughout most of Western Europe, and brought a peace and security that marked an end to the turmoil that had begun with the Germanic invasions of the Western Roman Empire at the beginning of the fifth century. Moreover, the Carolingians appear to have been consciously trying to restore some of the cultural and economic greatness that they associated with the long-vanished Roman Empire. Each of the monarchs was careful to associate with himself one of the outstanding intellects of the period: Charles Martel's chief minister was St. Boniface; Charlemagne brought in Alcuin to set up a school system, and to manage his administration; Louis the Pious worked with Benedict of Aniane to make Benedictine monasticism a progressive and civilizing force throughout western Europe; and even Charles the Bald, who ruled during the disintegration to the empire, had John Scotus Erigena to direct his administration and to help plan his actions.

The result of this steady collaboration of political and intellectual power permitted the Carolingians to bring about a rise in culture and learning far greater than the political bases of their power would otherwise have permitted. Pepin the Short, the Carolingian Mayor of the palace, had deposed the Merovingian monarch because central authority had declined steadily under the Merovingian kings as a result of their almost constant civil wars. They insisted on dividing the realm at the death equally among their heirs and civil wars were the regular result. In his deposition of the Merovingians, Pepin gained the support and close cooperation of the Church, and this added to the Carolingians ability to bring about reforms. But, by and large, the Carolingians did not solve any of the basic problems of western Europe. There was still the great differences between the Latin and relatively urban South, with its princely bishops and need for a stable administrative system, and the Germanic and overwhelmingly rural North, with its missionary monks and need for well-defended frontiers. The Carolingians strained their resources in developing military force capable of conquering and then holding their empire. Most important of all, however, was the fact that they had not abandoned gavelkind. Charlemagne ruled alone only because of the abdication of his brother, Carloman, and Louis the Pious obtained an undivided empire because of the untimely death of his elder brother. The unity of the Frankish Kingdom under its Carolingian rulers lasted less than a century, from the accession of the Carolingians in 751 to the death of Louis in 841 and the division of the kingdom that followed.

One wonders what sort of a spirit motivated these men and where they thought that their efforts were leading. Quite simply, they believed that they were ushering in a new age. For centuries, people had looked about them for signs that the predicted end of time was at hand and the Day of Judgment was near. Most of the Carolingians had quite a different view of things. If you read Alcuin's *Life of Saint Vedastus* carefully, you will find that Alcuin is telling you about his world, and you will be able to catch a glimpse of his confident and optimistic spirit.

3.2 Christian Church in the Middle Age

Christianity had spread throughout the Roman world and the church had set up its own government by the time the Western Roman Empire fell. As time went by differences in practices as well as in beliefs arose between the church in the western Mediterranean areas and the church in the eastern Mediterranean area. They even did not use the same language. After 1054, the church was divided into the Roman Catholic Church and the Eastern Orthodox Church. In order to develop a civilization based on Christianity, the Catholic church made Latin the official language and helped to preserve and pass on the heritage of the Roman Empire.

The church owed its influence not only to the maneuverings of the popes but also to the tireless work of the clergy and the powerful effect of Christian beliefs. By this time in its history, the church had evolved an elaborate organization to carry out its work. The pope, as the spiritual leader of Christianity, stood at the head of a strict hierarch. Supporting him was the papal curia—a staff of administrators, financial experts, secretaries, clerics, and legal advisers. A system of ecclesiastical courts handled the church's judicial functions and interpreted canon law, the church's law code based on *The Bible*. These courts were technically restricted to cases involving clerical personnel, but in actuality their jurisdiction was broader because of the huge number of people enmeshed in the workings of the church. The church's judicial branch rivaled the feudal courts in jurisdiction, and canon law sometimes challenged the authority of feudal law. Tithes, taxes, and special collections provided funds for the church's daily operations and its charitable obligations. The system was relatively efficient, and as long as the church spent the funds wisely, the populace kept up its generous contributions.

3.2.1 The Pope and Break between Eastern and Western Churches

From these early governing officials, who often merged their administrative abilities with more spiritual gifts and functions, there developed the government of the Church. This is a hierarchical organization, headed by the pope, who is Bishop of Rome, and who claims authority over all the other bishops. This claim, however, was denied almost from the first by the bishops of such great centers of eastern Christianity as Antioch, Alexandria, and later Constantinople; it never quite established itself in the East. But in the West it was very firmly established by the time of the breakup of the Roman Empire and the Germanic invasions, and was to be a major factor in the growth of western civilization.

The strength of its organization was one of the reasons for the triumph of the church of Rome. Many forces were working toward the elevation of the ecclesiastical center of Rome to an exceptional position. *The prestige* of Rome, the city of cities, would perhaps alone have insured this result. The final success of Rome also owes a great deal to the prestige of Peter and Paul. *The Gospels* report Jesus as saying to Peter, "Thou art Peter, and upon this rock I will build my church." This celebrated sentences is, incidentally, a pun. It is one of the foundations for the Petrine theory of the power of the Popes, who are the successors of Peter as Bishop of Rome. In the fourth century, with the setting up of Constantinople in the East as new administrative center, the pope gradually began to free himself from imperial controls. Finally, as the barbarian invasions became general after the sack of Rome in 410, the pope appeared more and, ore as the embodiment of those Roman regularities and certainties that were being threatened.

The division of Christendom into Eastern and Western churches has its roots in the early Middle Ages. The division was due in part to linguistic and cultural differences between the Greek East and the Roman, Latin-speaking West, a novel combination of

Greek, Roman, and Asian elements shaped Byzantine culture, giving Eastern Christianity more of a mystical orientation than western Christianity. Compared with their western counterparts, eastern Christians seemed to attribute less importance to life in this world and to be more concerned abut questions affecting their eternal destiny. This strong mystical orientation toward the next world may also have permitted the eastern patriarchs to submit more passively than western popes could ever do to royal intervention in church affairs.

The Emperor Leo's direct challenge of the pope coincided with a renewed threat to Rome and the Western church from the Lombards of northern Italy. Assailed on two fronts, the Roman papacy seemed surely doomed. There has not, however, been a more resilient and enterprising institution in Western history than the papacy. Since Gregory the Great, who 150 years earlier had negotiated a treaty with the Lombards, popes had recognized the Franks of northern Gaul as Europe's ascendant power and seen in them their surest protectors. In 754, Pope Stephen Ⅱ (752—757), initiating the most fruitful political alliance of the Middle Ages, enlisted the Franks and their ruler, Pepin Ⅲ, to defend the church against the Lombards and as a western counterweight to the eastern emperor. This marriage of religion and politics created a new western church and empire; it also determined much of the course of Western history into present.

3.2.2 Monastic Reform

Monasticism is the ancient style of vowed religious life which typically includes community, prayer, common worship, silence, and labor. It is governed by a monastic rule, or way of life, which involves a choice to live apart from society and the world, and so to witness in a radical way to Jesus Christ.

From the fifth to the eleventh century in western Europe lords and churchmen recognized two main goals: the conversion of pagans to Christianity and the establishment of proper order within the Christian community. The expansion of Frankish power and Christianity under Charlemagne, and Charlemagne's insistence upon clerical reform and education, illustrate both goals at a moment in early medieval history when they seemed closest to achievement. In spite of the disasters of the late ninth and tenth centuries, the process of conversion went on, including that of the Viking and Hungarian invaders. By the end of the eleventh century, most western European pagans had become converted to Christianity and one of the religious aims of the early Middle Ages had been accomplished. One sign of this change is the decreasing frequency with which ecclesiastical writers described forbidden pagan customs and superstitions in their works on penance in the twelfth century; they concentrated instead upon the proper attitudes of Christians within Christian society.

The period between the tenth and the late twelfth centuries, designated Romanesque by historians of art. Witnessed a new stage of European religious consciousness, one that reflects a heightened awareness of the proper ordering of Christian society. At the end of the long duel with paganism, Romanesque religion face the problem of order inside the Christian world. One of the main aspects of this problem was the monastic life.

The first signs of the new temper are to be found in the strongest centers of early medieval Christianity, the monasteries. Perhaps the most influential and best-known center of monastic reform was the monastery of Cluny in Burgundy. Established in 910 by Duke William the Good of Aquitaine, Cluny was exceptional from its very origins, for the duke gave the monastery not to an individual abbot of lay protector but directly to Saint Peter. The monastery was therefore independent of all local ecclesiastical and lay authority and directly subordinate only to the pope. The power of the spiritual attraction of Rome was considerable even in the dark days of the tenth century, and some Cluny's early prestige may have derived from its particular connection with Rome.

A series of extraordinarily distinguished abbots supervised the development of Cluny into a reformed and remarkably influential monastery. The closely regulated life of the monks at Cluny made them models of monastic devotion. The monastery greatly emphasized liturgical reforms, and its liturgy became a model for monastic liturgies throughout western Europe. Local and distant nobles came under the influence of this dynamic institution, and asked for instructions about reforming their own monasteries along Cluniac lines. Many other monasteries were slowly under the direct control of Cluny, and the Cluniac influence began to reach out into corners of Europe where there had been little previous hope of ecclesiastical reform.

The abbot of Cluny was the only abbot in the order; all other monasteries controlled by Cluny were governed by subordinate officials called priors. The fact that the abbot could select his own successor and that he was the single abbot among the 1,500 or so monasteries that were attached to Cluny enabled the houses of the Cluniac system to work together for reform and to coordinate their activities closely. The abbots traveled extensively, and they were as familiar in Rome and northern Italy as they were in France. The kidnapping of Saint Mayeul by Arab raiders in the Alps appeared to have been the rallying point for the final southern French assault that destroyed the powerful

Arab stronghold of La Garde Freinet toward the end of the tenth century.

There is no greater monument to the synthesis of aristocratic reform monasticism represented by Cluny than the great monastic church, now destroyed, called Cluny Ⅲ. Begun in 1088 and finance largely by gifts of King Alfonso Ⅵ of Leon-Castile, the building was completed after many delays in 1130. Until the rebuilding of St. Peter's Church in Rome in the sixteenth century, Cluny Ⅲ was the largest church building in Latin Christendom. It was a church in which not only monks but clergy and laity alike could see God worshiped with devotion, elegance, and purity of ritual highly and was all too aware of the distractions of secular life on other "men of prayer", Cluny and its great church offered the fulfillment of the Carolingian ideal of enlightened lay patronage and protection that enabled disciplined men of religion to perfect the art of liturgical prayer, to struggle against the forces of darkness in their unceasing liturgies, and to accept and shelter the bodies of their patrons and pray for their souls after death.

The abbots of Cluny also invoked images of an earlier, more peaceful, Christian world in their work toward the renewal of their own society. But they were not the only monastic reformers of the late tenth and eleventh centuries, nor was their form of monasticism the only model followed by their contemporaries. At Camaldoli in Italy and elsewhere a rigorously ascetic form of monasticism was developed and, in conjunction with this, new forms of the religious life of hermits and anchorites. These practices often sacrificed the earlier ideals of study and manual labor in favor of a life of silence and contemplation. In order to fulfill the needs of some of these rigorous communities, groups of lay brothers were admitted. These figures became a major art of monastic life in the late eleventh and twelfth centuries.

3.2.3 The Roman Curia and Papal-imperial Struggle

The Roman Curia, usually called the Vatican, is the administrative apparatus of the Holy See, coordinating and providing the necessary organization for the correct functioning of the Catholic Church and the achievement of its goals. It is generally considered as representing the international government of the Catholic Church. Curia in medieval and later Latin usage means "court" in the sense of "royal court" rather than "court of law." The Roman Curia, then, sometimes anglicized as Roman court, is the Papal Court, and assists the Pope in carrying out his functions. The Roman Curia can also be loosely compared to cabinets in governments of countries with a Western form of governance, though it only includes a Foreign ministry, the secular internal affairs being handled by separate institutions of the Vatican City State, unlike the earlier Papal States.

The Roman Curia was originally established in the 16th Century by Pope Sixtus V and had both religious and civil functions, though the latter were greatly transformed in the 19th century when the expansion of the Piedmontese State to include the greater part of Italy included the seizure of most of the Papal States in 1860 and the city of Rome itself in 1870, and hence effectively ended much of the Papacy's temporal power. An agreement was reached on this issue when in 1929 the Holy See concluded the Lateran Treaties with the Italian State, which had since 1919 occupied the whole of thc peninsula, plus Sicily and Sardinia. By this act, the Roman Curia gave up any claim to an administrative role in the defunct Papal States, though it has such with regard to the successor Vatican City State. In practice, the Curia is now mainly dedicated to the support of the Pope's ecclesiastical responsibilities.

It should be noted that it is normal for every Latin Catholic diocese to have a curia in its administration. For the Dioceses of Rome, these functions are not handled by the Roman Curia, but by the Vicariate General of His Holiness for the City of Rome, as provided by the Apostolic Constitution ecclesia in Urbe. The Vicar General, traditionally a Cardinal, and his deputy the Vicegerent, who holds the personal title of Archbishop, supervise the governance of the diocese by reference to the Pope himself, but with no more dependence on the Roman Curia as such than other Catholic dioceses throughout thc world.

The imperial office also changed during the later part of the struggle. The emperors of the Romans were also the kings of Germany, and the Investiture Conflict had revealed that the two offices were not as separate in fact as they might be in theory. The needs of the kingdom of Germany colored both the functions of the imperial office in the later twelfth and thirteenth centuries and the policy of the kings of Germany, emperors of the Romans. Although much of the earlier prestige and memory of the emperors from Charlemagne to Henry V survived in imperial policy and propaganda, the actual facts of imperial rule changed nearly as much as the actual problems of papal governance.

3.3 The Revival of Western Europe in the Twelfth Century

3.3.1 Rise of Universities and Development of Secular Disciplines

The schools of Paris in the days of Peter Abelard and for decades afterward consisted of assemblies of students grouped around individual masters, the students paying the masters individually. These assemblies came under the ecclesiastical jurisdiction of the bishop of Paris and his chancellor. In Paris and Bologna the experience of individuals coming together to study in a strange city far from their homes was a social and legal novelty, and the very presence of the schools and their lack of legal status rendered the students vulnerable to much of the hostility generated by the inveterate localism of the twelfth century. Unprotected by citizenship, status, or privilege, students were subject to price and rent gouging, a lack of legal protection, and the perennial distresses of under—financed strangers.

In 1158 the emperor Frederick Barbarossa issued *the Authenticum Habita*, in which he extended his protection to students in imperial territories. In particular, the document granted students free travel and legal immunities, and recognized that their study profited the emperor and his subjects. As a professional social consciousness grew among teachers and students, so did formal recognition of the status that formal study conferred. In the late twelfth century there appeared the ceremonial inception, a public defense of one's learning that has parallels in the formal rites of initiation into the order of knighthood, the oath of citizenship in the corporation of citizens of a town, and the ritual recognition of the status of master in a craft guild.

The universities prospered because society needed them. The Church, faced with increasing business at Rome and in the great dioceses after the Investiture Conflict, felt an increasing need for capable, loyal, trained assistants, and it had the great power to attract the men it needed. The twelfth century was probably no more fond of legal disputes than the eleventh, but the new law courts of the towns and the courts of kings and princes and prelates had to be staffed. Moreover, lesser princes and prelates began to find that when their clerical business was not kept up, their revenues and status declined perceptibly. All of these potential patrons helped generate a new demand for learning and letters.

The development of secular disciplines is an aspect of the high-medieval education boom. At first the cathedral schools existed almost exclusively forth basic training of priests, with a curriculum designed to teach only such literacy necessary for reading the Church offices. But soon after 1100 the curriculum was broadened, for the growth of both ecclesiastical and secular governments created a growing demand for trained officials who had to know more than how to read a few prayers. The revived reliance on law especially made it imperative to improve the quality of primary education in order to train future lawyers. Above all, a thorough knowledge of Latin grammar and composition began to be inculcated, often by studying some of the roman classics such as the works of Cicero and Virgil.

3.3.2 Revival of Roman Law

The development of early European legal in stitutions had produced a body of law very different in complexity and purpose from Roman law. From the earliest Germanic law codes to the customary legal arrangements of individual manors, villages and towns, early European law possessed little of the philosophical and professional attraction of Roman law. In addition, the fragmenting of political authority in the ninth and tenth centuries had tended to turn legal institutions into the private property of lords who controlled law courts, pocketed the fines they awarded, and administered a heavy-handed kind of local justice. Some legal systems, such as that of Anglo-Saxon England, were relatively highly developed, but Anglo-Saxon law was subsumed under the oppressive legal practices of William the Conqueror's Norman aristocrats. In most of the principalities that made up eleventh and twelfth-century France, regional customs determined legal practice. Moreover, much law operated under heavy procedural limitations and according to the theory of immanent justice—the belief that in certain cases divine intervention is required to indicate the guilt or innocence of the accused. Thus, various forms of the ordeal and trial by combat were practiced because it was believed that in them the will of God was revealed.

But the same intellectual revolution that had affected rhetoric and logic, Bible study and philosophy, also came to influence the law. The revolution had both ecclesiastical and secular sides. On the secular side, the revolution of learned law is generally attributed to the Bolognese rhetorician Irnerius, who began to expound the text of Justinian's Digerst, rediscovered relatively recently, to his students. As the explanation of this written, philosophical lawbook grew beyond the stage of simply explaining the meaning of obscure words, the great achievements of roman law began to generate independent interest, and schools devoted exclusively to the study of Roman law, first at Bologna and later throughout western Europe, began to grow up.

By the mid twelfth century the "Four Doctors", Martinus, Bulgarus, Rogerius and Hugo, had developed the techniques of explaining the texts of the law by writing marginal glosses, composing short treatises on legal reasoning, and writing summaries of individual titles in Justinian's collection. Medieval teachers of Roman law believed that the law was binding throughout Italy and the Empire and the cities of Pavia and Bologna became especially well known as centers of roman legal study. After more than a century of scholarship on Roman law, the jurist Accursius arranged the long tradition of commentary on the law into a single systematic commentary that became known as the glossa ordinaria, the ordinary gloss, of Roman law. In time the glossa ordinaria was routinely taught in schools of Roman law along with the text of the law itself.

The revival of Roman law coincided with a growing distaste for the confusion and archaism that many thinkers found in eleventh and twelfth-century European law. Even in those legal systems that formally remained outside the orbit of Roman law, such as the common law of England, the rationality, systematization, and regularity of Roman law made a great impact. Twelfth-century theologians protested against the use of the ordeal and trial by battle, on the grounds that they tempted God and were and of blasphemy. When the Fourth Lateran Council in 1215 forbade clerics to participate in the administration of the ordeal, the older legal procedure was well on its way of becoming a dead letter. In its place theologians approved the collection o evidence, its analysis, and a decision based upon rational process. So did the teachers and students of Roman law, who also worked as scribes, agents, judges, lawyers, and consultants for the towns, principalities, and monarchies of western Europe. Even those students who did not intend to become lawyers often studied Roman law for a time in order to acquire the intellectual training and discipline that the study of Roman law offered. The recovery of Roman law in the late eleventh and early twelfth centuries was one of the most important changes in the schools and the judicial systems of Europe. It touched abstract legal learning, helped rationalize the practice of law throughout Europe, and habituated many to solving disputes by rational procedures.

3.3.3 Prosperity of Theology and Scholasticism

The revival of Roman law and the slow spread of its influence to the customary laws of different regions in Europe illustrate the appeal that systematic, consistent thought exerted upon a society that had suddenly become aware of its own lack of system and the inconsistencies of its own law. The growth of theology in the twelfth century also reflects that perception.

With the spread of learning and the production of more manuscripts, thinkers became aware of the inconsistencies that also existed in the vast body of religious literature that the eleventh and twelfth centuries had inherited from the past. Peter Abelard's *Sic Et Non* was an ambitious attempt to illustrate the conflicts in interpretation in the sources and to devise a reliable method for resolving them. In spite of opposition to Abelard's theology, his method attracted more and more followers, for it offered an irresistible tool for solving the problems that thinkers had become more acutely aware of. In addition to Abelards logical study there was, as we have seen, a transformation of the substance and temper of theology illustrated in Saint Anselm's linking of reason and faith and in Abelard's sophisticated psychological analysis of intention and consent. Moreover, such theologians as Saint Bernard paved new ways in devotional literature, sharing with Saint Anselm and even with Abelard a new sense of the love between God and humankind, a fascination with the human Jesus, and a new emotional dimension to theological thought. It is in the light of these three developments that the rise of the study of theology out to be considered.

Around 1150, Peter the Lombard, a master in the Paris schools and later bishop of Paris, produced his book of *Sentences*, a systematic collection of scriptural texts and writings of Church fathers and masters that dealt topically with theological problems. The works of Gratian and Peter Lombard became the schoolbooks for the study of law and theology, and in some cases they were used until the beginning of the twentieth century. Arising in the schools and from masters such as Abelard, Gratian, and Peter Lombard, the principles of selecting, ordering, and typologizing diverse texts were now applied to the disciplines of law and theology.

Thus, the masters of theology in the schools moved further and further away from traditional methods of explaining Scripture. The language of theological definition and explanation became more and more that of the schools of logic and the philosophers, and less that of the meditative and literary traditions of the past. Not only did the new language and the new systematizing of thought and exposition explore further dimensions of the relationship between God and creation, it opened vistas in the definition of the human personality.

As the tools of logic and philosophy became the tools of theology, specialization, training, and formal expression became necessary for theological study. At the Fourth Lateran Council in 1215, the number of the sacraments was finally set at seven and their nature was defined; the complex questions of nature, grace, sin, and salvation now received firm definitions. In teaching theology the master now proceeded to treat texts, no matter how traditionally authoritative, in terms of the questions they illuminated, and the choice of these questions and their complexity directed the thrust of study. In time, such questions became the principal form of theological exposition.

The story of the high-medieval encounter between Greek and Arabic philosophy and Christian faith is basically the story of the emergence of Scholasticism. This word can be, and has been, defined in many ways. In its root meaning Scholasticism was simply the method of teaching and learning followed in the medieval schools. That meant that it was highly systematic and also that it was highly respectful of authority. Yet Scholasticism was not only a method of study: it taught that there was a fundamental compatibility between the knowledge humans can obtain naturally, i. e., by experience or reason, and the teachings imparted by Divine Revelation. Since medieval scholars believed that the Greeks were the masters of natural knowledge and that all revelation was in the Bible, Scholasticism consequently was the theory and practice of recording classical philosophy with Christian faith.

Scholastics quarreled over the proper relationship between philosophy and theology. The problem between philosophy and theology arose because, in Christian eyes, there was a lot of heresy in Aristotle's writings, especially as his teaching was interpreted by certain Islamic commentators. These commentators did not treat his work as a handmaiden to Christianity. For example, Aristotle believed in the eternality of the world. This plainly called into question the Judeo-Christian teaching that the world had been created in time, as stressed in the book of *Genesis*. Aristotle also taught that intellect, or mind, was ultimately one, a seeming denial of individuality and hence of Christian teaching about individual responsibility and personal immortality.

When the ologians took the logic and metaphysics of Aristotle over into their theologies, some critics believed it posed a threat to biblical teaching and traditional Church authority. Berengar of Tours, for example, was a scholastic who applied logic to the sacrament of the Eucharist; and before long he found himself questioning the Church's teaching on transubstantiation. Peter Abelard tried to subject the Trinity to logical examination. He found that, by Aristotle's logic, three could not be one nor one three, in contrast to the church's teachings about the unity of God; the Father, Son, and Holy Ghost.

The boldness of these new logicians shocked conservatives. Monastic leaders especially wondered whether the liberal arts course of study, dominated by Aristotle's writings, was more foe than ally of theological study. The love of learning had clearly gotten in the way of the love of God as far as the critics of Scholasticism were concerned.

A century of such suspicion and criticism of Aristotle's alleged undermining of Christian theology culminated in 1277 when the bishop of Paris condemned 219 philosophical propositions. The condemnation was directed against scholars who seemed to the authorities to be more interested in secular philosophy than in Christian truth. It chilled the relationship between learning and religion. Reason and revelation thereafter became two very different spheres of knowledge, much as Church and state were then also being forced apart in the world of secular politics. William of Ockham represented conservative opinion on the issue and signaled its future direction when he denied that essential matters of theology could be addressed as if they were empirical. To know God's mind, Christians must content themselves with biblical revelation; reason could not know God directly.

Chapter 4 The Change to Modern Western Culture

4.1 The Falling of the Medieval Civilization

4.1.1 The Feudalism Crisis and Capitalism Shoot in Western Europe

The late Middle Ages saw almost unprecedented political, social, and ecclesiastical calamity. France and England grappled with each other in a bitter conflict known as the Hundred Year's War (1337—1453), an exercise in seemingly will-full self-destruction that was made even more terrible in its later stages by the introduction of gunpowder and the invention of heavy artillery. Bubonic, plague, known to contemporaries as the Black Death, swept over almost all of Europe, killing as much as one-third of the population in many regions between 1348 and 1350 and transforming many pious Christians into believers in the omnipotence of death. A schism emerged within the Church that lasted thirty-nine years (1378—1417) and led, by 1409 to the election of no fewer than three competing popes and colleges of cardinals. In 1453 the Turks marched seemingly invincibly through Constantinople and toward the West. As their political and religious institutions buckled, as disease, bandits, and wolves attacked their cities in the wake of war, and as Islamic armies gathered at their borders, Europeans beheld what seemed to be the imminent total collapse of Western civilization.

Medieval governments were by no means all-powerful and secure. The rivalry of petty lords kept localities in turmoil and dynastic rivalries could plunge entire lands into war, especially when power was being transferred to a new ruler, and woe to the ruling dynasty that failed to produce a male heir.

To field the armies and collect the revenues that made their existence possible, late medieval rulers depended on carefully negotiated alliances among a wide range of lesser powers, Like kings and queens in earlier centuries, they too practiced the art of feudal government, but on a grander scale and with greater sophistication. To maintain the order they required, the Norman kings of England and the Captain kings of France fine-tuned traditional feudal relationships, stressing the duties of lesser to higher power and the unquestioning loyalty noble vassals owed the king. The result was a degree of centralized royal power unseen before in these lands and a nascent "national" consciousness that equipped both France and England for international warfare.

4.1.2 The Rising Nation-state and Declining Authority of Pope

The late medieval evolution from Christendom toward nationhood was not so much a transformation as a shift in balance. Even during the High Middle Ages the idea of a Christian commonwealth, guided by pope and clergy, had never been fulfilled. At best, popes could win momentary political victories over kings and could achieve an uneasy equilibrium between royal and clerical authority. By the late thirteenth century the balance was already tipping in favor of monarchies such as Edward I of England and Philip the fair of France. The trend accelerated during the late Middle Ages until 1500, the papacy had become much weaker as an international force and the monarchies stronger. "Nationhood" by any strict definition, had not yet come, but papal authority over the churches of the various kingdoms was becoming tenuous. The princely electors of Germany had long before denied the papacy and role in imperial elections or coronations, and papal influence in the appointment of French, English, and Spanish prelates had ebbed. More important still, the late Middle Ages witnessed a collapse of papal spiritual prestige and a widening chasm between Christian piety and the organized Church.

If any western European city of around 1200 epitomized Europe's greatest new accomplishment it was Paris: that city was not only a bustling commercial center and an important center of learning, it was also the capital of what was becoming Europe's most powerful government. France, like England and the new Christian kingdoms of the Iberian Peninsula, was taking shape in the twelfth and thirteenth centuries as a national monarchy, a new form of government which was to dominate Europe's political future. The developing national monarchies were the most successful and promising European governments. Until their emergence there had been two basic patterns of government in Europe: city-states had the advantage of drawing heavily upon citizen participation and loyalty and thus were able to make highly efficient use of their human potential. But they were often divided by economic rivalries and they were not sufficiently large of militarily strong to defend themselves against imperial forces. The empires, on the other hand, could win battles and often had the resources to support an efficient bureaucratic administrative apparatus, but they drew on little voluntary participation and were too far-flung of rapacious to inspire any deep loyalties. The new national monarchies were to prove the "golden mean" between these extremes. They were large enough to have adequate military strength and they developed administrative techniques that would rival and eventually surpass those of the roman or Byzantine Empires. More than that, building at first upon the bases of feudalism, they drew upon sufficient citizen participation and loyalty to help support them in times of stress when empires would have founded. By about 1300 the monarchies of England, France, and the Iberian Peninsula had gained the primary loyalties of their subjects, superseding loyalties to communities, regions, or to the government of the Church. For all these reasons they bought much internal peace and stability of large parts of Europe where there had been little stability before. Thus they contributed greatly to making life fruitful. The medieval national monarchies were also the ancestor of the modern nation-states—the most effective and equitable governments of our day. In short, they were one of Middle Ages' most beneficial bequests to modern times.

4.1.3 Heresy and Mysticism

The surge of popular piety also resulted in a flood of criticism against the Church itself. It was not that churchman had grown worse, but rather that the laity had begun to judge them by more rigorous standards. Popular dissatisfaction toward the workaday Church spurred the rush toward the austere twelfth-century monastic orders. Yet the majority of Christians could not become monks or nuns, and, for them, certain heretical doctrines, old and new, begun to exert a powerful appeal.

The heresies of the High Middle Ages flourished particularly in the rising towns of southern Europe. The eleventh-century urban revolution had caught the Church unprepared. The new towns were becoming centers of a burgeoning lay piety, yet the church, with its roots in the older agrarian order, seemed unable to minister effectively to the vigorous and widely literate new burgher class. Too often the urban bishops appeared as political oppressors and enemies of burgher independence rather than spiritual directors. Too often the Church of failed to understand the town dwellers' problems and aspirations or to anticipate their growing suspicion of ecclesiastical wealth and power. Although most townspeople remained loyal to the Church, a minority in the south, turned to new, anticlerical sects. In their denunciation ecclesiastical wealth, these sects were doing nothing more than St. Bernard and the Cistercians had done. But some of the anticlerical sects crossed the narrow line between orthodox reformism and heresy by preaching without Episcopal or papal approval. Far more important, they denied the exclusive right of the priesthood to perform sacraments.

One such sect, the Waldensians, was founded by a merchant of Lyons named Valdez, later known as Peter Waldo. Around 1173, Valdo gave all his possessions to the poor and took up a life of apostolic poverty. He and his follows sought the Church's permission to preach in the towns. The Church refused, after some confusion and delay, because of its uneasiness about the preaching untrained laypeople that, among the Waldensians, included women as well as men. The Church preferred to leave religious instruction in the hands of ordained males. But Peter Waldo and his follows continued their preaching. This act of defiance, along with their growing doubts about the special spiritual status of the priesthood, earned them the condemnation of the Church.

Similar groups, some orthodox, some heretical, arose in the communes of Lombardy and were known as Humiliati. These groups proved troublesome to the local ecclesiastical hierarchies, but generally they escaped downright condemnation, unless they themselves took the step of denying the authority of the Church. Many of them did take that step, however, and by the opening of the thirteenth century, heretical, anticlerical sects were spreading across northern Italy and southern France, and even into Spain and Germany.

4.2 The Times of the Renaissance

4.2.1 Humanism

The word "humanism" has many meanings. It can refer to a tradition of classical scholarship, anything humanitarian, of a philosophy focusing on the significance of human activity. Renaissance humanism encompassed these definitions but above all was a form of education and culture based upon the study of the classics. Humanists were less bound to recent tradition; they did not focus all their attention on summarizing and comparing the views recognized authorities on a text or question, but went directly to the original source themselves. And their most respected sources were classical and biblical, not the medieval philosophers and theologians. Avidly searching out manuscript collections, Italians Humanists mad the full sources of Greek and Latin antiquity available to scholars during the fourteenth and fifteenth centuries. Mastery of Latin and Greek was the surgeon's tool of the Humanist.

They focus on the important role played by the individual in society. Individual fulfillment became a leading Renaissance idea and remains a central notion in western thought today. During the Renaissance, the growing emphasis on the individual resulted in a more optimistic assessment of human nature—a development that in time led to a rejection of Christianity's stress on original sin.

Fourteenth century humanists such as Petrarch had glorified intellectual activity pursued in a life of solitude and had rejected a life of action in the community and family. Petrarch (1304—1374) has often been called the father of Italian Renaissance humanism. He was the first intellectual to characterize the Middle Ages as a period of darkness. Philosophy, he argued, should be the "art of virtuous living", not a science of logic chopping. The humanistic pursuits of Petrarch were best received in Florence. By the end of the fourteenth century, a whole circle of humanistic scholars had emerged in that city. Although some were connected to monastic orders, many were simply laymen. In fact, the latter were responsible for humanism gaining a powerful momentum at the beginning of the fifteenth century when it became closely tied to Florentine civic spirit and pride, giving rise to what one modern scholar has labeled "civic humanism". In the busy civic world of Florence, Florentine intellectuals began to take a new view of the role of intellectuals, a trend that intensified when the city's liberty was threatened at the beginning of the fifteenth century by the Milanese tyrant, Giangaleazzo Visconti. The Roman statesman and intellectual Cicero became their model. Civic humanism emerged in Florence but soon spread to Renaissance. Civic humanism intensified the involvement of humanist intellectuals in government and guaranteed that the rhetorical disciple they praised would be put to the service of the state. It is no accident that humanist served the state as chancellors, councilors, and advisers. Rhetoricians had become diplomats.

4.2.2 The Spreading of Renaissance in Europe

The renaissance originated in Italy for several reasons. The most fundamental was that Italy in the later Middle Ages encompassed the most advanced urban society in all of Europe. Unlike aristocrats north of the Alps, Italian aristocrats customarily lived in urban centers rather than in rural castles and consequently became fully involved in urban public affairs. Moreover, since the Italian aristocracy built its palaces in the cities, the aristocratic class was less sharply set off from the class of rich merchants than in the north. Hence whereas in France or Germany there was never any appreciable variation from the rule that aristocrats lived off the income from their landed estates while rich town dwellers gained their living from trade, initially so many town-dwelling aristocrats engaged in banning or mercantile enterprises and so many rich mercantile families imitated the manners of the aristocracy that by the fourteenth and fifteenth centuries the aristocracy and upper bourgeoisie were become virtually indistinguishable. The results of these developments for the history of education are obvious: not only was there a great demand for education in the skills of reading and counting necessary to become a successful merchant, but the richest and most prominent families sought above all to find teachers who would impart to their offspring the knowledge and skills necessary to argue well in public arena. Consequently, Italy produced a large number of secular educators, many of whom not only taught students but demonstrated their learned attainments in the production of political and ethical treaties and works of literature. The schools of these educators, moreover, created the best educated upper-class public in all of Europe and inevitably there with a considerable number of wealthy patrons who were ready to invest in the cultivation of new ideas and new forms of literary and artistic expression.

A second reason why late-medieval Italy was the birthplace of an intellectual and artistic Renaissance lay in the fact that it had a far greater sense of rapport with the classical past than any other territory in western Europe. Give the Italian aristocratic commitment to an educational curriculum which stressed success in urban politics, the best teachers understandably sought inspiration from ancient Latin and Greek texts because politics and political rhetoric were classical rather than medieval arts. Elsewhere, resort to classical knowledge and classical literary style might have seemed intolerably antiquarian and artificial, but in Italy the classical past appeared most "relevant" because ancient roman monuments were omnipresent throughout the peninsula and ancient Latin literature referred to cities and sites that Renaissance Italians recognized as their own. Moreover, Italians became particularly intent on reappropriating their classical heritage in the fourteenth and fifteenth centuries because Italians then were seeking to establish an independent cultural identity in opposition to a Scholasticism most closely associated with France. Not only did the removal of the papacy to Avignon for most of the fourteenth century, and then the prolonged Great Schism from 1378 to 1415, heighten antagonisms between Italy and France, but during the fourteenth century there was an intellectual reaction against Scholasticism on all fronts which made it natural for Italians to prefer the intellectual alternatives offered by classical literary sources. Naturally too, once Roman literature and learning became particularly favored in Italy, so did Roman art and architecture, for Roman models could help Italians create a splendid artistic alternative to French Gothicism just as Roman learning offered an intellectual alternative to French Scholasticism.

Finally, the Italian Renaissance obviously could not have occurred without the underpinning of Italian wealth oddly enough, the Italian economy as a whole was probably more prosperous in the thirteenth century than it was in the fourteenth and fifteenth. But late medieval Italy was wealthier in comparison to the rest of Europe than it had been before, a fact which meant that Italian writers and artists were more likely to stay at home than seek employment abroad. Moreover, in late-medieval Italy unusually intensive investment in culture arose from an intensification of urban pride and the concentration of per capita wealth. Although these two trends overlapped somewhat, most scholars tend to agree that a phase of predominantly public urban support for culture came first in Italy from roughly 1250 to about 1400 or 1450, depending on place, with the private sector taking over thereafter. In the first phase the richest cities vied with each other in building the most splendid public monuments and in supporting writers whose role were to glorify the urban republics in letters and speeches as full of magniloquent Ciceronian prose as possible. But in the course of the fifteenth century, when most Italian city-states succumbed to the hereditary rule of princely families, patronage was monopolized by the princely aristocracy. It was then that the great prines—the Visconti and Sforza in Milan; the Medici in Florence; the Este in Ferrara; and the Gonzaga in Mantua—patronized art and literature in their courts to glorify themselves, while lesser aristocratic families imitated those princes on a smaller scale. Not least of the great princes in Italy from about 1450 to about 1550 were the popes in Rome, who were dedicated to a policy of basing their strength on temporal control of the Papal States. Hence the most worldly of the Renaissance popes—Alexander Ⅵ (1492—1503; Julius Ⅱ (1503—1513); and Leo X (1513—1521), son of the Florentine ruler Lorenzo de' Medici—obtained the services of the greatest artists of the day and for a few decades made Rome the unrivaled artistic capital of the Western world.

4.2.3 Social Lives in the Renaissance

The Renaissance inherited from the Middle Ages a hierarchic and organic conception of society. Society was fundamentally divided into three estates: the clergy, shoes preeminence was grounded in the belief that society should be directed to a spiritual end; the nobility, whose privileged position rested on the theory that it provided protection and justice for society; and the third estate, which consisted of the peasants and inhabitants of the towns and cities. This social order experienced certain adaptations in the Renaissance, which we can see by examining the second and third estates.

Almost everywhere in western Europe, the landholding nobles were faced with declining real incomes during the greater part of the fourteenth and fifteenth centuries, while the expense of maintaining noble status was rising. It was once assumed that this decline of the nobility in the Late Middle Ages led to the triumph of the middle class, whose fortunes were made in trade, banking, and industry. But, in fact, members of the old nobility survived, while new blood infused its ranks. A reconstruction of the aristocracy was well underway by 1500.

As a result of these recons, the nobles, old and new, managed to dominate society as they had done in the Middle Ages, holding important political posts and serving as advisers to the king. Increasingly in the sixteenth century, members of the aristocracy pursued education as the means to maintain their role in government. One noble in the Low Countries, in a letter outlining how his son should be formally educated, stated that, due to his own lack of learning, he dared not express his opinions in the king's council and often "felt deep shame and humiliation" at his ignorance.

4.3 The Times of Reformation

4.3.1 Martin Luther and German Religious Reformation

Martin Luther was born on November 10, 1483, into a peasant family, although his father raised himself into the ranks of the lower bourgeoisie by going into mining. His father wanted him to become a lawyer, so Luther enrolled at the University of Erfurt where he received his bachelor's degree in 1502. In 1505, after becoming a master in the liberal arts, the young Martin began to study law. Luther was not content with the study of law and all along had shown religious inclinations. In the summer of 1505 enroute back to Erfurt after a brief visit home, he was caught in a ferocious thunderstorm and vowed that if he were spared, he would become a monk. He then entered the monastic order of the Augustinian Hermits in Erfurt, much to his father's disgust. While in the monastery, Luther focused on his major concern, the assurance of salvation. The traditional beliefs and practices of the church seemed unable to assuage his obsession with this question, especially evident in his struggle with the sacrament of penance or confession. The sacraments were a Catholic's chief means of receiving God's grace; that of confession offered the opportunity to have one's sins forgiven. Luther spent hours confessing his sins, but he was always doubtful. Had he remembered all of his sins? Even, more, how could a hopeless sinner be acceptable to a totally just and all-powerful God?

Despite his herculean efforts, Luther achieved no certainty and even came, as he once expressed it, to hate "this just God who punishes sinners".

Luther's dilemma had derived from his concept of the justice of God, which interpreted as a punitive justice in which God weighs the merits of good works per formed by humans as a necessary precondition for salvation. To Luther it appeared that the church was saying that one must earn salvation by good works. In Luther's eye, human beings weak and powerless in the sight of an almighty God, could never do enough to justify salvation in these terms. Through his study of the Bible, especially his work on Paul's Epistle to the Romans, Luther rediscovered another way of viewing the justice of God:

Night and day I pondered until I saw the connection between the justice of God and the statement that "the just shall live by his faith." Then I grasped that the justice of God is that righteousness by which though grace and sheer mercy God justifies us through faith. Thereupon I felt myself to be reborn and to have gone though open doors into paradise.

To Luther, the "justice of God" was now not a punitive justice but the grace of God that bestows salvation freely to humans, not through their good works, but through the sacrifice of Christ on the cross. Even faith on the power of belief is a product of divine grace or a gift of God. The doctrine of justification by grace through faith along became the primary doctrine of the Protestant Reformation. Since Luther had arrived at this doctrine from his study of the Bible, it became for Luther as for all other Protestants the chief guide to religious truth. Justification by faith and the Bible as the sole authority in religious affairs were the twin of the Protestant Reformation.

The event that propelled Luther into an open confrontation with church officials and forced him to see the theological implications of justification by faith along was the indulgence controversy. In 1517, Pope Leo X had issued a special jubilee indulgence to finance the ongoing construction of the new Saint Peter's Cathedral. This special indulgence, however, was connected to political and ecclesiastical affairs in Germany.

Luther was greatly distressed by the sale of indulgence, certain that people were simply guaranteeing their eternaldam nation by relying on these pieces of paper to assure them of salvation. In response, he issued his *Ninety-five Theses*, although scholars are unsure whether he nailed them to a church door in Wittenberg, as is traditionally alleged, or mailed them to his ecclesiastical superior. In either case, his theses were a stunning indictment of the abuses in the sale of indulgences. A German translation of *Ninety-Five Theses* was quickly printed in thousands of copies and received sympathetically in a Germany that had a long tradition of dissatisfaction with papal policies and power.

The controversy reached an important turning point with the Leipzig Debate in July 1519. There Luther's opponent, the clever and capable Catholic theologian Johann Eck, forced Luther to move beyond indulgences and question the authority of popes and councils. In effect, Luther was compelled to see the consequences of his new theology. At the beginning of 1520, he proclaimed: "Farewell, unhappy, hopeless, blasphemous Rome! The Wrath of God has come upon you, as you deserve. We have cared for Babylon, and she is not healed: let us then, leave her, that she may be the habitation of dragons, specters, and witches." At the same time, Luther was convinced that he was doing God's work and had to proceed regardless of the consequences. To friend who had urged moderation, he exclaimed: "Let there be a new and great conflagration, who can resist the counsel of God? Who knows whether these insensate men are not predestined by Him as the means of revealing the truth?... God alone is in this business. We are carried away by Him. We are led rather than lead."

In three pamphlets published in 1520, Luther moved toward a more definite break with the Catholic Church. *The Address to the Nobility of the German Nation* was a political tract written in German. The papacy, Luther averred, had used three claims to prevent reform: that the church is superior to the state, that only the pope can interpret Scripture, and that only the pope can call a council. All three were false, and he called upon the German princes to overthrow the papacy in Germany and establish a reformed German church. *The Babylonian Captivity of the Church*, written in Latin for theologians, attacked the sacramental system as the means by which the pope and church had held the real meaning of the Gospel in captivity for a thousand years. He called for the reform of monasticism and for the clergy to marry. While virginity is good, Luther argued, marriage is better, and freedom of choice is best. *On the Freedom of A Christian Man* was a short treatise of the doctrine of salvation. It is faith along, not good works, which justifies, frees, and brings salvation through Christ. But the Christian, saved and freed by his faith in Christ, is not free from good works, but performs good works out of gratitude to God. "Good works do not make a good man, but a good man does good works." from faith flows love and from love a free spirit that is disposed to serve one's neighbor voluntarily. Hence, "a Christian man is the most free lord of all, and subject to none; a Christian man is the most dutiful servant of all, and subject to everyone."

Unable to countenance Luther's forcefully worded dissent from traditional Catholic teachings, the church excommunicated him in January 1521. He was also summoned to appear before the imperial diet or Reichstag of the Holy Roman Empire, convened by the newly elected emperor Charles V (1519—1556). Expected to recant the heretical doctrines he had espoused, Luther refused and made the famous reply that became the battle cry of the reformation:

Since then Your Majesty and your lordships desire a simple reply, I will answer without horns and without teeth. Unless I am convicted by Scripture and plain reason—I do not accept the authority of popes and councils, for they have contradicted each other—my conscience is captive to the Word of God. I cannot and I will not recant anything, for to against conscience is neither right nor safe. Here I stand, I cannot do otherwise. God help me. Amen.

Luther's heroic stand at Worms was once viewed as a step in the development of religious freedom, but that interpretation overlooked an important consideration. While Luther clearly placed his conscience above the authority of the church, he also believed that he had arrived at the truth, from which others were not allowed to deviate. Luther once expressed: "I have neither the power nor the will to deny the Word of God. If any man has a different opinion concerning me, he does not think straight or understand what I have actually said."

4.3.2 John Calvin and the French Reformation

Of the second generation of Protestant reformers, one stands out as the systematic theologian and organizer of the Protestant movement—John Calvin (1509—1564). Born a generation later than Luther, Calvin reached manhood when Christian unity had for all intents and purposes already disappeared. Although his basic doctrinal positions were similar to Luther's, their different backgrounds resulted in significant differences as well.

John Calvin began his academic training in 1523 at the University of Paris, but switched to the study of law at Orleans and Bourges from 1528 to 1531, while simultaneously studying Greek. In 1531, he returned to Paris to concentrate on his humanistic pursuits. In his early development, Calvin was also influenced by Luther's writings, which were being circulated and read by French intellectuals as early as 1523. Up to 1533, then, Calvin had received a remarkably diverse education. In that same year, he experienced a religious crisis that determined the rest of his life's work. He described it in these words:

God, by a sudden conversion, subdued and brought my mind to a teachable frame, which was more hardened in such matters than might have been expected from one at my early period of life. Having thus received some taste and knowledge of true godliness, I was immediately inflamed with so intense a desire to make progress therein, although I did not leave off other studies, I yet pursued them with less ardor.

Calvin's conversion was solemn and straightforward. He was so convinced of the inner guidance of God that he became the most determined of all the Protestant reformers.

After his conversion and newfound conviction, Calvin was no longer safe in Paris since King Francis I periodically persecuted Protestants. Eventually, Calvin made his way to Basel, where in 1536, he published the first edition of the *Institutes of the Christian Religion*, a masterful synthesis of Protestant thought, a manual for ecclesiastical organization, and a work that immediately secured Calvin's reputation as one of the new leaders of Protestantism.

On most important doctrines, Calvin stood very close to Luther. He adhered to the doctrine of justification by faith alone to explain how humans achieved salvation. But Calvin also placed much emphasis on the absolute sovereignty of God or the "power, grace, and glory of God."

Like other reformers, Calvin believed in predestination. Although it was but one aspect of his doctrine of salvation, predestination became the central focus of succeeding generations of Calvinists. This "eternal decree", as Calvin called it, meant that God had predestined some people to be saved and others to be damned.

Calvin identified three presumptive tests to assure his followers of their possible salvation: an open profession of faith, a "decent and godly life", and participation in the sacraments of baptism and communion. In no instance did Calvin ever suggest that worldly success or material wealth was a sign of election. Most importantly, although Calvin stressed that there could be no absolute certainty of salvation; his followers did not always make this distinction. The practical psychological effect of predestination was to give later Calvinists an unshakable conviction that they were doing God's work on earth. Thus, Calvinism became the militant international form of Protestantism.

The absolute sovereignty of God had another implication as well. If only God is sovereign. Then no human being, even a king, can lay claim to absolute power. Calvin separated church and state and gave to the state the duty to maintain peace and order including the prevention of public offenses against religion. Calvin followed Luther in calling for obedience to legally constituted governments. Even if the ruler wasn't unbridled despot, his subjects must "obey and suffer." Yet, Calvin foresaw instances in which obedience to a ruler might mean disobedience to God. In that case, he argued, we must follow the biblical injunction to "obey God rather than men". This resistance, however, was not to be undertaken by private individuals but by representative assemblies. Over the next seventy-five years, Calvinist minorities would use this suggestion by Calvin to justify armed rebellion in France, Scotland, the Netherlands, and England against "licentious kings" who persecuted their faith.

A third corollary of Calvin's emphasis on the absolute sovereignty of God was that God exerted his sovereignty through his church. The church, then, was a divine institution largely independent of state power. It had two primary functions; to preach the pure word of God and administer the sacrament of the Lord's Supper, but only in a spiritual sense. Christ is at the right hand of God, but to the believer, Christ is spiritually present in the Lord's supper. Finally, Calvin agreed with other reformers that the church had the power to discipline its members. This element seemed to get out of control at times when Calvin finally had the opportunity to establish his church in Geneva.

Up to 1536, John Calvin had essentially been a scholar. In that year, however, he found himself temporarily in Geneva where the local Protestant reformer, William Farrell, asked him to stay and assist in reforming the city. Calvin was reluctant to do so, wishing instead to pursue the quiet life of a scholar. But Farrell's warning that it was God's will persuaded Calvin to take up a ministry in Geneva that lasted until his death in 1564.

Calvin achieved his first major success when the city council accepted his new church constitution known as *the Ecclesiastical Ordinances* in 1541. This document established four orders or offices; pastors, teachers, elders, and deacons. The duties of the pastors or ministers were to preach the Gospel, administer the sacraments, and correct un-Christian behavior. To the teachers or doctors was given the responsibility to "instruct the faithful in sound doctrine, in order that the purity of the Gospel may not be corrupted." The elders or presbyters were laymen, chosen from and by the city magistrates, whose function was to maintain discipline: "to have oversight of the life of everyone, to admonish amicably those whom they see to be erring or to living a disordered life, and ... to enjoin fraternal corrections." The deacons were also laymen who were responsible for the care of the poor, widows, and orphans and the administration of the city's hospitals.

4.3.3 The Reformation in England

The English Reformation was initiated by an act of state. King Henry Ⅷ (1509—1547), with the approval of Parliament, severed the ties of allegiance that bound the church of England to the Roman Catholic church, establishing a national church and proclaiming himself to be the "supreme head" of the church in place of the pope.

At one time, such a Reformation in England would have been unthinkable. Antipapal feeling ran high since many Englishmen resented pope; influence in English affairs, especially in matters of taxation and justice, Anticlericalism was rife as people wealth in ostentatious extravagance. One layman charged that "these are not the shepherds, but the ravenous wolves going in shepherds' clothing, devouring the flock."

Anticlericalism and antipapal feelings were not the only manifestations of religioussentiment in early sixteenth-century England. A deep craving for spiritual expression fostered the spread of Lutheran ideas, encouraged in part by two different traditions of dissent. Heretical Lollardy, stressing the use of the Bible in the vernacular and the rejection of papal supremacy, continued to exert influence among the lower classes, while Christian humanism with its calls for reform influenced the English middle and upper classes. People influenced by Lollardy and Christian humanism were among the first to embrace Lutheran wrings when they began to arrive in England in the 1520s.

Despite these factors, there might not have been a Reformation in England if it had not been for the king and his consuming desire to divorce his first wife Catherine of Aragon.

Henry relied upon Cardinal Wolsey, the highest ranking English church official and lord chancellor to the king, to obtain an annulment of his marriage from Pope Clement Ⅶ. Normally, the pope might have been willing to oblige, but the sack of Rome in 1527 had made the pope dependent upon the Holy Roman emperor Charles B, who happened to be the nephew of Queen Catherine. Discretion dictated delay in granting the English king's request. Impatient with the process, Henry dismissed Wolsey in 1529.

Two new advisers now became the king's agents in fulfilling his wishes. These were Thomas Cranmer (1489—1540), who became archbishop of Canterbury in 1532, and Thomas Cromwell(1485—1540), the king's principal secretary after the fall of Wolsey. They advised the king to obtain an annulment of his marriage in England's own ecclesiastical courts. The most important step toward this goal was the promulgation by Parliament of an act cutting off all appeals from English church courts to Rome, a piece of legislation that essentially abolished papal authority in England. Henry no longer needed the pope to attain his annulment. He was now in a hurry, since Anne Boleyn had become pregnant and he had secretly married her in January 1533 to legitimize the expected heir.

In 1534, Parliament moved to finalize the break of the Church of England with Rome. The Act of Supremacy of 1534 declared that the king was "taken, accepted, and reputed the only supreme head on earth of the church of England". A position that gave him control of doctrine, clerical appointment, and discipline. Parliament also passed a Treason Act making it punishable by death to deny that the king was the supreme head of the church. These additional enactments by the Reformation Parliament nor only legalized church. These additional enactments by the Reformation Parliament nor only legalized Henry's actions and repudiated papal authority but created the "autonomous sovereignty of the English government". Few challenged the new order. One who did was Thomas More, the humanist and former Lord Chancellor, who saw clearly to heart of the issue. To accept the new settlement meant that "Therefore am I not bound... to conform my conscience to the Council of one realm against the general council of Christendom". As he proclaimed at his trial, More's conscience refused to accept the victory of the national state over the church; a Christian could not bow his head to a secular ruler in matters of faith. More was beheaded in London on July 6th, 1535.

Above all others, Thomas Cromwell worked out the details of the Tudor government's new role in church affairs based on the centralized power exercised by the king and Parliament. Cromwell came to the extravagant king's financial rescue with a daring plan for the dissolution of the monasteries. About four hundred religious houses were closed in 1536 and their land and possessions confiscated by the king. Many were sold to bobbies, gentry, and some merchants. The king received a great boost to his treasury as well as creating a group of supporters who now had a stake in the new Tudor order.

Although Henry Ⅷ had broken with the papacy, little change occurred in matters of doctrine, theology, and ceremony.

The last decade of Henry's reign was preoccupied with foreign affairs, factional intrigue, and a continued effort to find the perfect wife. In religious affairs, Henry managed to hold the Church of England in line with Catholic doctrine, but after his death the movement toward Protestantism grew much stronger under his successor, the son of his third wife, Jane Seymour, the underage and sickly Edward VI(1547—1553).

Since the new king was only nine years old at the time of his accession to the throne, real control of England passed to a council of regency guided by Edward's uncle, the duke of Somerset. Rather incompetent and incapable of handling the intricacics of royal administration complicated by conflicting aristocratic factions, Somerset was outmaneuvered by his archrival, the duke of Northumberland, and executed in 1551, Northumberland now assumed the leadership of the council of regency and became the virtual ruler of England.

Chapter 5 Modern Culture in the Age of Enlightenment

5.1 Western Culture in the 17th and 18th Century

5.1.1 Commercial and Economic Development

The decline in the available supply of gold and silver in the seventeenth century had created a chronic shortage of money that undermined the efforts of governments to meet their needs. The creation of new public and private bands and the acceptance of paper notes made possible an expansion of credit in the eighteenth century.

5.1.2 The New Political Power—Bourgeoisie

The Third Estate was composed of the bourgeoisie, peasants, and urban laborers. Although the bourgeoisie provided the leadership for the Revolution, its success depended on the support given by the rest of the Third Estate. The bourgeoisie consisted of merchant-manufacturers, wholesale merchants, bankers, master craftsmen, doctors, lawyers, intellectuals, and government officials below the top ranks. Although the bourgeoisie had wealth, they lacked social prestige. A merchant, despite his worldly success, felt that his occupation denied him the esteem enjoyed by the nobility "There are few rich people who at times do not feel humiliated at being nothing but wealthy." observed an eighteenth-century Frenchman.

Influenced by the aristocratic values of the day, the bourgeoisie sought to erase the stigma of common birth by obtaining the most esteemed positions in the nation and by entering the ranks of the nobility, whose style of life they envied. Traditionally, some bourgeoisie had raised socially either by purchasing a judicial or political office that carried with it a title of nobility or by gaining admission to the upper clergy and the officer ranks of the army. As long as these avenues of upward social mobility remained open, the bourgeoisie did not challenge the existing social structure, including the special privileges of the nobility.

But in the last part of the eighteenth century it became increasingly difficult for the bourgeois to gain the most honored offices in the land. Finding the path to upward mobility and social dignity blocked, the bourgeois came to resent a social system that valued birth more than talent. Increasingly, members of the bourgeoisie, imbued with the rational outlook of the Enlightenment, sought to abolish the privileges of birth and to open careers to talent.

Practical considerations of social prestige and economic gain, however, do not alone explain the revolutionary mentality of the bourgeoisie. When they challenged the Old Regime, the bourgeois felt that they wee fulfilling the ideals of the philosophers and serving all humanity. This idealism would inspire sacrifice and heroism.

5.2 The Enlightenment of the Western

5.2.1 The Development of Physical Science in Modern Times

In addition to the constitutional, demographic, political, economic, and international crises of the seventeenth century, we need to add an intellectual one. The Scientific Revolution questioned and ultimately challenged conceptions and beliefs about the nature of the external world and reality that had crystallized into a rather strict orthodoxy by the Late Greeks and Romans and grounded in Christian thought, the medieval worldview had become a formidable one. No doubt, the breakdown of Christian unity during the Reformation and the subsequent religious wars had created an environment in which Europeans had become accustomed to challenging both the ecclesiastical and political realms. Should it surprise us that a challenge to intellectual authority soon followed?

The Scientific Revolution brought Europeans a new way of viewing the universe and their place in it. The shift from an earth-century Enlightenment stands as the major force in the transition to the largely secular, rational, and materialistic perspective that has defined the modern Western mentality since its full acceptance in the nineteenth and twentieth centuries.

In one sense, the Scientific Revolution was not a revolution. It was not characterized by the explosive change and rapid overthrow of traditional authority that we normally associate with the word revolution. The Scientific Revolution did overturn centuries of authority, but only in a gradual and piecemeal fashion. Nevertheless, its results were truly revolutionary. While the Renaissance and Reformation might be viewed, as one historian of science has argued, as "a mere internal displacement within the system of medieval Christendom", the Scientific Revolution was the key factor in setting Western civilization along its modern secular and material path.

To say that the Scientific Revolution brought about dissolution of the medieval worldview is not to say that the Middle Ages was a period of scientific ignorance. Many educated Europeans took an intense' interest in the world around them since it was, after all, "God's handiwork" and therefore an appropriate subject for study Late medieval scholastic philosophers from Roger Bacon on had advanced mathematical and physical thinking in many ways, but the subjection of these thinkers to a strict theological framework. Unquestioning reliance on a few ancient authorities, especially Aristotle and Galen, limited where they could go. Many "natural philosophers", as medieval scientists were called, preferred refined logical analysis to systematic observations of the natural world. A number of historians have argued, however, that some of the natural philosophers developed ideas that came to friction in the seventeenth century. These historians have pointed out, for example, that Galileo's development of the science of mechanics was grounded upon the work of fourteenth-century scholastics. And yet, as other scholars have noted, there was still a great contrast between the "theoretical" approach of the scholastics and the "practical" experiments of Galileo that enabled him to make his case.

The historical debate over the issue of late medieval influence on the Scientific Revolution reminds us that historians have had a difficult time explaining the causes of the Scientific Revolution. They have pointed out, however, that a number of changes and advances in the fifteenth and sixteenth centuries may have played a major role in helping natural philosophers abandon their old views and develope new ones.

While medieval scholars had made use of Aristotle, Galen, and Ptolemy in Latin translations to develope many of their positions in the fields of physics, medicine, and astronomy, it was the Renaissance humanists who mastered Greek as well as Latin and made available new works of Galen, Ptolemy, and Archimedes as well as Plato and the pre-Socratics. These writings made it apparent that even the unquestioned authorities of the Middle Ages, Aristotle and Galen, had been contradicted by other thinkers. The desire to discover which school of thought was correct stimulated new scientific work that sometimes led to a complete rejection of the classical authorities. We know that Copernicus, for example, founder of the heliocentric theory, had read in Plutarch that

Phallus and a number of other ancients had believed that it was the earth and not the sun that moved.

Renaissance artists have also been credited with making an impacton scientific study. Their desire to imitate nature led them to rely upon a close observation of nature. Their accurate renderings of rocks, plants, animals, and human anatomy established new standards for the study of natural phenomena. At the same time, the "scientific" study of the problems of perspective and correct anatomical proportions led to new insights. "No painter," one Renaissance artist declared, "can paint well without a thorough knowledge of geometry." Renaissance artists were frequently called upon to be practicing mathematicians as well. Leonardo da Vinci devised "war machines" while Albrecht Diurer made designs for the fortifications of cities.

5.2.2 The Formation of Bourgeois' Ideology in Modern Times

With the exception of Machiavelli in the Renaissance and Thomas Hobbes and the republicans during the English Revolution, the Enlightenment produced the greatest originality in political thought witnessed in the West up to that time. Three major European thinkers and a host of minor ones wrote treaties on politics that remain relevant to this day: John Locke, *Two Treatises of Government* (1690); Baron de la Brede et de Montesquieu, *The Spirit of the Laws* (17480); and jean Jacques Rousseau, *The Social Contract* (1762). All repudiated the divine right of kings and were concerned with checking the power of monarchy; each offered different formulas for achieving that goal. These major political theorists of the Enlightenment were also aware of the writings of Machiavelli and Hobbes and, although often disagreeing with them, borrowed some of their ideas.

Machiavelli had analyzed politics in terms of power, fortune, and the ability of the individual ruler; he did not call in God to justify the power of princes or to explain their demise. Machiavelli had also preferred a republican form of government to monarchy, and his republican vision did not lose its appeal during the Enlightenment. Very late in the century, most liberal theorists recognized that the republican form of government, or at the least the virtues practiced by citizens in a republic, offered the only alternative to the corruption and repression associated with absolutist monarchy.

Enlightenment political thinkers were ambivalent toward much of the writing of Thomas Hobbes (1588—1679). All, however, liked his belief that self-interest is a valid reason for engaging in political activity and his refusal to bring God into his system to justify the power of kings. Hobbes said power did not rest on divine right but arose out of a contract made among men who agreed to elevate the state, and hence the monarch, to a position of power over them. That contract, once made, could not be broken. As a consequence, the power of the government, whether embodied in a king of a parliament, was absolute.

Hobbes published his major work, Leviathan, in 1651, soon after England had been torn by civil war; thus, he was obsessed with the issue of political stability. He feared that, left to their own devices, men would kill one another; the "war of all against all" would prevail without the firm hand of a sovereign to stop it. Hobbes's vision of human nature was dark and forbidding. In the state of nature, the original men had lived lives that could only have been "nasty, brutish, and short." Their only recourse was to set up a power over themselves that would restrain them. For Hobbes the state was, as he put it, a "mortal god", the only guarantee of peace and stability. He was the first political thinker to realize the extraordinary power that had come into existence with the creation of strong centralized governments. Most Enlightenment theorists, however, beginning with John Locke, denied that governments possessed absolute power over their subjects, and to that extent they repudiated Hobbes. Many European thinkers of the eighteenth century. Including Rousseau, also rejected Hobbes's gloomy view that human nature is greedy and warlike. Yet Hobbes lurks in the background of the Enlightenment. He is the first wholly secular political theorist and he sounded the death knell for theories of the divine right of kings. The Elightenment theorists started where he left off.

Probably the most widely read political philosopher during the first half of the eighteenth century was John Locke. His *Two Treaties of Government* was seen as a justification for the Revolution of 1688—1689 and the notion of government by consent of the people.

Locke's theory, in its broad outlines, stated that the right to govern derived from the consent of the governed and was a form of contract. When people gave their consent to a government, they expected it to govern justly, to protect their property, and to ensure certain liberties of the propertied. If a government attempted to rule absolutely and arbitrarily—if it violated the natural rights of the individual—it reneged on its contract and forfeited the loyalty of its subjects. Such a government could legitimately be overthrown. Locke believed that a constitutional government that limited the power of rulers was the best defense of property and individual rights. He also advocated religious toleration for those religious groups whose beliefs did not threaten the state. Locke denied toleration to Catholics because of their association with the Stuarts, and to atheists because their oaths to God could not be trusted. He also promoted the necessity for education, particularly for those who saw themselves as the natural leaders of society. And not least, he advocated commerce and trade as one of the foundations of England's national strength.

Late in the eighteenth century, Locke's ideas were used to justify liberal revolutions in both Europe and America. Indeed, the importance of Locke's political philosophy was not simply his recourse to contract theory as a justification of constitutional government; it was also his assertion that the community could take up arms against its sovereign in the name of the natural rights of liberty and property. Locke's ideas about the foundation of government had greater impact on the Continent and in America during the eighteenth century than they did in England.

Baron de la Brideet de Montequieu (1689—1755) was a French aristocrat who, like Voltaire, visited England late in the 1720s and knew the writings of Locke. Montesquieu had little sympathy for revolutions, but he did approve of constitutional monarchy. His primary concern was to check the unbridled authority of the French kings. In opposition to the Old Regime, Montesquieu proposed a balanced system of government, with an executive branch offset by a legislature whose members were drawn from the landed and educated elements in society. Montesquieu genuinely believed that the aristocracy possessed a natural and sacred obligation to rule and that their honor called them to serve the community. He also aimed to fashion a government that channeled the interests and energies of its people, a government that was not bogged down in corruption and inefficiency. In stressing the rule of law and the importance of nonmonarchical authority, Montesquieu became a source for legitimating the authority of representative institutions. Hardly an advocate of democracy, nonetheless Montesquieu was seen as a powerful critic of royal absolutism. His writings, particularly *The Spirit of the Laws*, established Montesquieu both as a major philosopher who possessed republican tendencies and as a critic of the Old Regime in France. Once again, innovative political thinking highlighted the failures of absolutist government and pointed to the need for some kind of representative assembly in every European country. In addition, Montesquieu's ideas on a balanced system of government found favor in the new American republic.

Not until the 1760s did democracy find its champion in Jean Jacques Rousseau (1712—1778). Rousseau based his politics on contract theory—the people choose their government and, in so doing, effectively give birth to civil society. But Rousseau further demanded that the contract be constantly renewed and that government be made immediately and directly responsible to the will of the people. *The Social Contract* opened with this stirring cry for reform: "Man is born free; and everywhere he is in chains," and went on to ask how that restriction could be changed. Freedom is in the very nature of man: "to renounce liberty is to renounce being a man, to surrender the rights of humanity and even its duties."

In *The Social Contract*, Rousseau tried to resolve the conflict between individual freedom and the demands of the state. His solution was a small state, modeled after the Greek city-state. Such a state, said Rousseau, should be based on the general will which is best for the community, which expresses its common interests. Rousseau wanted laws of the state to coincide with the general will; he felt that people have the wisdom to arrive at laws that serve the common good, but to do so they have to set aside selfish interests for the good of the community. For Rousseau, freedom consisted of obeying laws prescribed by citizens inspired by the general will. Citizens themselves must constitute the law-making body; law making cannot be entrusted to a single person or a small group.

For Rousseau, those who disobey laws—who act according to their private will rather than in accordance with the general will as expressed in-law-degrade themselves and undermine the community. Therefore, government has the right to force citizens to be obedient—to compel them to exercise their individual wills in the proper way. Rousseau believed that government has the right to force freedom. But he did leave the problem of minority rights unsolved.

No philosopher of the Enlightenment was more dangerous to the Old Regime than Rousseau. His ideas were perceived as truly revolutionary—as a direct challenge to the power Kings, churches, and aristocrats. Although Rousseau thought that many leaders of the enlightenment had been corrupted by easy living and the life of the salons, with their attendant aristocrats and dandies, he nevertheless earned an uneasy place in the ranks of the philosophers. In the French Revolution, his name would be invoked to justified democracy, and of all the philosophers, Rousseau would probably have been the least horrified by the early phase of that revolutionary upheaval.

The Enlightenment's emphasis on property as the foundation for individual rights and its search for uniform laws inspired by Newton's scientific achievement led to the development of the science of economics. Appropriately, that intellectual achievement occurred in the most advanced capitalistic nation in Europe, Great Britain. Not only were the British in the vanguard of capitalist expansion; by the third quarter of the eighteenth century, which expansion had bought on the stat of the Industrial revolution. Its new factories and markets for the manufacture and distribution of goods provided a natural laboratory where theorists, schooled in the Enlightenment's insistence on observation and experimentation, could observe the ebb and flow of capitalist production and distribution. In contrast to its harsh criticisms leveled against existing institutions and old elites, the Enlightenment on the whole approved of the independent businessman—the entrepreneur. And there was no one more approving than Adam Smith (1732—1790), whose *Wealth of Nations* became a kind of bible for those who regarded capitalist activity as uniformly worth-while, never to be inhibited by outside regulation.

Throughout the seventeenth century in England there had been along tradition of economic thought. The resulting ideology stressed independent initiative and the freedom of market forces to determine the value of money and the goods it can buy. By 1700, English economic thought was already well ahead of what could be found on the Continent, with the exception of some Dutch writings. That sophistication undoubtedly reflected the complexity of market life in cities like London and Amsterdam.

One important element in seventeenth-century economic thought, as well as in the most advanced thinking on ethics, was the role of self-interest. Far from being viewed as crude of socially dangerous, it was seen as a good thing, to be accepted and even encouraged. In the mid-seventeenth century, Hobbes took the view that self-interest lay at the root of political action, and by the end of the century, Locke argued that government, rather than primarily restraining the extremes of human greed and the search for power, should first reflect the interests of its citizens. By the middle of the eighteenth century, enlightened theorists all over Europe—especially in England, Scotland, and France—had decided that self-interest was the foundation of all human actions and that at every turn government should assist people in expressing their interests and thus in finding true happiness.

5.2.3 Literature in the Age of Enlightenment

Pope was the great poet and verse satirist of the 18th century. This so-called "Augustan Age" in English literature produced no greater satirical poetry than that of Alexander Pope, and no other poet in the history of English literature had handled the heroic couplet with comparable flexibility and brilliance. Pope became renowned for his translations of Homer and for his biting counterattacks on the criticisms of his literary enemies. He represented the rationalistic neoclassical tendency in literature and has often been called the spokesman I verse of the Age of Reason. He wrote many works, but he is chiefly remembered for the following titles: *Essay on Criticism*, *The Rape of the Lock*, *Dunciad*, and *Essay on Man*.

In 18th century England, two writers must be mentioned as far as the periodical essay is concerned: Joseph Addison (1672—1719), an essayist, poet and statesman and, Richard Steele (1672—1729), an essayist, dramatist and politician. Both Addison and Steele contributed to *The Tatler* (1709—1711) and *The Spectator* (1711—1712), two series of periodical essays, which dealt with almost all the aspects and types of character in the town life of the times, in an attempt to reform the manners of the age. These essays had strong influence on the English writing style in those days, as Samuel Johnson said: "Whoever wishes to attain an English style, familiar but not coarse, and elegant but not ostentatious, must give his days and nights to the volumes of Addison."

In German, Lessing—a philosopher, dramatist, and critic—was the first dramatist of lasting importance and the most brilliant representative of the German Enlightenment. He stood on the threshold of the Storm and Stress movement, and his works reveal the two guiding principles of his own life-truth and reason. *Minna Von Barnhelm* (1767) was his most brilliant dramatic work.

Immanuel Kant was the key figure of the German classical philosophy. He is sometimes called the "waterhead of modern philosophy." He proposed the well-known "nebular hypothesis" and offered an analysis of speculate and moral reason and the faculty of human judgment. He exerted an immense influence on the intellectual movements of the 19th and 20th centuries. No other modern philosopher has been so widely studied as he was, or is subject to so much debate among rival interpreters. Kant started as a natural scientist. His major works are: *General History of Nature and theory of the heavens, Critique of Pure Reason, Critique of Practical Reason, and Critique of Judgment.*

Chapter 6 Western Culture in Industrialization

6.1 Technological Progress and Industrialized Society

If we speak of western culture in industrialized period, we must firstly talk about the Industrial Revolution. The process of Industrialization began from Western Europe for a number of reasons. Western Europe was wealthier than much of the world, and its wealth was spread across more classes of people. This wealth and accumulated slowly over the centuries, despite the devastations of famine, plague, and war. The widespread production of diverse rural handicrafts, such as weaving, leather tanning. Jewelry making, for the preceding two centuries provided the foundation for the comparatively rapid expansion of trade, both overseas and on the continent, during the 16th and 17th centuries. This expansion resulted from an aggressive search for new markets rather than from new methods of production; it built on the capitalist practices of medieval and Renaissance bankers and merchants, and tapped the wealth of much larger area of the world than the Mediterranean lands accessible to earlier generations. Thus the resources of the New World and of Africa, both human and material, fueled Europe's accumulation of wealth. Western agriculture, which differed from that of the Orient in many ways, also contributed greatly to the coming of the industrial age in Europe. Western agriculture was comparatively thrifty of land, capital, and human labor. Grain crops could grow on lands that varied in fertility and contour and did not require the costly irrigation ditches, dam, and canals of rice cultivation. Over the centuries, the decline of serfdom and manorial obligations and the increasing efficiency of agriculture freed people from new forms of labor, there was no development in Western Europe of state power comparable to that of Canada or Russian, which kept labor tied to the land.

6.1.1 The Inventions in Industry

The Industrial Revolution brought a change from handicrafts to machine manufacture and from human or animal power to other forms of energy, such as steam and the internal combustion engine. This important technological inventions in this period brought immense influence to the Europe and ultimately the world.

1. Development of the Steam Engine

The invention and perfection of the steam engine provided a dependable and efficient source of power for the new industrial machinery.

About 1700, Thomas Savery, an English inventor, built a practical steam pump. A few years later, Thomas Newcomen (1663—1729) built a steam engine that was first used in 1712 to pump water from a coalmine. Although it was wasteful of fuel, the Newcomen steam engine met a need, and by 1760 about one hundred Newcomen engines were operating in Great Britain.

In 1769, James Watt (1736—1819) patented a more efficient version of the Newcomen engine. Watt's steam engine required substantially less fuel.

While most of the early steam engines were used to pump water, by 1800 several hundred steam engines powered machinery in cotton textile mills and other factories.

2. The Revolution in Transportation

(1) Roads and Canals

The revolution in transportation began with improvements in road construction and the expansion of canal systems. About 1815, John McAdam (1756—1836), a Scotsman, developed a durable road surface made of crushed stones cemented by stone dust and water. These macadam roads, as they were known, represented a marked improvement over the dirt roads then generally in use. Extensive canal systems were built in both Europe and America. In 1869, the great Suez Canal, linking the Mediterranean Sea with the Indian Ocean by way of the Red Sea, was opened to shipping.

(2) Railroads

The development of the steam engine and improvements in the quality of iron led to the creation of railroads. For several generations, horse-drawn carts, operating on wooden rails, had been used to move coal and iron. During the eighteenth century, iron replaced wood for both the rails and the wheels of the carts.

The next step was to develop a steam-powered locomotive to pull the carts. George Stephenson (1781—1848), a British inventor, was the first to develop an economically successful locomotive. In 1825, a Stephenson locomotive was put into operation on the world's first real railroad, running some forty miles from the coalfields around Darlington in northern England to the port of Stockton. In 1830, Stephenson's famous locomotive, the

Rocket, demonstrated its speed on the new Liverpool to Manchester railway, running twelve miles in fifty-three minutes.

A great boom: railroad construction began. In 1830, only a few miles of railroads were in operation. By 1870, European railway mileage totaled almost 900,000.

(3) Electricity and Petroleum

Thomas A. Edison (1847—1931):

In 1879, the American genius Edison developed the first successful incandescent electric light bulb. In 1882, he designed a plan for the construction of central electric power stations. The major urban centers of America and Europe soon became electrified, and electric light replaced kerosene and gas lighting. Electricity was used increasingly to power industrial machinery.

(4) The Use of Oil for Power

The first commercially important oil well was drilled in Pennsylvania in 1859, and petroleum gradually began to be used instead of coal to power steam engines. In 1892, Rudolf Diesel (1858—1913), a German inventor, patented an engine that burned oil directly in its cylinders to produce power, instead of using it to make steam. Diesel engines were far more efficient than coal-burning steam engines, although they did not come into wide-spread use until after World War Ⅰ.

3. The Revolution in Communications

Innovations introduced during the nineteenth century made rapid long-distance communication possible for the first time in human history.

(1) The Telegraph

In 1836, Samuel F. B. Morse (1791—1872), an American, invented the telegraph and eight years later, in 1844, sent a message from Washington to Baltimore. In 1851, a telegraph cable was laid the first successful transatlantic cable joining the United States and Great Britain.

(2) The Telephone

In 1876, Alexander Graham Bell (1847—1922), an American, invented the telephone, and the Bell Telephone Co. was founded the following year. In 1884, telephone service began between New York and Boston, and by the 1890s, a telephone network was taking shape in Europe.

(3) The Radio

During the 1890s, Guglielmo Marconi (1874—1937), an Italian inventor, began experiments in wireless telegraphy. In 1899, Marconi sent a message across the English

Channel and 1901, across the Atlantic Ocean. Radio, the wireless transmission of voices and music, developed on the eve of World War Ⅰ, based largely on research undertaken by Sir John A. Fleming (1849—1945), an Englishman, and Lee de Forest (1873—1961), an American. Regularly scheduled radio broadcasting began in the years following World War Ⅰ.

6.1.2 The Development of Natural Science

The climax of a century of advances in all fields of science came in the discoveries of the great physicists between 1890 and 1914, which destroyed the very concept of nature as described by laws that scientists like Newton had so successfully uncovered.

In the early nineteenth century the scientific field in which the most significant break thought occurred was chemistry, largely because of refinements in laboratory experimentation. Chemists like the French pioneer Antoine Lavoisier and the English experimenter Joseph Priestley concentrated on Aristotle's theory that matter comprised four elements, and they were able to prove, that phenomena such as burning and rusting involved a combination of some element with oxygen. And the scientists were successfully beginning to draw up a list of the basic chemical elements.

After 1800, however, a major advance was made by considering the elements as composed of atoms. John Dalton, an English schoolteacher, was correct in assuming that future progress lay in ascertaining the exact atomic weight of the different elements, although he mistakenly assumed that the simplest compound of two elements would contain only one atom of each element. During the following sixty years, chemists were able to designate the atomic makeup of a large number of compounds, both by letters and by structures based on grouping of the atoms in the molecule. High explosives evolved through the discovery of nitrocellulose in 1846. Organic chemistry was one basic force in industrial progress in the second half of the nineteenth century.

Equally important advances were made in the study of energy. In the eighteenth century, scientists had been unable to find the connection between heat, light, electricity, and magnetism. Instead, they assumed that heat, electricity, and so on were substances-material fluids that flowed in and out of other material substances but were weightless. At the end of the eighteenth century, Rumford was able to show that heat in unlimited quantities could be produced by friction, and that since matter cannot be produced limitlessly, heat cannot be matter. By the 1830s it was generally conceded that light was not a substance but rather wave motion of energy. And in the 1840s, through the work of an English physicist, James Joule, and a German, Hermann von Helmhotz, the convertibility of one form of energy into another, such as electricity into another, but the total amount of energy in the world will always remain the same. And it reached its most effective use in the twentieth century with the harnessing for destructive as well as peaceful uses of the energy contained within the atom.

Advances in biology in the mid-nineteenth century caused a public furor because they challenged the description of creation given in the *Bible* in the Book of *Genesis*—that the earth and all the living things were created by God in six days.

With the fast development of natural science, great changes have taken place in western countries at the end of the 18th century and at the beginning of the 19th century, and it also indirectly implicates a greater challenge in western society.

6.1.3 Transformation of the Society

The change in agricultural production, business organization, and technology had revolutionary consequences for society. People were drawn from the countryside into cities and from one country to another. Traditional ways of life changed for Europeans.

European society before industrialization was based on kinship. Property in the form of land formed the basis of social class and social power, which was usually exercised on a local or provincial level. Industrialization brought a new world with many forms of property and several kinds of power, and the nation ultimately became more important than the province, region, or local area. In its new world, individuals were increasingly important than the province, region, or local area. In this new world, individuals were increasingly important before the law, in trade and in political thought, but in trying to make their way through day-to-day adversity they came to feel small, powerless, and isolated-cut adrift from families and villages. In a sense, the breakdown of family and town controls made individuals freer, but towns and families had offered irreplaceable support in time of need, such as unemployment of illness.

1. Cites grew in number, size, and population as a result of industrialization.

No longer just seats of government and commerce, manufacture and industry as well. Before 1800, about 10 percent of the European population lived in cities. Halfway through the nineteenth century, 52 percent of the Britain lived in cities, although only 25 percent of the French, 36 percent of the Germans, 7 percent of the Russians, and 10 percent of U S. inhabitants did. Most of the shift from rural to urban living in Europe's urban population during the 1800s was acute in its influence.

Industrial cities in the nineteenth century, particularly in England, grew rapidly, without planning or much regulation by locator national governments. Government and business were often reluctant to use taxation to finance remedies for poor working and living conditions. Civic pride and private patronage were too weak to cobalt the effects of unregulated private enterprise. On the European continent, where industrialization came later, states were more willing to regulate industrial and urban development; they also had the bureaucracy for planning and regulation, but such efforts were still inadequate. So much growth with little planning or controlled to cities with little sanitation, no lighting, wretched housing, poor transportation, and little security. Cities had grown without planning before, but they had not been home and workplace for such large numbers of people, many of them new arrivals. Rich and poor alike suffered in this environment of disease, cried, and ugliness, although the poor obviously bore the brunt of these evils.

2. Change in Social Structure

The Industrial Revolution destroyed forever the old division of society into clergy, nobility, and commoners. The development of industry and commerce caused a corresponding development of a bourgeoisie, a middle class comprised of people of common birth who engaged in trade and other capitalist ventures. The middle class was made up of several economic layers. The wealthiest bourgeois were bankers, factory and mine owners, and merchants but the middle class also included shopkeepers, manages, lawyers, and doctors. The virtues of work, thrift, ambition, and caution characterized the middle class as a whole, as did the perversion of these virtues into materialism, selfishness, callousness, harsh individualism, and smugness.

From the eighteenth century on, as industry and commerce developed, the middle class grew in size, first in England and then throughout Western Europe. But its increase did not automatically bring increased power. The Industrial Revolution had begun in a pre-industrial, agrarian society characterized by centuries, old political organizations and social classes.

During the nineteenth century, the social changes resulting from industrialization brought the middle class greater power and social respectability. By the end of the century, bourgeois politicians held the highest offices in much of Western Europe and shared authority with aristocrats, whose birth no longer guaranteed them the only political and social power in the nation.

Although the urbanization of Europe and America had barely begun, people were aware of the problems of industrialization and were trying to adopt reform measures. Sometimes the social thought of liberals, conservatives, and radicals was brilliantly prescient about the problems facing modern industrial society. But some social thinkers were nostalgic for the good old days when "a master knew his man" and both had obligations to one another. Faith in progress, inspired in part by the achievements exhibited in the Great Exhibition, convinced other reformers that they could develop the tools to resolve the era's problems. Still others, "revolutionary realist" as they liked to call themselves, distrusted the sentimental social thinkers and the believers in progress, though the realist incorporated in their vision of the future a romantic nostalgia for working conditions that had not existed for more than a century. Yet these social thinkers of the nineteenth century supplied the ideas and analysis with which, until deep into the twentieth century, men and women tried to understand and to mold their industrializing world.

6.2 Thoughts in Industrialized Society

The history of 19th century Europe was to a great extent shaped by the interplay of the forces of thoughts, mainly liberalism, conservatism and so on. The people of France, England, Germany, Italy, Poland, and the Austrian Empire espoused a set of doctrines reflecting their concerns and interests In this part, we shall exam the western thoughts in Industrialization.

6.2.1 Conservatism and Liberalism

1. Conservatism

The post-revolutionary period also permeate philosophy and political thought, particularly conservatism and liberalism. To the traditional rulers of Europe, kings, aristocrats, clergy, the French Revolution was a great evil that had had inflicted a near-fatal wound on civilization. Disgusted and frightened by the revolutionary violence, terror, and warfare, the traditional rulers sought to refute the philosophers' world-view that had spawned the revolution. To them, natural rights, equality, the goodness of man, and perpetual progress were perverse doctrines that had produced the Jacobin "assassins." In conservatism they found a political philosophy to counter the Enlightenment Ideology.

Edmund Burk's *Reflections on the French Revolution* (1790) was instrumental in shaping conservative thought. Burke (1729—1797), a British philosophy and statesman, wanted to warn his countrymen of the dangers inherent the ideology if the revolutionaries. Burke developed a coherent political philosophy that served as a counterweight to the ideology of the Enlightenment and the Revolution.

To conservatives, who like the romantics venerated the past, this was supreme arrogance and wickedness. They regarded the revolutionaries as presumptuous men who recklessly severed society's inks with ancient institutions and traditions and condemned venerable religious and moral beliefs as ignorance.

For conservatives, human beings wren to by nature good. Human wickedness was not due to a faulty environment, as the philosophers had proclaimed, but was at the core of human nature, as Christianity taught. Evil was held in check not by reason but by tried and tested institutions, traditions, and beliefs.

For conservative, God and history were the only legitimate sources of political authority; states were not made but were an expression of the nation's moral, religious, and historical experience. No legitimate or sound constitution could be drawn up by a group of assembled people for that purpose. Scraps of paper with legal terminology and philosophic visions could not produce an effective government; instead, a sound political system evolved gradually and inexplicable in response to circumstances.

For conservatives, society was not a machine with replaceable parts but a complex and delicate organism, tamper with its vital organs, as the revolutionaries had done, and it would die. Conservatism pointed to a limitation of the Enlightenment. It showed that human beings and social relationships are far more complex than the philosophers had imagined. People do not always accept the rigorous logic of the philosopher and are not eager to break with ancient ways, however illogical they appear to the intellect. The granite might of tradition remains an obstacle to all the visions of reformers.

2. Liberalism

The decades after 1815 saw a spectacular rise of the bourgeoisie. Talented and ambitious bankers, merchants, manufactures, professionals, and officeholders wanted to break the stranglehold that the landed nobility, the traditional elite held in political power and social prestige; they also wanted to eliminate restrictions on the free pursuit of profits.

The political philosophy of the bourgeoisie was most commonly liberalism. While conservatives sought to strengthen the foundations of traditional society, which had been severely shaken in the period of the French Revolution and Napoleon, liberalism. While conservatives sought to strengthen the foundations of traditional society, which had been severely shaken in the period of the French Revolution and Napoleon, liberal wanted to alter the status quo and to carry out the promise of the Enlightenment and the French Revolution. Conservatives extolled the community, but liberals gave central concern to individual freedom. Conservatives tried to preserve a social hierarchy based on inherited aristocracy, but liberals insisted that a person's value was measured not by birth but by achievement. Conservatives held that the state rests on tradition, but liberals sought the rational state in which political institutions and procedures were based on intelligible principles. Conservatives wanted individuals, inherently evil, to obey their betters. Liberals, on the other hand, had confidence in the capacity of individuals to control their own lives.

In the long view of Western civilization, liberalism is an extension and development of the democratic practices and rational outlook that originated in ancient Greece. The French philosophers were instrumental in the shaping of liberalism. From Montesquieu, liberals derived the theory of the separation of powers and of checks and balances, principles intended to guard against autocratic government. The American and French revolutions were crucial phases in the history of liberalism.

The liberal's primary concern was the enhancement of individual liberty. They agreed with the German philosopher Immanuel Kant that every person exists an end in himself or herself and not as an object to be used arbitrarily by others. If uncovered by government and churches and properly educated, a person could develop into a good, productive, and self-directed human being. People could make their own decisions, base actions o universal moral principles, and respect one another's rights.

In the tradition of the philosophers, liberals stressed the pre-eminence of reason as the basis of political life. Unfettered by ignorance and tyranny, the mind could eradicate evils that had burdened people for centuries and begin an age of free institutions and responsible citizens. For this reason, liberals supported the advancement of education.

Liberals attacked the state and other authorities that prevented the individual from exercising the right of free choice, that interfered with the right of free expression, and that prevented the individual from self-determination and self-development. They agreed with John Stuart Mill, the British philosopher, who declared that "over his won body and mind, the individual is sovereign... that the only purpose for which powered can be rightly exercised over any member of a civilized community, against his will, is to prevent harm to others."

6.2.2 Liberals' Economic Theory and Malthus' *An Essay on the Principle of Population*

Liberals held that the economy, like the state, should proceed according to natural laws rather than the arbitrary fiat of rulers. Adopting the laissez-faire theory of Adam Smith, they maintained that a free economy, in which private enterprise was unimpeded by government regulations, was as important as political freedom to the well-begin of the individual and the community. When people acted from self-interest, the liberals said, they worked harder and achieved more; self-interest and natural competitive impulses spurred economic activity and ensured the production of more and better goods at the lowest possible price, thereby benefiting the entire nation. For this reason, the government must neither block free competition nor deprive individuals of their property, which was their incentive to work hard and efficiently. The state contributed to the nation's prosperity when it maintained domestic order; it endangered economic development when it tampered with the free pursuit of profits. Believing that individuals were responsible for their own misfortunes, liberals were often unmoved by the misery of the poor and they considered social reforms to alleviate poverty as unwarranted and dangerous meddling with the natural laws of supply and demand.

Two attitudes emerged from liberal economic principles, one optimistic, hoping for the expansion of human productivecapacities and the end of want; and the other pessimistic, predicting a cycle of increasing pressure on scarce resources and deepening competition among workers for the necessities of life. For the first half of the nineteenth century, Thomas Malthus (1766—1834), author of *An Essay on the Principle of Population*, had an impact as great as Adam Smith's on the lives of workers and the thought of reformers. Malthus argued that population increased would outstrip increases in food productions, which suggested that the poverty of the working class was permanent, Malthus reasoned that if wages were raised, workers' families would grow and the extra wages would be used to support the added members. This doctrine was called Malthusianism and seemed to supply "scientific" justification for opposing governmental action to aid the poor. Poverty, argued Malthusians, was an iron law of nature, the result of population pressure on resources; it could not be eliminated by government reforms.

Economist David Richard (1772—1823) used Malthus's idea to form another theory that also made poverty seem inevitable and irremediable. Wages, he said, tend to remain at the minimum needed to maintain workers. An increase in wage encouraged laborers to increase their families. As the supply of workers increased, competition for jobs also increased, causing wages to decline. Richard's disciples made his law inflexible—an "Iron Law of wages" offered dismal prospects.

Many workers felt the new science of economics offered little hope for them. They argued that the liberals were only concerned with their class and national interests, that they were had, callous, and apathetic toward the sufferings of the poor. The liberals responded that the cure for the evils of industrialization was more industrialization.

6.2.3 Utopian Socialism

The socialist movement either in the form of communism or social democracy has been one of the major political forces twentieth-century Europe but 150 years age it had no significant following. Early socialists often applauded the productive capacity of industrialism while denying that the free market could adequately produce and distribute goods. An unregulated industrial system, they believed, resulted in mismanagement, low wages, poor tribulation, and widespread suffering. Socialists proposed that human society be organized as a community, not a community, not an aggregate of atomistic, selfish individuals.

6.2.4 Classical Philosophy in France

France has a long and quite distinctive history of philosophy. With the English Revolution of 1640, the British Empiricists were free from the bounds of feudalism long before the French Revolution (1789) and the French began with a strongly Rationalist philosophy, but in preparing for the violent overthrow of the French aristocracy, the French bourgeoisie drew heavily on their British counterparts, particularly John Locke and David Hume, in the form of Sensationalist philosophy and overtly wielded the weapon of Reason and knowledge in their struggle against the autocracy. Thus the French were the first to disclose the social character of knowledge, and seizing power in the Revolution the French bourgeoisie attempted to apply reason to society, legislation Rousseau's contract social. Thus in France philosophy and politics have always been closely linked and it was in France that the beginnings of Socialist theory arose.

The French poet, dramatist, historian, and philosopher, was an outspoken and aggressive enemy of every injustice such as tyranny, bigotry, cruelty, but especially of religious intolerance. He was noted for his characteristic wit, satire and critical capacity.

His works are an outstanding embodiment of the principle of the French Enlightenment. Of all his writings, two books must be mentioned here.

Letters Anglaise : a product of the author's years of exile in England has been called "the first bomb dropped on the Old Regime".

Candid(1758) is the most famous of Voltaire's novels. It is a satire on the previous adventure novels of the age, an attack upon the claims of unlimited optimism. It is the story of a nave and innocent young man who becomes gradually disillusioned. The family teacher was always telling him that the world they live in was the best of all possible worlds. But he was turned out of the castle for falling in love with the baron's daughter. Through misfortunes and hardships in this word. He realized that the secret of happiness is to "cultivate one's garden."

In his early writing, Rousseau contended that man is essentially good, a "noble savage" when in the "state of nature", and that good people are made unhappy and corrupted by their experiences in society He viewed society as "artificial" and "corrupt" and that the furthering of society results in the continuing unhappiness of man. Rousseau's essay, *Discourse on the Arts and Sciences* (1750), argued that the advancement of art and science had not been beneficial to mankind.

Perhaps Rousseau's most important work is *The Social Contract* that describes the relationship of man with society. Contrary to his earlier work, Rousseau claimed that the state of nature is brutish condition without law or morality, and that there are good men only a result of society's presence. *The Social Contract* is the "compact" agreed to among men that sets the conditions for membership in society.

Rousseau was one of the first modern writers to seriously attack the institution of private property, and therefore is considered a forebear of modern socialism and communism. Rousseau also questioned the assumption that the will of the majority is always correct. He argued that the goal of government should be to secure freedom, equality, and justice for all within the state, regardless of the will of the majority.

Rousseau's ideas about education have profoundly influenced modern educational theory. He minimizes the importance of book learning, and recommends that a child's emotions should be educated before his reason. He placed a special emphasis on learning by experience.

6.3 Romanticism and Realism

Romanticism was a movement in literature, philosophy, music and art that developed in Europe in the late 18th century and early 19th century. Literature took the full force of Romanticism. It brought a full flowering of literary talents. Later, realism as a literature movement began. These two periods' literature had their own characteristics and achievements.

6.3.1 Traits and Achievement of Romantic Literature

The essence of romanticism is particularly difficult to describe because romanticism is much more conned with broad general attitudes than with specific stylistic features.

Second, emphasis on emotion rather than intellect led to the expression of subjective rather than objective visions; after all, the emotions known best are the ones we have experienced.

This in turn produced a third attitude of romanticism: its love of the fantastic and the exotic, which made it possible to probe more deeply into an individual's creative imagination.

A fourth characteristic is a mystical attachment to the world of nature that was also the result of the search for new sensations.

German literature had a strong romantic strain. The storm and stress movement prepared the way for European Romanticism. *The Tower Fighter* of Johann Wolfgang von Goethe spans the transition from neoclassicism to romanticism in literature like a colossus. So great was the range of his genius that in the course of along and immensely productive life he wrote works in a bewildering variety of styles. One of the first writers to rebel against the principles of neoclassicism. He used both poetry and prose to express the most turbulent emotions. The climax of his life is represented by his novel—*The Surrows of Young Werther*. In the years around the turn of the century, he wrote the classical drama *Iphigeneia in Tauris*. He was best known for the work *Faust*. Like Goethe, Schiller started as a Romantic. In his first play *The Robbers*, he expressed a strong resentment against the repressive feudal rule, but I was *Love and Intrigue* that mad him the best dramatist for the "Storm and Stress" idea. In this tragedy, Schiller gave full voice to his thoughts of idealism, his longing for freedom and love.

The second wave of romantic writers appeared in Germany was the Schlegel brothers, August W. von Schlegel's greatest achievement was in the field of translation. Friedrich von Schlegel attempted to do away with the distinctions between different modes of writings, blending poetry, criticism, oratory and philosophy into a whole. And Heinrich Heine's *Book of Songs* was a lyric poetry combined natural imagery with a mixture of sentiment and irony.

The most influential romantic poet was Walt Whitman, his *Leaves of Grass* was the product of American Romanism peak, and other outstanding writers were Aleksander Pushkin in Russian, Adam Micliewicz in Poland.

6.3.2 Traits and Achievement of Realistic Literature

Realism, the dominant movement in literature in the mid-19th century, opposed the romantic veneration of the inner life and romantic sentimentality. The romantics' exalted passion and intuition let their imaginations transport them to a presumed idyllic medieval past, and sought subjective solitude amid nature's wonders. Realists, on the other hand, were preoccupied with the external world, with social conditions and contemporary manners, with the familiar details of everyday life. With clinical detachment and meticulous care, they analyzed how people looked, worked, and behaved. Like scientists, realist writers carefully investigated the empirical world. Romantic writers had written lyrics, for lyric poetry is the language of feeling; the novel, because it lends itself admirable to depicting human behavior and social conditions, was the literary genre used by realist writers. Many realist novels were serialized in the inexpensive newspapers and magazines that the many newly literate common people could read. Thus the commoners' interests helped to shape the content of the novels. Seeking to portray reality as it is, realist writers frequently dealt with social abused and the sordid aspects of human behavior and social life.

Realism literature reflects a social reality whose phenomena serve as a model for the work of art, there alist gives a complete and correct account of observed social reality, and thus is able to uncover the driving forces of history, the principles governing social change. It became clear to some of the realists, however, as they attempted to represent the "real world" in art, that all they could represent was what structuralism theorists call a "reality effect": that they were using language, that is, a symbol system, and that they were placing humans in complex systems of social relations and of material conditions which could be represented only by signs, and then only briefly and selectively.

The period of realism in England literature corresponds roughly to the latter half of the reign of Queen Victoria, and this is the period when England was at the peak of its power. Charles Dickens, the son of an impoverished government clerk, captured the public and dumbfounded the critics with *Pickwick Papers*. After writing the historical novel, *A Tale of Two Cities*, he devoted himself to the novel of social conditions, an indictment of the society in his time. He wrote *Oliver Twist*, *A Christmas Carol*, *Hard Times* and *Bleak House* has the most intricate, complicated plot, while *Hard Times* gives an intensely focused picture of an English industrial town in the heyday of capitalist expansion. His best book was *David Copperfield*, a kind of autobiographical romance, in which his power over our everyday emotion is unrivalled. Of the first rank among Victorian novelists, George Eliot's masterpiece *Middlemarch* is regarded by some critics as the finest English novel of the 19th century; *The Mill on the Floss* evokes the freshness of the novelist's own childhood and its unsatisfied need for love. Together with her other novels Adam Bede and Silas Marker, it established her as a novelist of warm sympathy for the humble and is grace. Hardy was a solitary man, the most important of his classically constructed tragic novels are: *Far from the Madding Crowd*, *The Return of the Native*, *The Mayor of Caster bridge*, *Tess of the D' Urbervilles*, and *Jude the Obscure*. George Gerard Shaw won the Nobel Prize in 1925, and his plays cover a wide range of modes; *Heartbreak House*, about the decadence of pre-war English society; the romantic historical drama St. Joan; the philosophical *Man and Superman*; the tragic *The Doctor's Dilemma*; and a examination of monarchy, *The Apple Cart*. His best comedies include *Pygmalion and Major Barbara*.

The beginning of modern Russian literature is to be traced to the Napoleonic wars. People expressed themselves in the form of literature which became the voice of the people. Nikolai Gogol was the first master of fiction in Russia to leave romantic conventions and to life for his subjects. His main works were: *The Inspector general*, *Dead Soul*.

After the American Civil War, a new generation of writers grew up in literary world. Harriet Beecher Stowe's *Uncle Tom's Cabin* was acclaimed the greatest of all antislavery manifestoes. Mark Twain was the pioneers of realms in the United States. With the publication of *The Celebrated Jumping Frog of Calaveras Country*, he was famous as humorist and storyteller. Mark twin was justly called "the Lincoln of American Literature", his novel, *The Adventures of Huckleberry Finn*, *The Adventures of Tom Sawyer*, *The Prince and the Pauper*. One of the greatest realists of all, the Angle-American novelist Henry James, drew much inspiration from his mentors, Eliot and Howells. James' concern with character motivation and behavior led to the development of subgenera, the psychological novel. He was hailed as "the Master beyond all masters." His works included *The Portrait of a Lady*, *The Passionate Pilgrim and other stories*, *Daisy Miller*, *The Gold Bow.* Some of his long short stories such as *The beast in the Gungle* are also superb.

6.3.3 The Arising of the American National Literature

The early history of the art in America was intimately linked to developments of Europe. England, in particular, by virtue of its common tongue and political connections, exerted an influence in literature that even the War of Independence did not end. American writers sought publishers and readers there, and molded their style on that of English writers, and some went to Europe to study, sometimes with less than happy results. In the case of literature, the French Revolution provided a change of direction, for revolutionary ties inevitably resulted in the importation of neoclassicism into America. With the dawning of the Romantic Era, however, American writers for the first time gave an authentic voice of their own.

In a land where daily existence was lived so close to the wildness and beauty of nature, the romantic attachment to the natural world was bound to make a special appeal. The romantic concept of the transcended unity of humans and nature was quickly taken up in the early 19th century by a whole group of American writers who even called themselves the Transcendentalists. Borrowing ideas from Kant and from his English followers such as Coleridge and Wordsworth, they developed notions of an order of truth that transcends what we can perceive by our physical senses and which unites the entire world. One of their leading representatives, Ralph Waldo Emerson (1803—1882), underlined the particular importance of the natural world for American writers in his essay *The American Scholar*, first published in 1837. In calling for the development of a national literature, Emerson laid down as a necessary condition for its success that his compatriots should draw their inspiration from the wonders of their own country.

Emerson always tried to make his own work "smell of pines and resound with the hum of insects", whose masterpiece *Walden* (1854) uses his day-to-day experiences as he lived in solitude on the shore of Walden Pond to draw general conclusions about the nature of existence. Thoreau's passionate support of the freedom of the individual led him to active in the antislavery movement, and by the end of his life he has moved from belief in passive resistance to open advocacy of violence against slavery.

Ideas of freedom, tolerance, and spiritual unity reached their most complete poetic expression in the works of America's first great poet, Walt Whitman (1819—1892). His first important collection of poems was published in 1855 under *The Title Leaves of Grass*. From then until his death he produced edition after edition, retaining the same title but gradually adding many new poems and revising the old ones.

The essential optimism of the transcendentalists, especially as interpreted by Whitman, is absent from the work of the two great American novelists of the 19th century, Nathaniel Hawthorne (1804—1864) and Herman Melville (1819—1891), Hawthorne in particular was deeply concerned with the apparently ineradicable evil in a society dedicated to progress. In *The Scarlet Letter* (1850), his first major success, and in many of his short stories he explored the conflicts between traditional values and the drive for change.

Melville imitated Hawthorne's example in combining realism with allegory and in dealing with profound more issues. His subjects and style are both very different, however. *Moby Dick* (1851), his masterpiece, is often hailed as the greatest of all American works of fiction. It shares with Goethe's *Faust* the theme of the search for truth and self-discovery, which Melville works out by using the metaphor of the New England whaling industry. Both Melville and Hawthorne were at their greatest when using uniquely American settings and characters to shed light on universal human experience.

6.4 Music in Romantic Era

A few general observations may be made about the technical differences between Romantic and Classic music. Long sections, even entire movements may continue in one unbroken rhythmic pattern, with the monotony and, when successful, the cumulative effect of an incantation. Highly developed Classic genres, like the symphony or sonata by Chopin of Schumann, for example, is like novel by Tiech or Novalis, a series of picturesque episodes without any strong bond of formal unity within the work. Quite often, however, a Romantic symphony or oratorio achieved a new kind of unity by using the same themes, identical or transformed, in different movements. The Romantic treatment of shorter forms is usually quite simple and clear.

6.4.1 Music in Romantic Era

1. Beethoven

For many of the romantics, music was the supreme art. Free from the intellectual concepts involved ill language and the physical limits inherent in the visual arts, it was capable of the most wholehearted and intuitive expression of emotion. Since Ludwig van Beethoven(1170—1827), widely regarded as the pioneer of musical romanticism, also manifested many characteristically romantic attitudes, such as love of nature, passionate belief in the freedom of the individual, and fiery temperament, it is not surprising that he has come to be regarded as the prototype of the romantic artist. When he wrote proudly to one of his most loyal aristocratic supporters—"There will always be thousands of princes, but there is only one Beethoven", he spoke for a new generation of creators.

Although Beethoven's music served as the springboards for the Romantic Movement in music, his own roots were deep in the classical tradition. He pushed to the limits classical forms like the sonata allegro. In spirit, furthermore, his work is representative of the Age of Enlightenment and the revolutionary mood of the turn of the century, as is proved by both the words and music of is opera *Fidelio*, *Op. 72. A* complex and many-sided genius, Beethoven transcended the achievements of the age in which he was born and set the musical tone for the 19th century.

One of the first pieces to express the characteristically Beethovenian spirit of rebellion against Fate and the determination to struggle on is his *Piano Sonata NO. 8 in C minor*, *Op.* 13, generally known as the "Pathetique". As is often the case, the significance of Beethoven's music is as easy to grasp on hearing as it is difficult to express in words. The heavy, foreboding chords seem to try to pull themselves up, only to fall back again and again in defeat, until finally they culminate in a burst of defiant energy that sets the main allegro portion of this movement on its stormy way. Just before the very end of the movement the ghost of the slow introduction returns briefly, as if to emphasize the odds against which the struggle has been—and will be—waged.

It is important to understand precisely how Beethoven used music in a new and revolutionary way. His music tells us how he feels, what his succession of moods is, and what conclusion he reaches. It does other things at the same time, and at this early stage in his career for the most part it self-consciously follows classical principles of construction, but the vivid communication of personal emotions is its prime concern. That Beethoven's range was not limited to anger and frustration is immediately demonstrated by the beautiful and consoling middle slow movement of the "Pathetique", with its lyrical main theme, but the final movement returns to turbulent passion.

Parallels for the turbulent style of the "Pathetique" can be found in other contemporary arts, especially literature, but although to some extent Beethoven was responding to the climate of the times, there can be no doubt that he was also expressing a personal reaction to the terrible tragedy that had begun to afflict him as early as 1796 his hearing had grown very weak, and by 1802 he was virtually totally deaf.

Nonetheless, although obviously affected by his condition. Beethoven's music was not exclusively concerned with is own fate. The same heroic attitude with which he faced his personal problems was also given universal expression, never more stupendously than in the *Symphony No.* 3 subtitls *The Eroica*, *The Heroic Symphony*. As early as 1799 the French ambassador to Vienna had suggested that Beethoven write a symphony in honor of Napoleon Bonaparte. But in 1804, the year of its completion, Napoleon had himself crowned Emperor. When Beethoven heard the news he angrily crossed out Napoleon's name on the title page. The first printed edition, which appeared in 1806, bore only the dedication "to celebrate the memory of a great man."

The second movement of the Eroica is a worthy successor toes the first. A funeral march on the same massive scale, it alternates a mood of epic tragedy, which has been compared with the impact of the works of the Greek playwright Aeschylus, with rays of consolation that at times achieve a transcendental exaltation.

The third and fourth movements relax the tension. For the third, Beethoven replaces the stately minuet of the classical symphony with a scherzo, the word literally means joke and is used to describe a fast-moving, generally lighthearted piece of music. The last movement is a brilliant and energetic series of variations on a theme Beethoven had composed a few years earlier for a ballet he had written on the subject of Prometheus, who defied the ancient gods by giving mortals the gift of fire, for which he was punished by Zeus, a final reference to the heroic mod of the entire work.

6.4.2 Program Music

Program music is music intended to evoke extra-musical ideas, images in the mind of the listener by musically representing a scene, image or mood. The term is almost exclusively applied to works in the European classical music tradition, particularly those from the Romantic music period of the 19th century, during which the concept was popular, but pieces that fit the description have long been a part of music. The term is usually reserved for purely instrumental works, and not used, for example, for Opera or Lieder.

6.4.3 National Music

Nationalism as a force in nineteenth-century music is a complex phenomenon, the nature of which has often been distorted. A sense of pride in a language and its literature was an ingredient in the national consciousness that led to the unification of Germany and Italy. Up to a point, the choice of subject matter by Wagner and Verdi was a reflection of their patriotic feelings, but neither one was narrowly national in this respect. Verdi, as we saw, became a symbol for national unity, but this was for reasons other than the character of his operas. Neither of these composers cultivated a style that could be identified as ethnically German or Italian. Brahms made arrangements of German folksongs and wrote melodies that resemble folksongs; Haydn, Schubert, Schumann, Strauss, Mahler, all consciously made use of folk idioms, not always the folk idioms of their own native countries. The Polish elements in Chopin, of the Hungarian-Gypsy ones in Liszt and Brahms were for the most part exotic accessories to fundamentally cosmopolitan styles. Nationalism was not really an issue in their music.

In England, France, United States, Russia, and the countries of Eastern Europe, where the dominance of German music was felt as a threat to indigenous musical creativity, the search for an independent, native voice was one facet of nationalism. Another was the ambition of composers to be recognized as equals of those in the Austro-German orbit. These aspirations were often in conflict. The best way to gain recognition, particularly at home, was to imitate the foreign composers and to compete with them on their terms. Products of this kind of imitation were also most exportable, but they lacked ethnic identity. By employing native folksongs and dances or imitating their character in originally inverted music one could develop a style that had ethnic identity but might notes acceptable to traditional audiences and the European public in general. Still, music that had a national color was often found attractive because of novel exotic elements.

6.5 Painting in Nineteenth Century of the West

The political revolution in France, the Napoleonic glory and the subjugation of other European countries in its wake, the movement for independence in Europe and elsewhere left their unmistakable marks on the paintings of the period. Just as there was an obvious reaction against the established order in all phases of life, there was in the artistic world an effort to be free from traditional authority. Artists regarded themselves as their own masters, choosing for themselves new messages and inventing dozens of new styles. Here was a generation of artist who chose real events as subjects for their paintings and introduced into the artistic world an element of realism that was never found on former ages.

6.5.1 Romanticism

Just as Beethoven and his Romantic successors rejected the idealizing and universal qualities of classical music to achieve a more intense and personal communication, so painters began to abandon the lofty, remote world of neoclassical art for more vivid images. In the case of painting, however, the question of style was far more related to political developments. Neoclassicism had become, as it were, the official artistic dress of the Revolution, so it was not easy for a painter working in France, still the center of artistic life, suddenly to abandon the revolution style. The problem is particularly visible in the works of Jacques Louis David(1748—1825), whose *Oath of the Horatii* had been inspired by the pre revolutionary longing for austere Republican virtue. By the end of the Revolution, David had come to appreciate the averages of peace. The subject is drawn from Roman mythology and focuses on that moment when Hersilia, wife of the Roman leader Romulus, interrupts the battle between Romans and Sabines and begs for an end to war. The style, however, remains firmly neoclassical, not only in the choice of subject but also in its execution. The two opponents, with their heroic figures and noble brows, are idealized along typically neo-classical lines. The emotional gestures of Hersilia and others are also stylized and frozen. The painting is powerful, but it depicts a concept rather than individual human feelings.

6.5.2 Realism

In 1855 two of the major works of Courbet for the Paris International Exhibition were rejected. The reason given was that the subjects and figures were too coarsely materialistic and too large. They were unsuitable for artistic representation. Courbet, rejected by the exhibition jury, set up his own gallery outside the grounds, and called it the Pavilion of Realism. With the unplanned collaboration of Millet and Daumier, Courbet challenged the whole world of stock classicism, and empty heroics that made up much of the Academy's art and summoned public attention to what the French poet and art critic Charles Baudelaire in 1846 called "the heroism of modern life."

The greatest French painters of the second half of the 19th century were realists, who used the everyday events of the world around them to express their views of live. One of the first realist artists was Honord Daumier (1808—1879), who followed the example of Goya in using his work to criticize the evils of society in general and government in particular. In *The Legislative Body*, or more accurately, Belly, he produced a powerful image of the greed and corruption of political opportunists that has lost neither its bitterness nor, unfortunately, its relevance.

Equally political was the realism of Gustave Courbet (1819—1877), a fervent champion of the working class, whose ability to identify with ordinary people won him the label of Socialist. Courbet tried to correct this political impression of his artistic and philosophical position in a vast and not entirely successful allegorical work, *The Studio*. Like Goya's royal portrait, the painting deliberately evokes memories of Velasquez' *Las Meninas*, although the artist is now placed firmly in the center of the picture, inspired by a nude model who may represent Realism or Truth.

Millet was born in the country and brought up in the fields. His works generally depict one or domestic toil. The atmosphere he created was calm, gentle and profound. In his paintings there was not the kind of brutality and vulgarity one finds in Courbet because Millet was completely outside the circle of politics. Millet's way of portrayal is close to sculpture, in which the eye, the nose and mouth do not have clear outline. *The Sower and Gleaners* are his famous works.

The two great American painters of the later 19th century, Winslow Homer (1836—1910) and Thomas Eakins (1844—1916), both used the luminist approach to realism as a basis for their own very individual styles. In the case of Homer, the realism of his early paintings was in large measure the result of his work as a documentary artist, recording the events of the Civil War. His style underwent a notable change as he became exposed to contemporary French impressionist painting. His mysterious Eagle Head is certainly far more than a naturalistic depiction of three women and a dog on a beach. By the way in which he has positioned the figures, Homer suggests rather than spells out greater emotional depths than initially meet the eye.

Thomas Eakins used realism as a means of achieving objective truth. His pursuit of scientific accuracy led him to make a particular study of the possibilities of photography. Animals and, more particularly, humans in motion continually fascinated him. This trait can be observed in *The Swimming Hole* where the variety of poses and actions produces a series of individual anatomical studies rather than a unified picture. In his own day Eakins' blunt insistence on accuracy of perception did not endear him to a public that demanded more glamorous art. In his portraits he returns the romantic tradition of expressing emotions by depicting g them. The sitter in *Miss Van Buren*, as in most of his portraits, turns her eyes away from us, rapt in profound inner contemplation. The artist's own emotional response to the mood of his subject is made visible in his painting.

Painters such as Homer and Eakins, and other writers discussed here, are important in the history of American culture not only for the value of their individual works. Their achievements demonstrated that American society could at last produce creative figures capable of absorbing the European cultural experience without losing their individuality. From this time on there could be no doubt that American artists and writers had their own distinctive contribution to make to the Western cultural tradition.

6.5.3 Impressionism

Impressionism was a form of artistic expression in the 19th century. It was most pervasive in painting, but is also found in literature and art. Impressionism in painting, which began in the mid-19th century Paris, was a school or movement only in a very general sense. It took its subject matter whenever I found it, usually in the, more public aspects of the middle class pleasures and distractions that became fashionable in the reign of the French Louis Napoleon. The artists frequented the scenes they portrayed: seaside resorts, forests and rivers, sidewalk cafes, racetracks, and the theatre and ballet. Freed from such authority of traditional themes as biblical, historical, or allegorical stories, the impressionists assumed a new and subjective position relate to their subject matter. The individual sensations of the artist under the influence of a specific transitory experience, such as a particular time of day or a condition of weather, became a dominant theme of the impressionists.

The term "impressionism" first appeared in 1847 in a newspaper review of an exhibition held in the studio by a group of young painters. It was taken directly from the title of Monet's *Impression: Sunrise* (1872). Between 1874 and 1886 the impressionists held their exhibitions in various art galleries in Paris. The chief characteristics of the impressionist style were first seen the Monet's landscapes in which the forms are broken by loose brush strokes and the colours of objects are reflected into other objects throughout the painting. By about 1880 a pervasive coloured atmosphere was dissolving objects into hovering and shimmering images.

In a sense, impressionists were realists, for they were determined to paint only what they saw, and they were vitally interested in the scientific interpretation of nature. But impressionist technique was different form that of the older realist painters, scenes from the world around them were not depicted as if the results of careful study. On the contrary, the works of impressionists sought to reveal immediate sense impressions, leaving it to the mind of the observer to fill in additional details. This often resulted in a type of work appearing at first glance to be non-naturalistic. Figures were commonly distorted; a few significant details were made to represent an entire object; and dabs of primary color were placed side by side without a trace of blending. Convinced that light is the principal factoring determining the appearance of objects, the impressionists left the studio for the woods and fields in an attempt to capture the fleeting alterations of a natural scene with each transitory shift of sunlight and shadow. From science they had learned that light is composed or a fusion of primary colors visible in the spectrum. Accordingly, they decided to use these colors almost exclusively. They chose, for example, to achieve the effect of the green in nature by placing daubs of pure blue and yellow side by side, allowing the eye to mix them.

Impressionism differs from realism in one other important respect. In these new paintings artists remained detached from their subject. They didn't paint to evoke pity, or to teach a lesson. They painted to proclaim the value and importance of painting as painting. In doing so, the artist was not deliberately setting out to exclude the viewers. It was clear, however, that the viewer must not expect to understand a painting except on the artist's terms. Probably the greatest of the impressionists were the Frenchmen Claude Monet(1840—1926) and Auguste Renoir(1841—1919). Monet was perhaps the leading exponent of the new mode of interpreting landscapes. His painting have little structure or design in the conventional sense; they suggest, rather than depict, the outlines of cliffs, trees, mountains. And fields. Intensely interested in the problem of light. Monet would to out at sunrise with a armful of canvases in order to paint the same subject in a dozen momentary appearances. It has been said in one of his masterpieces "light is the only important person in the picture." Renoir's subjects include not only landscapes but portrait and scenes fro contemporary life. He is famous for his pink and ivory nudes, which, as expressions of frank sexuality, represented and additional threat to middle-class sensibilities.

The freedom explicit in the work of the impressionists encouraged other upon the impressionists, objecting to their preoccupation with the momentary aspects of nature and their indifference of meaning. Expressionists wren to arguing a return to meaning in the sense of "message." They were instead insisting that a painting must represent the artist's particular intellect. Here again, they were making art a private matter, removing it yet another step from the public. The artist who laid the foundations of expressionism was Paul Cezanne(1839—1906), now recognized as one of the greatest painters who ever lived. A native of southern France, Cezanne labored to express a sense of order in nature that he believed the impressionists had ignored. To achieve this end, he painted objects as a series of planes, each plane expressed in terms of a color change. While Cezanne was in this way equating form with color, he also began to reduce natural forms to their geometrical equivalents, hoping thereby to express the basic shapes of existence itself. He distorted form into geometrical regality until abstraction became reality. In all this Cezanne was declaring the painter's right to recreate nature in such a way as t express an intensely personal vision.

In a word, the impressionists aimed at capturing the fleeting image of a scene taken in by the eye in real life and recreating the transitory experience with brush strokes which are eventually transformed into a web of infinitely varied, tiny units that dissolve solid objects into a dense, cored atmosphere. Specifically, the impressionist gaiters mad explorations in different directions, each creating distinct style of their own.

Chapter 7 Western Culture in the First Half of the 20th Century

As the world entered into the 20th century, the first single event of any significance it witnessed was a global disaster for mankind, World War I. It took place from 1914 to 1918. It began in Europe and was fought principally on that continent but eventually involved all the continents of the world. By the end of the war, on estimated 93% of the world's population was in some degree involved. Ten million people were killed or missing and many more were wounded during the war.

After the First World War, the problems of the capitalist world were far from being solved. On the contrary, economic crisis in all the imperialist countries deepened. All aspects of Western culture, including art, literature, theater, education and science were shaken and given new directions.

This worldwide economic disaster gave rise to a most ugly phenomenon, Hitler and his Nazi party came into power in Germany. The result was even more horrible and disastrous for mankind; The Second World War.

Fought between 1939 and 1945, World War II was the most destructive war in history. This time, the war was not confined to the European continent. Military operations were conducted also in Asia, Africa, and even on some Pacific islands. More than 17 million members of the armed forces of the various countries were killed. Although the war turned out to be a victory for democracy over fascism, it strained the economic capabilities of the major nations and left many countries on the verge of collapse.

7.1 Great Development of Science and Technology in the Early Age of the 20th Century

The beginning of the 20th century saw a rapid development in all fields of technology at a speed the world had never see. The highest point of the development was represented by Einstein, who revolutionized science with his theory of relativity, represented the highest point of this development.

7.1.1 Einstein and Relativity

Albert Einstein was born on March 14, 1879 in Ulm, Wurttemberg, Germany. Einstein contributed more than any other scientist since Sir Isaac Newton to our understanding of physical reality.

The most well known of these works in Einstein's 1905 paper proposing *The Special Theory of Relativity*. He based his new theory on the principle that the laws of physics are in the same form in any frame of reference. As a second fundamental hypothesis. Einstein assumed that the speed of light remained constant in all frames of reference.

1. Special Relativity

Einstein's *Special Theory of Relativity* describes the motion of particles moving at close to the speed of light. In fact, it gives the correct laws of motion for any particle. This doesn't mean Newton was wrong; his equations are contained within the relativistic equations. Newton's "laws" provide a very good approximate form, valid when V is much less than C. For particles moving at slow speeds, the differences between Einstein's laws of motion and those derived by Newton are tiny. That's why relativity doesn't play a large role in everyday life. Einstein's theory supersedes Newton's, but Newton's theory provides a very good approximation for objects moving at everyday speeds.

Einstein's theory is now very well established as the correct description of motion of relativistic objects, that is, those traveling at a significant fraction of the speed of light.

2. Theoretical Basis for Special Relativity

Einstein's theory of special relativity results from two statements—the two basic postulates of special relativity:

The speed of light is the same for all observers, no matter what their relative speeds.

The laws of physics are the same in any inertial frame of reference. This means that the laws of physics observed by a hypothetical observer traveling with a relativistic particle must be the same as those observed by an observer who is stationary in the laboratory.

Given these two statements, Einstein showed how definitions of momentum and energy must be refined and how quantities such as length and time must change from one observer to another in order to get consistent results for physical quantities such as particle half-life. To decide whether his postulates are a correct theory of nature. Physicists test whether the predictions of Einstein's theory match observations. Indeed many such tests have been made—and the answers Einstein gave are right every time!

Later in 1905 Einstein showed how mass and energy were equivalent expressing it is the famous equation: This equation became a cornerstone in the development of nuclear energy.

Einstein received the Nobel Prize in 1921 but not for relativity, rather for his 1905 work on the photoelectric effect. He worked on at Princeton until the end of his life on an attempt to unify the laws of physics. Why is he so important to the age? Not because he personified brainpower, not because he was "an Einstein", but rather because he demonstrated that the imagination is capable of coming to terms with experience. Simply by gazing into existence, he concluded that time and space could be warped. That mass and energy were interchangeable. He understood that the world was a puzzle created for deciphering and, more, that a person's place in the order of things was to solve as much of the puzzle as possible. This is what makes a human, and this is what makes the governing elements of morals and humor.

Einstein also contended that mass is a variable, with the mass of a body depending on its rate of motion. A body's mass increases as its speed increases with the speed of light providing a theoretical limit. In addition, Einstein proposed the idea of the equivalence of mass and energy, which he expressed in his famous formula $E = mc^2$. In this formula, E represents energy, while m is mass and c is the speed of light. According to this formula, if matter could suddenly be transformed into energy, only small quantity of matter world be required to produce a great quantity of energy. The concept received a practical expression in the first atomic explosion in 1945.

7.1.2 Planck and Quantum Theory

The German physicist Max Karl Ernst Ludwig Planck (1858—1947) developed the concept of the quantum, or fundamental increment of energy, basic to quantum mechanics, and a cornerstone of modern physics. After receiving his Ph. D. from the University of Munich in 1879, Planck taught at the University of Kiel (1885—1889) and the University of Berlin (1889—1926). His appointment at the latter institution included the directorship of the Institute of Theoretical Physics that was newly founded for him.

Planck began studying black body radiation in 1879 and discovered that at very short wavelengths it did not obey the distribution laws given by Wilhelm Wien. In trying to understand this spectrum suing Wien's laws, Planck ran smack into an "ultraviolet catastrophe." A black body would give off an infinite amount of energy at the ultraviolet end of the spectrum. That was impossible.

After working on this problem unsuccessfully for several years, he took a fateful step in late 1900 that he eventually called "an act of desperation." Planck cautiously proposed that, contrary to classical wave theory, matter emits and absorbs radiation in tiny discrete packets or bundles called "quanta"—not continuously, as everyone had assumed.

Initially Planck was not comfortable with this explanation and fully expected the idea to be disproved by further research. Instead quantum theory, which gained Planck the Nobel Prize for physics in 1918, was used by Albert Einstein to explain (1905) the photo electric effect and by Niels Bohr to propose (1913) a model of the atom with quantified electronic states; the theory was later developed into quantum mechanics. Understanding the implications of quantum mechanics leads directly to the development of atomic energy and the semiconductor industry.

Quantum theory is the theoretical basis of modern physics that explains the nature and behavior of matter and energy on the atomic and subatomic level. In 1900, physicist Max Plank presented his quantum theory to the German Physical Society. Planck had sought to discover the reason that radiation from a glowing body changes color from red, to orange, and, finally, to blue as its temperature rises. He found that by making the assumption that energy existed in individual units the same way that matter does, rather than just as a constant electromagnetic wave, as had been formerly assumed, and was therefore quantifiable, he could find the answer to his question. The existence of these units became the first assumption of quantum theory.

Max Planck made many contributions to theoretical physics, but his fame rests primarily on his role as originator of the quantum theory, which won him the Nobel Prize for Physics in 1918. This theory revolutionized our understanding of atomic and subatomic processes, just as Albert Einstein's theory of relativity revolutionized our understanding of space and time. Together they constitute the fundamental theories of 20th-century physics. Both have forced man to revise some of his most cherished philosophical beliefs, and both have led to industrial and military applications that affect every aspect of modern life.

7.1.3 Morgan's Genetics

Morgan, Thomas Hunt, American zoologist and geneticist, is famous for his experimental research with the fruit fly by which he established the chromosome theory of heredity. He showed that genes are linked in a series on chromosomes and are responsible for identifiable, hereditary traits. Morgan's work played a key role in establishing the field of genetics. He received the Noble Prize for physiology of Medicine in 1933.

Morgan apparently began breeding Drosophila in 1908. In 1909 he observed a small but discrete variation known as white-eye in a single male fly in one of his culture bottles. Aroused by curiosity, he bred the fly with normal females. All of the offspring were red-eyed. Brother-sister matins among the F1 generation produced a second generation with some white-eyed flies, all of which were males. To explain this curious phenomenon, Morgan developed the hypothesis of sex-limited, today called sex-linked characters, which he postulated were part of the X-chromosome of females. Other genetic variations arose in Morgan's stock, many of which were also found to be sex-linked. Because all the sex-linked characters were usually inherited together, Morgan became convinced that the X-chromosome carried a number of discrete hereditary units, or factors. He adopted the term gene, which was introduced by the Danish botanist Wilhelm Johannes in 1909, and concluded that genes were possible arranged in a linear fashion on chromosomes. Much to his credit, Morgan rejected his skepticism about both the Mendelian and chromosome theories when he saw from tow independent lines of evidence, breeding experiments and cytology, that one could be treated in terms of the other.

In recognition of his work on chromosomes, Morgan was awarded the Nobel Prize in Physiology of Medicine in 1933. The Nobel Prize recognized Morgan's two fundamental scientific contributions; the development of the chromosome theory of heredity, a theory of the gene that proved to be the driving biological concept of the twentieth century, and the creation of a new biology based on a rigorous experimental method.

7.2 Introvert Philosophy and Positive Philosophy

The 20th century brought with it upheavals that produced a series of conflicting developments within philosophy over the basis of knowledge and the validity of various absolutes. With classical certainties thought to be overthrown, and new social, economic, scientific, ethical, and logical problems, 20th-century philosophy was set for a series of attempts variously to reform, preserve, alter, abolish previously conceived limits.

New studies in philosophy of science, philosophy of mathematics, and epistemology furthered seemingly antagonistic tendencies in accounting for consciousness and its objects, as expressed in the profound differences between analytic and continental philosophy, both of which had foundations in place at the beginning of the century. Advances in relativity, quantum, and nuclear physics, generative sciences like cognitive science, cybernetic, genetics, and generative linguistics, rich literary output, and the emergence of the motion picture as an art form greatly enriched philosophical subject matter.

7.2.1 Schopenhauer(1788 –1860) and Nietzsche(1844—1900)

Schopenhauer, German post-Kantian philosopher, Schopenhauer's philosophical reputation has never been assured, either in his lifetime or in more recent thought, the prevailing and, in his view, partly through his trivalent attitude to academic philosophy in general. Yet there is some truth in his own belief that, o fall the post-Kantians, he provided the most lucid and penetrating development of Kant's philosophy.

Schopenhauer's earliest work was *Uber die vierfache Wurzel des Satzes vom zureichenden Grunde*(1831), a Kantian delimitation of the kinds of reasons legitimate in philosophical explanation of why anything is as it is. His major contribution was *Die Welt als Wille und Vorstellung* published in 1818 and again, in a considerably amplified edition, in 1844. Later work was largely an application of his ideas in the field of moral philosophy.

The essence of Schopenhauer's theory, which relates to Kant's division of the phenomenal and noumenal worlds, is that there are two aspects of the self: the self as it appears phenomenally as an object of perception and the self ways: for instance, in its antidualistic conception of man as a single entity viewed under the aspects either of body or of will; and—an idea which was to stimulate Feud—in its pessimistic emphasis upon the distorting and covert forces of the will. In this latter respect, a focal point of Schopenhauer's attention was art, conceived as the sole arena of human endeavor in which man may escape subjection to the will in free aesthetic contemplation.

Schopenhauer wrote elegantly, a style notably free of jargon and obscurity, and it was as an essayist, in his collection *Parerga und Paralipomena* (1851), that he first commanded wide attention. He subsequently attracted such figures as Tolstoy, Conrad, Proust, Mann, and Freud. It remains true, if regrettable, that Schopenhauer is still more often read for his cultivated aphoristic writings than for his metaphysics.

Friedrich wihelm Nietzsche is a German writer and philosopher born at Rochen, the son of a Lutheran pastor. Educated at the famous Schulpforta and at the Universities of Bonn and Leipzig, he was an outstandingly brilliant student, who at the age of 24 was appointed professor of classics at the University of Basel. Here Nietzsche had the historian Jacob Burchkhardt as a colleague and Richard and Cosima Wagner, who lived nearby, were among his friends. Recurrent psychosomatic illness forced him to give up his chair in 1879. He spent most of the next ten years at resorts in Italy, France, and Switzerland, trying to recover his health. He became insane in January 1889, after which his sister, Elizabeth, looked after him until his death in 1900. The following are the most significant of his numerous writings: *Die Geburt der Treagodie* (1872), *Unzeitgemasse Betrachtungen* (1873—1876), *Die Frohliche Wissenschaft* (1882), *Also Sprach Zarathustra* (1883—1892), *Jenseits Von Gut Und Bose* (1886), *Zur Genealogie der Moral* (1887), and *Der Antichrist* (1895).

In the English-speaking world Nietzsche has only rarely been considered an important philosopher. Instead, he is still popularly seen as, at best, an impressive aphorist whose psychological apercus partly anticipated the theories of Freud, and at worst, as one of the latest and perhaps the most inflammatory of a long line of German opponents of the ideals of liberal enlightenment. Nietzshe's ambiguous reputation is not undeserved In particular, his contemptuous dismissal of democracy in favor of the aristocratic ideal of the Ubermensch or overman; his atheism, expressed with unprecedented vehemence in *Der Antichrist*; his attacks on Christian and utilitarian ethics, notably in *Jenseits Vou Gut Und Bose* and *Zur Genealogie der Moral*; his stress, from the time of his first book—*Die Geburt der Tragodie*—on the unconscious, voluntaristic, orgiastic, and self-destructive sides of human nature, seemingly at the expense of the calm, conscious, individuated, and rational sides; to which might be added his non-squeamishly chauvinistic attitude towards women—all these elements in

Nietzsche's thought have acted as barriers to his obtaining anything like general acclaim in the English-speaking world.

For various reasons, Nietzsche is not to interpret objectively. In reading him due account has to be taken of the deceptively informal structure of his books, and of his manifold use of irony. His bold display of personal obsessions can easily lead one to forget that be can also think objectively and reason cogently. Nietzsche's delightful intimacy of tone, which unhappily degenerates into megalomania in later works, and his frequent shifts I mood and emphasis, are further characteristics that give his books a very special place in the modern literature of ideas. It is certainly a mistake simply to bracket Nietzsche with professional German philosophers. Because of their peculiarities of form and intention, Nietzsche's writings are best seen as belonging to the great tradition of European moral essayists and aphorists, beginning with Montaigne, continuing in the 17th and 18th centuries with writers like La Rochefoucauld and Vauvenargues, and later, during Nietzsche's formative years with the essays of Schopenhauer and R. W. Emerson. Nietzsche studied all these writers carefully and learned more form them than he ever did from, say, Kant or Hegel.

Although Nietzsche's books defy easy summary there are at least three central and closely connected areas of his thought that are of genuine philosophical interest.

7.2.2 Bergson(1859—1941)'s Life Philosophy

French philosopher who was awarded the Noble Prize for Literature in 1927, Bergson Henri argued that the intuition is deeper than the intellect. His *Creative Evolution*(1907) and *Matter and Memory*(1896) attempted to integrate the findings of biological science with a theory of consciousness. Bergson's work was considered the main challenge to the mechanistic view of nature. He is sometimes claimed to have anticipated features of relativity theory and modern scientific theories of the mind.

"In reality, the past is preserved by itself automatically. In its entirety, probably, it follows us at very instant; all that we have felt, thought and willed from our earliest infancy is there, leaning over the present which is about to join it, pressing against the portals of consciousness that would fain leave it outside." (From Creative Evolution)

"There is nothing in philosophy which could not be said in everyday language". Bergson told once in an interview. In spite of his good intentions, his ideas were often high-flown and difficult to follow. in his first major work, *Time and Free Will*(1889), Bergson aimed to show how pseudo-problems about the will and its freedom have arisen from a false phenomenology of mental states-essentially, a tendency to conceive and describe them in spatial terms. Human experience does not perceive real life as a succession of demarcated conscious states, progressing along some imaginary line, but rather a continuous flow. Bergson made the distinction between the concept and experience of time. While the physicist observes objects and events in succession, time is presented to consciousness as duration, not through separate operations of instinct and the intellect.

In *An Introduction to Metaphysics*, Bergson saw that the intuition, the direct apprehension of process, as the discoverer of truth-intuition, not analysis, reveals the real world. Sometimes intuition in Bergson referred to getting bright ideas; sometimes it was the method of philosophy like intellect is of mathematics. His concept of e lan vital, "creative impulse" of "living energy", was developed in Creative Evolution.

In 1914 all of Bergson's writings, but most especially *Creative Evolution*, were placed upon the list of books devout Catholics were forbidden to read. After its appearance twenty-five years elapsed before Bergson published another major work. *The Two Sources of Morality and Religion* (1932), Dealing with Einstein's theory of relativity. Bergson had opposed in 1911 Einstein's ideas, but then his view had changed and he introduce the concept of non-linear time. Bergson is generally regarded as having lost his public debate with Einstein, but some of the leading physicists have devoted articles to his work.

7.2.3 Freud(1856—1939)'s Psychoanalysis

All the major figures of late-nineteenth-century science, art, and philosophy were driven to probe beneath the surfaces of things of atoms, of reason, of codes of respectability, and of human relationships. Their work dispelled smugness and complacency, but it also undercut self-confidence; such was the effect of psychoanalysis. Most significant of all the developments the study of human behavior was the work of Sigmund Freud(1856—1939) and those influenced by him.

Sigmund Freud, a Viennese physician, founded psychoanalysis at the turn of the century. He came to believe the certain forms of emotional disturbance like hysteria were traceable to earlier forgotten episodes of patients' lives. After first trying various techniques such as hypnosis, which he soon abandoned, he employed free recall. If patients could be helped to bring these suppressed experiences into conscious recall, the symptoms of illness would often disappear. From these beginnings Freud and his followers explored the role that the unconscious played in all human behavior, he himself stressing the sexual drives. His books entitled *The Interpretation of Dreams*, *Three contributions to the Sexual Theory* and *The Ego and the Id* had a profound influence upon the modernist movement. In his theory, the unconscious in emphasized and human sexuality is given prime importance in analyzing human behavior. His discovery opened up a new dimension for the modernists, who later strove to explore this new "inner" reality in many of their works of art.

In 1900, Freud published his most important book, *The Interpretation of Dreams* (1900). It combined his theory of infantile sexuality with another idea; the psychic significance of dreams. He stressed dreams as a key to understand the subconscious. As a rationalist, Freud believed that apparently irrational phenomena, like dreams, must have reasonable, scientific explanations. He concluded that dreams are expressions of unconscious wishes, desires, and derives that waking consciousness suppressed. While awake, the mind censors, certain thoughts fundamental to an individual's psychological makeup, but during sleep it expressed them cloaked in symbols. Freud argued that these unconscious drives and desires were clues explaining certain conscious behaviors.

7.3 The Development of Economics

In the beginning, as the monologist scanning the slide would say, there was Marshall. Alfred Marshall occupied the heights of the late Victorian economics to the end of World War Ⅰ as firmly as Ricardo had been encamped between about 1820 and 1850, and as Keynes cornered the post-World War Ⅱ period. To be sure, there were delicate finishing touches to the opinions of the masters, and there were delicate finishing touches to the opinions of the masters, and there were rebellious streams. In the Marshallian age the pragmatic American empirical school made the deepest penetration, with the exemplary statistical studies of the disequilibrium cyclical economy under the skillful literary and technical wisdom of Wesley Clair Mitchell. Sustenance also came from the iconoclastic vim, over laden with a liberal dose of sarcasm, which flowed from the gifted pen of Thorstein Veblen, supported by the philosophic overtones of John Dewey. Historical and descriptive appraisals emerged from that other branch of American realism, namely the institutionalists, who may even again, on a new set of issues, be poised to launch a new assault on irrelevant theorizing. The earlier aversion to rigid and outdated theorizing drew some of its inspiration from the ascendant German Historical school of the Hohenzollern empire.

7.3.1 Marshall's Neoclassical Economics

Neoclassical economics is an approach to economics that relates supply and demand to an individual's rationality and his or her ability to maximize utility or profit. It also increased the use of mathematical equations in the study of various aspects of the economy. This approach was developed into the late-nineteenth century, based on books by William Stanley Jevons, Carl Menger and Leon Walras.

Recall that "improving the allocation of resources" is one of the five ways we might increase the wealth of a nation. "Allocation of resources" is a key concept especially for microeconomics. Almost all economists would agree that the allocation of resources is an important aspect of economic thinking and of real economic systems.

However, there has been a school of thought in economics in the twentieth century, enormously influential especially in the United States, for which the allocation of resources is more than just one of the considerations. This school of thought is called "neoclassical economics", and the "neo" means that they differ in important ways from the "classical economists" of the previous century.

Neoclassical economists share some of the following points in common.

1. For neoclassical economics, economics is the study of the allocation of resources. In this school of thought, economics is defined as "the study that considers human behavior as a relation between scarce means and alternative ends."

2. Almost all neoclassical economists are positive economists, though there are some positive economists who aren't neoclassical. Thus, neoclassical economists regard the study of the allocation of resources as essentially a scientific, not a normative, study.

3. Neoclassical economists believe that free markets usually bring about an efficient allocation of resources.

4. Conversely, efficient allocation is the important thing about free markets. In those more or less rare cases when markets "fail" to bring about an efficient allocation of resources, it is appropriate for the government to intervene to correct the situation. If it can.

With this strong focus on the allocation of resources and on the role of markets, neoclassical economists have indeed learned an enormous amount about these topics, and will have much to teach us. Neoclassical economists have led the way in clearing up some key concepts almost all economists would rely on.

7.3.2 Pigou's Welfare Economics

Arthur C. Pigou(1877—1959),a British economist,graduated from King's College, Cambridge. He was a lecturer at University College,London,and at Cambridge. He was professor of political economy at Cambridge from 1908 to 1943. Pigou taught straight Marshallian economics,often insisting to his students "it's all in Marshall." Pigou was throughout his life an avid free trader.

In 1908 he was appointed to Marshall's chair in economics at the age of thirty. He served as a member of the committee on currency and foreign exchange(1918)and of the royal commission on income tax(1919). He was a leading exponent of the theory that economic waste due to unemployment,poor health,and poor housing is a responsibility of society, which should bear the costs. Among his many works are *Wealth and Welfare* (1912), *The Economics of Welfare*(1920), *The Political Economy of War*(1921; new ed. 1941), *The Theory of Unemployment*(1933), *Socialism versus Capitalism*(1937), and *Income:An Introduction to Economics*(1946).

Pigou is best known for his work in welfare economics. In his book *The Economics of Welfare*, Pigou developed Alfred Marshall's concept of externalities, costs imposed or benefits conferred on others that are not taken into account by the person taking the action. He argued that the existence of externalities was sufficient justification for government intervention. The reason was that if someone was creating a negative externality, such as pollution, he would engage it too much of the activity that generated the externality. Someone creating a positive externality say, by educating himself and making himself more interesting to other people, would not invest enough in education because he would not perceive the value to himself as being as great as the value to society.

To discourage the activity that caused the negative externality, Pigou advocated a tax on the activity. To encourage the activity that created the positive externality, he advocated a subsidy. These are now called pigovian taxes and subsidies.

The Economics of Welfare occupies a privileged position in economics. It contributed to the professionalization of economics, a goal aggressively and effectively pursued by Pigou's predecessor and teacher Alfred Marshall, *The Economics of Welfare* also may be credited with establishing welfare economic, by systematically analyzing marker departures and their potential remedies. In writing *The Economics of Welfare*, Pigou built a bridge between the old and the new economics at Cambridge and in Britain. Much of the book remains relevant for contemporary economics. The list of his analyses that continues to play an important role in economics is impressive. Some of the more important include: public goods and externalities, welfare criteria, index number problems, price discrimination, the theory of the firm, the structure of relief programs for the poor ad public finance.

7.3.3 Keynesian Economics

Keynesian economics derives from the work of John Maynard Keynes (1883—1946), perhaps the most famous economist of the twentieth century and one of the greatest figures in the whole history of economic inquiry. His book, *The General Theory of Employment, Interest and Money*, published in 1935, revolutionized economic thinking in the field of macroeconomic theory and policy; that is, the theory of the working of the overall economy and of the policy measures to maintain economic stability. Although developments in economic thinking since his day have modified considerably his theoretical ideas and the policy implications that seemed to flow from them, the gist of his reasoning can still find echoes in contemporary economic discussion.

Keynesian economics is a theory of total spending in the economy and its effects on output and inflation. Although the term is used to describe many things, six principal tenets seem central to Keynesianism. The first three describe how the economy works.

1. A Keynesian believes that aggregate demand is influenced by a host of economic decisions—both public and private—and sometimes behaves erratically. The public decisions include, most prominently, those on monetary and fiscal policy. Some decades ago, economists heatedly debated the relative strengths of monetary and fiscal policy, wit some Keynesians arguing that monetary policy is powerless, and some monetarists arguing that fiscal policy is peerless. Both of these are essentially dead issues today. Nearly all Keynesians and monetarists now believe that both fiscal and monetary policy affect aggregate demand. A few economists, however, believe in what is called debt neutrality-the doctrine that substitutions of government borrowing for taxes have no effects ion total demand.

2. According to Keynesian theory, changes in aggregate demand, whether anticipated or unanticipated, have their greatest short-run impact on real output and employment, not on prices. This idea is portrayed, for example, in Phillips curves that show inflation changing only slowly when unemployment changes. Keynesians believe the short run lasts long enough to matter. They often quote Keynes's famous statement "In the long run, we

are all dead. " to make the point

Anticipated monetary policy can produce real effects on output and employment only if some prices are rigid—if nominal wages, for example, do not adjust instantly. Otherwise, an injection of new money would change all prices by the same percentage. So Keynesian models greatly either assume or try to explain rigid prices or wages. Rationalizing rigid prices is hard to do because, according to standard microeconomic theory, real supplies and demands do not change if all nominal prices rise of fall proportionally.

3. Keynesians believe that prices and, especially, wages respond slowly to changes in supply and demand, resulting in shortages and surpluses, especially of labor. Even though monetarists are more confident than Keynesians in ability of markets to adjust to changes in supply and demand, many monetarists accept the Keynesian position on this matter. Milton Friedman, for example, the most prominent monetarist, has written: "Under any conceivable institutional arrangements, and certainly under those that now prevail in the United States, there is only a limited amount of flexibility in prices and wages. " In current parlance, that would certainly be called a Keynesian position.

No policy prescriptions follow from these three beliefs alone. And many economists who do not call themselves Keynesian-including most monetarists would, nevertheless, accept the entire list. What distinguishes Keynesians from other economists is their belief in the following three tenets about economic policy.

7.3.4 Schumpeter(1883—1950)'s Capitalism, Socialism and Democracy

Schumpeter led a melodramatic life(1883—1950), moving from Austria to England to Egypt to Germany before coming to Harvard for good in 1932. He was a phenomenally productive scholar, despite occasional forays into business and government in addition to a plethora of romantic liaisons that included three marriages. His first published article appeared in 1905, his last in 1950. His output included fifteen books, six pamphlets, about one hundred book reviews, and 148 articles, comments, and occasional pieces.

Long after his death, his influence continues to grow. *Massimo M. Augello's Jaseph Alois Schumpeter: A Reference Guide* appeared in 1990 and ran to over 350 pages. Since then, several dozen articles on Schumpeter have appeared, in addition to biographies by Robert Loring Allen, Richard Swedberg, and Wolfgang Stolper. All of this work has enriched our knowledge of this remarkable polymath.

Many scholars of business history, most totally Alfred D. Chandler, Jr., have looked to Schumpeter as the economist who best understood the rise of big business and the central roles of innovation and entrepreneurship. In economic history, the work of Nathan Rosenberg and William Lazonick, among others, is imbued with Schumpeterian insights. In the study of "business strategy", a term probably coined by Schumpeter in Capitalism, Socialism and Democracy, Michael Porter's seminal work places a distinctly Schumpeterian emphasis on relentless innovation as the essence of competitive strategy. Within economics, Schumpeter's influence n America is perhaps best exemplified by the work of F. M. Scherer and Richard R. Nelson, Scherer, a prolific scholar and author of a standard textbook in industrial organization, acknowledges his intellectual debts in a book entitled Innovation and Growth: Schumpeterian Perspectives. Nelson's Schumpeterian proclivities are on display In An Evolutionary theory of Economic Change, co-authored with Sidney G. winter. A few other economists have tried to implement parts of the Schumpeterian system, particularly those having to do with innovation.

As a scholar Schumpeter never advanced a program of economic reform. He believed that doing so compromised "scientific" work. In particular he criticized Keynes and other English economists for their "Ricardian Vice" of leaping into policy debates with abstract models as general prescriptions for change.

Schumpeter's core argument in Capitalism, Socialism, and Democracy is reducible to three major tenets:

1. The essence of capitalism is innovation in particular sectors. Certain standard tools of economics, such as static equilibrium and macroeconomic analysis, can therefore disguise reality and mislead scholars and students.

2. The virtues of capitalism—in particular its steady but gradual pattern of growth are long-run and hard to see; its defects, such as inequality and apparent monopoly, are short-run and conspicuously visible.

3. It is dangerous for economists to prescribe "general" recipes, because political and social circumstances are always changing.

Capitalism, Socialism, and Democracy was Schumptpeter's most popular success by far. Translated into at least sixteen languages, it still sells widely in paperback editions. Although the author often compared it unfavorably with his more scholarly books, it retains its seminal quality three generations after it appeared.

Despite the book's title, it contains little of lasting interest about either socialism or democracy. But it bursts with ideas about capitalism, and as a "performance"—a term

Schumpeter liked to apply to others' works—it may be the best analysis of capitalism ever written.

7.4 Modernist Literature and Art in the West

Modernism has been called "the tradition of the new". It was characterized by a conscious rejection of established rules, traditions and conventions. It strove to reflect 20th century's social and political changes, and anxieties, its rapid growth in technologies and psychological knowledge. It provided fresh ways of looking at man's position and function in the universe.

Modernism has also been called the "dehumanization of art." It pushes into the background traditional humanistic notions of the individual and society. Yet, it is not divorced from the past. It restates, in new terms, the same questions about existence and human nature found in 19th-century works of art and literature.

However, not all the people discussed this part is modern in that sense, for the modern tradition is pluralistic, marked by different ways, experimental and traditional, in which it embodies 20th century experience. Modernist literature represents a broad plexus of concerns that are variably represented in 120 years of European writing, notably experimentation, anti-realism, individualism and intellectualism. Styles within the movement—if movement it was—have varied from the dense formalism of Robert Lowell and Hart Crane to conversational looseness in Marianne Moore and William Carlos Williams. Everyone has their favorites, but these may be the better known poets: Wallace Stevens, E. E. Cummings, W. H. Auden, William Empson, Elizabeth Bishop, John Berrymean Sylvia Plath, James Wright, and Ted Hughes.

7.4.1 Modernist Literature—Mirror of Western Society

Modernist literature was at its height from 1900 to 1940, and featured such authors as T. S. Eliot, James Joyce, William Faulkner, Franz Kafka, Virginia Woolf, W. B. Yeats, F. Scott Fitzgerald, Ezra Pound, Gertrude Stein, Mennoter Braak, Marcel Proust, Thomas Mann and Ernest Hemingway.

Modernist literature attempted to move from the bonds of realist literature and introduce concepts as disjointed timelines. Modernism was distinguished by emancipator metanarrative. In the wake of modernism, and post-enlightenment, metanarrative tended to be emancipator, whereas beforehand this was not a definite, the rise of trade unionism, and a general discontent. Something had to perform a unifying function, and this was the point when culture became politically important.

Modernist literature is defined by its move away from romanticism, venturing into subject matter that is traditionally mundane—a prime example being *The Love Song of J. Alfred Prufrock* by T. S. Eliot. Modernist literature often features a marked pessimism, a clear rejection of the optimism apparent in Victorian literature. In fact, "a common motif in modernist fiction is that of an alienated individual—a dysfunctional individual trying in vain to make sense of a predominantly urban and fragmented society." However, many Modernist works like T. S. Eliot's *The Waste Land* are marked by the absence of a central, heroic figure; I rejecting the solipsism of romantics like Shelley and Byron, these works reject the subject of Cartesian dualism and collapse narrative and narrator into a collection of disjointed fragments and overlapping voices.

Modernist literature goes beyond the limitations of the realist novel with its concern for larger factors such as social or historical change; this is largely demonstrated in "stream of consciousness" writing. Examples can be seen in Virginia Woolf's *Kew Gardens and Mrs*. Dalloway, James Joyce's *A Portrait of the Artist as a Young Man* and *Ulysses*, Katherine Porter's *Flowering Judas*, and others.

Many Modernist works are studied schools today, from Ernest Hemingway's *The Old Man and the Sea*, *as a Young Man*.

Modernism, as literary movement, is seen, in large part, as a reaction to the emergence of city life as a central force in society.

7.4.2 Symbolism Literature and T. S. Eliot(1888—1965)

The poetic scene of the first years of 20th century was dismal and uninspired. With Whitman and Dickinson dead, the field was strewn with pieces of poetry extremely moralistic, sentimental and imitative of what had gone before, This was the situation that prevailed in 1900—1910. There was obvious disaffection widely felt, especially among the younger generation, some events took place that helped toward the evolution of modern poetry. *The Symbolist Movement in Literature* (1899) by Arthur Symons, an English critic, was exerting a profound influence on T. S. Eliot, Ezra Pound and practically everybody else who was interested in new voices in poetry. The years 1912—1914 witnessed the appearance of all kinds of innovations. T. S. Eliot, like other new poets wrote a poetry that defied most of the accepted rules, and dealt with subjects which had not been dealt with except, perhaps, by Whitman, thus pushing the boundaries of poetry further back. And they wrote in new ways and techniques. These people were in effect creating a poetic revolution in America, and also a very large American poetry reading audience. Within a little over two decades, it scored a complete triumph over old poetry. Pound, Eloot, Williams, Stevens, Sandburg, E. E. Cummings and Hart Crane, to name just a few, all made their presence felt, and Eliot became, by 1925, the acknowledged leader of the new verse and criticism both in America and Great Britain.

Thomas Stearns Eliot, American—born English poet and critics, was paradoxically, the most modern and the most traditional, the most influential and the most influenced, of poets in the 20th century. He was awarded the Nobel Prize in 1948 for his contribution to modern poetry.

7.4.3 Expressionism and Kafka

Expressionism is a term used to describe works of art and literature in which the representation of reality is distorted to communicate an inner vision. The expressionist transforms nature rather than imitates it. In literature, expressionism is often considered a revolt against realism and naturalism. Seeking to achieve a psychological or spiritual reality rather than record external events in logical sequence. In the novel, the term is closely allied to the writing of Franz Kafka and James Joyce. The characters and scenes are presented in a stylized, distorted manner with the intent of producing emotional shock. The German painter Alfred Cubin, a member of Der Blaue Reiter, wrote one of the earliest expressionist novels, *Die Andere Seite*. He exerted a profound influence on the Czech novelist Franz Kafka and other writers. The early expressionist playwrights, August Strindberg of Sweden and Frank Wedekind of Germany, exerted an international influence on the next generation of playwrights. These included the Germans Georg Kaiser and Ernst Toller, the Czech Karel, and the Americans Eugene O'Neill and Elmer Rice. In the drama, Strindberg is considered the forefather of the expressionists, though the term is specifically applied to a group of early 20th-century German dramatists, including Kaiser, Toller, and Wedekind. Their work was often characterized by a bizarre distortion of reality. Playwrights not closely associated with the expressionists occasionally wrote expressionist drama, e. g. , Karel Capek's *R. U. R*(1921) and Eugene O'Neill's *The Emperor Jones*(1921). The movement, though short lived, gave impetus to a free form of writing and of production in modern theater.

Expressionist drama gave rise to a new approach to staging, scene design, and directing. The object was to create a totally unified stage picture that would increase the emotional impact of the production on the audience. Among prominent directors were the Germans Max Reinhardt and Erwin Piscator and the Russian Vsevolod Meyerhold. Set designers such as Edward Henry Gordon Graig of Britain and Robert Edmond Jones of the United States used techniques similar to those of expressionist painters to provide visual stimulation consonant with the dramas. Expressionist painting and drama also influenced the cinema, as can be seen in the German films *The Cabinet of Dr. Caligari* (1919), with its nightmarish perspectives and mask-like makeup, and *The Last Laugh* (1924), notable for the brilliant use of lighting and camera angles to convey the bitter story.

Franz Kafka(1883—1924), is an icon of dark existentialist and absurdist literature that often wrote about themes of isolation, alienation, and authoritarian oppression. His best-known work includes the short story *The Metamorphosis*, in which the main character transforms into a beetle, as well as *In the Penal Colony*, *The Hunger Artist*, and the novels *The Trial*, *The Castle*, and *The Unfinished America.* Also of note were the various autobiographical observations and literary ideas culled from his many journals as well as his famed "Letter to His Father", in which he attempted to explain their strained relationship and his emotional peculiarities.

Illness and physical limitation also plagued Kafka, yet another senseless extrusion of suffering which implied to him a callous universe or perverse creator. In addition to the tuberculosis that had first appeared in 1917, Kafka experienced frequent bouts of insomnia, migraine headaches, boils, constipation, and other ailments. He was a hypochondriac and possibly an anorexic, as his weight suffered wild fulgurations and his dietary peculiarities progressed through prodigious consumption of unpasteurized milk to a completely vegan diet.

Franz Kafka died in 1924 from complicationsrelated to tuberculosis. It has been noted that due to the great pain in his throat, from this condition, he was unable to eat and barely to drink in his last days. He often complained of thirst in his letters home to his father and at the end may have simply starved to death. His body is buried in Prague, in the Jewish section of the Strasnice cemetery. His mother and father are interred beside him. All three of his sisters were killed in Nazi concentration caps during World War Ⅱ.

7.4.4 "Stream of Consciousness" in Literature and Joyce

Stream of consciousness is a kind of narrative technique in non-dramatic fiction intended to render the flow of myriad impressions—visual, auditory, tactile, associative, and subliminal—that impinge of an individual consciousness. The term was first used by William James I *The Principles of Psychology* (1890) to describe the unbroken flow of thought and awareness of the waking mind. It is used to describe the narrative method where novelists describe the unspoken thoughts and feelings of their characters without resorting to objective description or conventional dialogue. To represent the mind at work. A writer may incorporate snatches of thought and grammatical constructions that do not seem coherent because they are based on the free association of ideas and images.

In the 20th century, writers attempting to capture the total flow of their characters consciousness commonly used the techniques of interior monologue, which represents a sequence of thought and feeling. Novels in which stream of consciousness plays an important role include James Joyce's *Ulysses* (1922), William Faulkner's *The Sound and the Fury* (1929), and Virginia Wolf's *The waves* (1931).

James Joyce, Irish writer, was perhaps the most important fiction writer in the 20th century, and the fountainhead of subjective movement of fiction. His works are characterized by experiment with language, symbolism and such narrative techniques as interior monologue and steam of consciousness.

An Irishman by birth, Joyce did not spend much time in that country. Upon graduation from the university, he went abroad and never returned. However, his country, family and church formed the basis on which he structured his art.

In 1916, Joyce wrote an autobiographical novel, *A Portrait of the Artist as a Young Man*. It projected the developing mind and consciousness of a certain Stephen Dedalus, who is shaped by his environment but at the same time rebels against it. It depicts Stephen in his immaturity, still trying to seek his identity. However, the depiction is done within the hero's mind. And the language in different parts of the book suits the different stages of the developing mind. This novel represented a turning point in modern English fiction.

Joyce's masterpiece is, however, *Ulysses* (1922). It is considered his most mature work and the single best fiction ever written since the beginning of the 20th century. The book had some censorship troubles but immediately became famous. The book's title alludes to Homer's epic *Odyssey*. He describes the event of a single day—June 16,

1904—in Dublin. In it Joyce used stream of consciousness skill profusely to depict the three main characters in great detail. Thematically, *The Odyssey* myth is employed to show modern man's voyage and adventures in life. Due to his innovations in narrative technique, the book is difficult to read. But an even more difficult book was to follow.

In 1939, Joyce's *Finnegans Wake* was published. In this book, Joyce was even more innovations. It is composed of many complex puns in more than 30 languages, and it is encyclopedic in allusions. Much research has been done on the interpretation of it in the West.

7.4.5 Lost Generation and Hemingway (1899—1961)

The term "lost generation", was coined by Gertrude Stein, a lost generation writer herself, in a remark to Ernest Hemingway. Group of U. S. writers who came of age during World War I and established their reputations in the 1920s; more broadly, the entire post-World War I American generation, is called Lost Generation. The writers considered themselves "lost" because their inherited values could not operate in the postwar world and they felt spiritually alienated from a country they considered hopelessly provincial and emotionally barren. Hemingway's book paints the image of a whole generation, the Lost Generation. This included the young English and American expatriates as well as men and women caught in the war and cut off from the old values and yet unable to come to terms with the new era when civilization had gone mad. The term embraces Hemingway, F. Scott Fitzgerald, John Dos Passos, E. E. Cummings, Archibald Macleish, and Hart Crane, among others.

Ernest Hemingway (1899—1961) novelist and short story writer was one of the most celebrated and influential authors of the 20th century. He was awarded the Nobel Prize in 1954 for his mastery of the art of modern narration.

Hemingway helped to accomplish a revolution in literary style and language. He tried to cut out all words that were not strictly necessary. His style is characterized by short and simple sentences with very few adjectives and adverbs. But they are full of emotion.

Hemingway wrote quite a few works of fiction, most of which are well known today. Among them are *The Sun Also Rises* (1926), *A Farewell to Arms* (1929), *For Whom the Bell Tolls* (1940) and *The Old Man and the Sea* (1952).

With the publication of *The Sun Also Rises*, Hemingway became the spokesman for what Gertrude Stein had called "a lost generation". The term was used to refer to the young men who survived the war physically but were afterwards spiritually and morally adrift. In this novel, he describes a group of Americans and Englishmen, who have suffered physically and emotionally during the war. Their aimless existence vividly expresses the spiritual bankruptcy and moral weakening of a entire generation.

Hemingway is probably one of the most celebrated authors of his time. Hemingway is well known for his fiction. His take on fiction is something invented or imagined. Main topics were centralized around his love of embellishment of the facts. Hemingway did not have the education as many other writers of his time, rebelling against his parents attempt to send him to colleges. His idea of education did not consist of lectures, and research papers, but of life experiences, and his love of reading. Hemingway's readings centered on Russian writers such as Tolstioy and Turgenev. Tolstoy was a primary influence in Hemingway's writings. WWI also had a profound impact on him as well, as he was an ambulance driver during the war. He hated the abstract, especially abstract words such as honor, glory, and courage. Hemingway held strong to old beliefs, and symbolism, as he used symbolism to depict the Protestant religion he could not accept. He used observation and description in his works, rather than rhetoric views. The concept of war fascinated Hemingway, as well as the experiences one could endure in a lifetime. One of the most famous works, *Farewell to Arms* depicted the uselessness for words such as honor and glory, because they were not the first things in a soldier's mind as he walked onto the battlefield. Hemingway's works were raw, and dealt with the notion that one could be inside the characters mind, the concrete, and not around in the abstract view of his works.

7.5 Changeable Western Social Science

The end of the nineteenth and the beginning of the twentieth century's mark the great age of sociological thought. The leading sociological thinkers of the period all regarded science as the only valid model for correct thinking and all claimed that their thought rested on a scientific foundation. They struggled with some of the crucial problems of modern society. How can society achieve coherence and stability when religion no longer unites people? What are the implications of the non—rational for political life? How can people preserve their individuality in a society that is becoming increasingly regimented?

Emile Durkheim(1858—1917), a French scholar of Jewish background, and heir to

Comte's positivism, was an important founder of modern sociology. Like Comte, he considered scientific thought the only valid model for modern society. A crucial element of Durkheim's thought was the effort to show that the essential ingredients of modern times—secularism, rationalism, and individualism—threaten society with disintegration.

In traditional society a person's place and function were determined by birth. Modern people, however, captivated by the principle of individualism, will not accept such restraints. They seek to uplift themselves and demand that society allow them the opportunity. In the process, they reject or ignore the social restraints that society so desperately requires, thereby giving rise to a spirit of anarchy.

The weakening of those traditional ties that bind the individual to society constituted, for Durkheim, the crisis of modern society. Without collective values and common beliefs, he felt, society was threatened with disintegration and the individual with disorientation. To a western world intrigued by scientific progress, Durkhieim emphasized the spiritual malaise of modern society. Modern people, said Durkheim, suffer from anomie—a collapse of values. They do not feel integrated into a collective community and find no purpose in life. In *Suicide* (1897) Durkheim maintained that the pathology of modern society is demonstrated by its high rate of suicide. Modern people are driven to suicide by intense competition and the disappointment and frustration resulting from unfulfilled expectations and lack of commitment to moral principles. People must limit their aspirations and exercise discipline over their desires and passions. They must stop wanting more. Religion once could spur people to do these things, but it no longer can.

Chapter 8 Western Culture after Two World Wars

World War Ⅱ ended in 1945 after untold horrors and suffering, with the unconditional surrender of the Axis. War crime trials punished Axis leaders for crimes against humanity. The United States and the Soviet Union emerged as the two superpowers at the end of the World War Ⅱ. While the United States led the democratic countries of Western Europe, the Soviet Union's forces occupied and dominated Eastern Europe. The two blocs confronted each other in the Cold War that followed, divided by an "iron curtain" that separated Communist governments established by Soviet forces in Eastern Europe from the nations of Western Europe, Soviet attempts to oust western occupation forces in Berlin, to destabilize Turkey, and to aid Communist rebels in Greece led to determined U. S. responses—in the Berlin airlift, the Truman Doctrine, and the formation of NATO—that checked Soviet expansion. Economic aid in the form of the Marshall Plan, followed by the formation of the Common Market, revived Western Europe's economy and made communism unattractive to most people in that region. The Soviet Union countered with Warsaw Pact, a military alliance of Eastern European nations, and COMECON, an economic alliance.

Huge quantities of new knowledge were added in all fields of physical science, from astronomy, to physics, to biology and chemistry. This knowledge was applied to medicine and space research as well as to such fields as psychology, archaeology, and anthropology.

The material lives of most people, especially those in the western world, improved dramatically in the twentieth century. Synthetic materials added to the array of goods; and new sources of energy such as petroleum and atomic energy enabled fast travel and spurred the growth of mammoth cities. In many countries, heavy smokestack industry has given way to high-technological and service industries. Conglomerates had given way to high-technological and service industries. Conglomerates and large corporations, or government-owned enterprises, have replaced small companies. Wars, as well as changing economic conditions, led to women entering the modern work force, which in turn brought them increased political rights and improved their economic status.

As a result of advances in knowledge in many fields, twentieth-centary and intellectual life became rich and varied. New ideologies developed in response to changing conditions. The most influential ideologies rooted in the nineteenth century but advanced in the twentieth, were nationalism, socialism, Marxist, conservatism, liberalism, and fascism.

Modernism described twentieth-century artistic developments in painting, sculpture, and music, rapid communications resulted in cross-cultural exchanges and the assimilation and transformation of themes and techniques from many different cultures. A popular culture also developed, led by the United States and transmitted by the mass media.

8.1 Great Achievements of Science and Technology

8.1.1 The Application of Nuclear Energy

An especially momentous breakthrough in technology was the peaceful use of nuclear energy, which now produces substantial proportions of the electricity consumed in industrial societies. But this, too, is a mixed blessing. Although atomic power plants provide cheap energy, the peril of accidental damage to reactors with resultant leaking of radiation is considerable. The explosions at the Chernobyl nuclear power plant in the Soviet Union in 1986 raised radiation levels in many parts of Europe and will have dire long-term consequences.

8.1.2 The Development of Spaceflight Technology

Technology made the twentieth century the age of flight. In 1909 Orville and Wilbur Wright flew a propeller-driven heavier-than-air craft for the first time. A viators in small airplanes conducted reconnaissance missions and dog fights in the First World War and carried the mails between the wars. In the Second world War the multi-engine bombing plane came into its own. After the war, jet-propelled airplanes became prevalent in both military and commercial aviation. Space exploration began in 1957, when the Soviet Union put the first artificial satellite, called "Sputnik", into orbit. By the 1980s American spacecraft landed on Mars, and Voyager Ⅱ photographed the outer planets and their moons. The entire age of flight, from Kitty Hawk to the moos of Uranus, has taken place within a single human lifetime.

8.1.3 Gene Project

Charles Darwin's theory of biological evolution through natural selection remains central to twentieth-century study of biology. However, biologists have modified Charles Darwin's basic evolutionary theory; some have argued that evolution is not a process of small changes adding up to large transformations over long periods, but rather of relatively rapid change interspersed with long, static periods of little change in any give species. Botanists and zoologist, especially those seeking to increase and improve the world's food supply, have accelerated the "natural selection" process. For example, now produces more than twice the yield I a shorter growing season than was possible fifty years ago.

Major new biological discoveries have revealed much about the genetic base of life and the ecological interaction of many species in a system of related life forms. At the microscopic level, biologists discovered DNA (deoxyribonucleic acid), which controls the chromosomes composing the nucleus of the living cell. DNA molecules, twisted around each other in a complicated "double helix" — that is, to perform all the basic processes of life. At a different level of organization of life, ecologists have studied how species of animals and plants interact with each other and with various aspects of their common environment. Their discoveries have emphasized the interrelatedness of all living matter, leading to more urgent warnings about the effects of altering that common environment.

Major new biological discoveries have revealed much about the genetic base of life and the ecological interaction of many species a system of related life forms. At the microscopic level, biologists discovered DNA, which controls the chromosomes composing the nucleus of the living cell. DNA molecules, twisted around each other in a complicated "double helix" pattern, program living tissue to develop and reproduce itself through cell division—that is, to perform all the basic processes of life. At a different level of organization of life, ecologists have studied how species of animals and plants interact with each other and with various aspects of their common environment. Their discoveries have emphasized the interrelatedness all living matter, leading to more urgent warnings about the effects of altering that common environment.

8.1.4 The Birth and Application of Computer

A very broad area of technological advance concerned the "computer revolution".

Computers, operating much more rapidly than the human brain and able to record and instantly retrieve immense quantities of information, were applied to an expanding variety of tasks, from recording airline reservations to guiding artificial satellites and shuttlecraft in their orbits. The Japanese and others "robotized" entire factories with computers. At present, Japanese and American scientists are in a keen competition to produce even more powerful computers.

Computer technology has enabled societies around the world to store, order, and retrieve vast amounts of knowledge. As the decades pass, raw data piles up in records repositories, on paper and film, on tapes and computer disks. Collections of statistical data alone furnish mountains of information unimaginable in the past. But in many ways, the resulting flood of knowledge has often been overwhelming. The twentieth century has become an age of specialization, a century of experts. As a result, people, even in the same society or nation, often do not share a common body of knowledge, the cultural values and belief systems of many societies have become increasingly fragmented and diverse.

Twentieth century technology has also brought great dangers. Modern industry pollutes the air and water; "acid rain" has defoliated large forest areas. Automobiles put a whole society on wheels; yet road accidents also have injured millions and killed tens of thousands annually. High technology raised as well the specter of earth-orbiting "Star Wars" weaponry. Atomic weapons, stockpiled in huge quantities by the superpowers, pose a very real threat of global annihilation.

8.2 The Philosophy Schools in the Western Countries

8.2.1 Sartre and Existentialism

Existentialists trace the roots of their worldview to such nineteenth-century thinkers as Nietzsche, who proclaimed the "Death of God" in the materialistic age. The French Writer Jean-Paul Sartre (1905—1980) expressed the existential mood of the mid-twentieth century in his play *No Exit* and novel *Nausea*. Sartre defined existentialism with the pithy phrase "existence precedes essence", meaning that material existence is the fundamental reality, and essences, or spiritual beings, are only myths. For existentialists, the harsh truth about human existence is the sheer meaninglessness or even absurdity. To many of the generation that had survived horrors of the Great

Depression and World War Ⅱ, absurdity and anguish seemed apt characterizations of the age.

Jean-Paul Sartre(1905—1980), whose philosophy takes its name from its doctrine that the existence of human beings as free individuals is the fundamental fact of life, argues that this freedom is of no help to humanity; instead it is a source of anguish and terror. Realizing, however, that they are free agents, morally responsible for all their acts, individuals fee themselves strangers in an alien world. They can have no confidence in a benevolent God in a universe guided by purpose, for, according to Sartre, all such ideas have been reduced to fictions by modern science. The only way of escape from despair is the path of "involvement", or active participation in human affairs. It should be noted that in addition to the atheistic existentialism of Sartre, there was also a prior Christian version, which had its origin in the teachings of Soren Kierkegaad (1818—1855), a Danish theologian of the mid-nineteenth century. Like its atheistic counterpart, Christian Existentialism also reaches that the chief cause of its freedom is original sin.

The philosophy that most persistently gripped the intellectual imagination of the western world in the postwar period was existentialism. Existentialism is more an attitude than a single philosophical system. Its direct ancestry can be traced to the 19th-century Danish theologian and religious thinker Stren Kierkegaard(1813—1855), who set out its main emphasis. Kierkegarard strongly reacted against the great abstract philosophical systems developed by such philosophers as Georg Hegel (1770—1831) in favor of an intense study of the individual person in his or her actual existing situation in the world. Kierkegaard emphasized the single individual "the crowd is untruth" that exists in a specific set of circumstances at a particular time in history with a specific consciousness. Philosophers like Hege, Kierkegaard once noted ironically, answer every question abut the universe except "Who am I?" "What am I doing here?" and "Where am I going?"

This radically subjective self-examination was carried on all through the last century by philosophers like Friedrich Nietzsche and novelists like Fyodor Dostoyevsky, who are regarded as forerunners of modern existentialist philosophy. In our own century writers like Franz Kafka, the German philosopher Martin Heidegger gave shaper focus to the Existentialism both as a philosophy and a style of life, however, was the French writer and philosopher Jean-Paul Sartre(1905—1980).

Sartre believed it's the task of the modern thinker to take seriously the implications of atheism. If there is not God, Sartre insisted, then there is no blueprint of what a person should be and there is no ultimate significance to the universe. People are thrown into life and their very aloneness forces them to make decisions about who they are and what they shall be. "People are condemned to be free," Sartre wrote. Existentialism was an attempt to help people understand their place in a absurd world, their obligation to face up to their freedom, and the kinds of ethics available to people in a world bereft of any absolutes.

The appeal of existentialism was its marriage of thought and action, its analysis of modern anxiety, and its willingness to express its ideas through the media of plays, novels, films, and newspaper polemics. After the close of the war in 1945 there was a veritable explosion of existentialist theatre in Europe. In the United States existentialist themes were eagerly taken up by intellectuals and writers who were attracted to its emphasis on anxiety and alienation.

The so-called beat writers of the 1950s embraced a rather vulgarized style of existentialism filtered through the mesh of jazz and the black experience. The existentialist ethic has remained alive mainly through the novels of Albert Camus. In works like *The Stranger* (1942), *The Plague* (1947) and *The Fall* (1956), Camus, who disliked being called an existentialist, continues to impress his readers with heroes who fight the ultimate absurdity of the world with lucidity and dedication and without illusion.

8.2.2 The Frankfurt School

The Frankfurt School refers to a group of German-American theorists who developed powerful anal lyses of the changes in western capitalist societies that occurred since the classical theory of Marx. Working at the Institute for Sozialforschung in Frankfurt, Germany in the late 1920s and early 1932s, theorists such as Max Horkheimer, T. W. Adorno, Herbert Marcuse, Leo Lowenthal, and Erich Fromm produced some of the first accounts within critical social theory of the importance of mass culture and communication in social reproduction and theory of the importance of mass culture and communication in social reproduction and domination. The Frankrut School also generated one of the first models of critical cultural studies that analyze the processes of cultural production and political economy, the polities of cultural tests, and audience reception and use of cultural artifacts (Kellner 1989 and 1995).

Moving from Nazi Germany to the United States, the Frankfurt School experienced at firsthand the rise of a media culture involving film, popular music, radio, television, and other forms of mass culture (Wiggershaus 1994). In the United States, where they found themselves in exile, media production was by and large a form of commercial entertainment controlled by big corporations. Two of its key theorists Max Horkheimer and T. W. Adorno developed an account of the "culture industry" to call attention to the industrialization and commercialization of culture under capitalist relations of production (1972). This situation was most marked in the United States that had little state support of film or television industries, and where a highly commercial mass culture emerged that came to be a distinctive feature of capitalist societies and a focus on critical cultural studies.

During the 1930s, the Frankfurt school developed a critical and transdisciplinary approach to cultural and communications studies, combining political economy, textual analysis, and analysis of social and ideological effects. They coined the term "culture industry" to signify the process of the industrialization of mass-produced culture and the commercial imperatives that drove the system. The critical theorists analyzed all mass mediated cultural attics within the context of industrial production, in which the commodities of the culture industries exhibited the same features as other products of mass production: co-modification, standardization, and massification. The culture industries had the specific function, however, of providing ideological estimation of the existing capitalist societies and of integrating individuals into its way of life.

Furthermore, the critical theorists investigated the cultural industries in a political context as a form of the integration of the working class into capitalist societies. The Frankfurt School theorists were among the first neo—Marxian groups to examine the effects of mass culture and the rise of the consumer society on the working classes which were to be the instrument of revolution in the classical Marxian scenario. They also analyzed the ways that the culture industries and consumer society were stabilizing contemporary capitalism and accordingly sought new strategies for political change, agencies of political transformation, and models for political emancipation that could serve as norms of social critique and goals for political struggle. This project required rethinking Marxian theory and produced many important contributions—as well as some problematical positions.

The Frankfurt school focused intently on technology and culture, indicating how technology was becoming both a major force of production and formative mode of social organization and control. In a 1941 article, Some Social Implications of Modern technology. Herbert Marcuse argued that technology in the contemporary era constitutes an entire "mode of organizing and perpetuating social relationships, a manifestation of prevalent thought and behavior patterns, an instrument for control and domination." In the realm of culture, technology produced mass culture that habituated individuals to conform to the dominant patterns of though and behavior, and thus provided powerful instruments of social control and domination.

The culture industry thesis described both the production of massified cultural products and homogenized subjectivities. Mass culture for the Frankfurt School produced desires, dreams homes, fears and longings, as well as unending desire for consumer products. The culture industry produced cultural consumers who would consume its products and conform to the dictates and the behaviors of the existing society. And yet, as Walter Benjamin pointed out (1969), the culture industry also produces rational and critical consumers able to dissect and discriminate among cultural texts and performances, much as sports fans learn to analyze and criticize sports events.

In retrospect, one can see the Frankfurt School work as articulation of a theory of the state of state and monopoly capitalism that became dominant during the 1930s. This was an era of large organizations, theorized earlier by Austro-Marxist Rudolf Hilferding as "organized capitalism" (1980), in which the state and giant corporations managed the economy and in which individuals submitted to state and corporate control. This period is often described as "Fordism" to designate the system of mass production and the homogenizing regime of capital which wanted to produce mass desires, tastes, and behavior. It was thus an era of mass production and consumption characterized by uniformity and homogeneity of needs, thought, and behavior producing a mass society and what the Frankfurt School described as "the end of the individual." No longer was individual thought and action the motor of social and cultural progress; instead giant organizations and institutions overpowered individuals. The era corresponds to the staid conformist, and conservative world of corporate capitalism that was dominant in the 1950s with its organization men and women, its mass consumption, and its mass culture.

During this period, mass culture and communication were instrumental in generating the modes of thought and behavior appropriate to a highly organized and massified social order. Thus, the Frankfurt School theory of the culture industry articulates a major historical shift to an era in which mass consumption and culture was indispensable to producing a consumer society based on homogeneous needs and desires for mass-produced products and a mass society based on social organization and homogeneity. It is culturally the era of highly controlled network radio and television, insipid top forty pop music, glossy Hollywood films national magazines, and other mass-produced cultural artifacts.

Of course, media culture was never as massified and homogeneous as in the Frankfurt school model and one could argue that the model was flawed even during its time of origin and influence and that other models were preferable, such as those of Walter Benjamin, Siegried Kracauer, Ernst Bloch, and others of the Weimar generation and, later, British cultural studies. Yet the original Frankfurt school model of the culture industry did articulate the important social roles of media culture during a specific regime of capital and provided a model, still of use, of a highly commercial and technologically advanced culture that serves the needs of dominant corporate interests, plays a major role in ideologically advanced culture that serves the needs of dominant corporate interests, plays a major role in ideological reproduction, and in enculturating individuals into the dominant system of needs, thought, and behavior.

8.2.3 From Structuralism to Deconstructuralism

Structuralism is a theory of humankind in which all elements of human culture, including literature, are thought to be parts of a system of signs. Critic Robert Scholes has described structuralism as a reaction to "modernist' alienation and despair".

European structuralist such as Roman Jakobson, Claude Levi-Strauss, and Roland Barthes attempted to develop a semiology, or language form the isolation in which they had been studied and to show that the laws that govern them govern all signs, form road signs to articles of clothing.

Structuralism was heavily influenced by linguistics, especially by the pioneering work of Ferdinand de Saussure. Particularly useful to structuralists was Saussure's concept of the phoneme and his idea that phonemes exist in two kinds of relationships: diachronic and synchronic. A phoneme has a diachronic, or horizontal, "relationship" with those other phonemes that precede and follow it in particular usage, utterance, or narrative—what Saussure, a linguist, called parole. A phoneme has a synchronic, or "vertical", relationship with the entire system of language within which individual usages, utterances, or narratives have meaning language. A means what it means in English because those of us who speak the language are plugged into the same system.

Following Saussure, Levi-Strauss, an anthropologist, studied hundreds of myths, breaking them into their smallest meaningful units which he called "mytehmes", Removing each form its diachronic relations with other mythemes in a single myth, he vertically aligned those mythemes that he found be homologous. He then studied the relationships within as well as between vertically aligned columns, in an attempt to understand scientifically, through ratios and proportions, those thoughts and processes that humankind has shared, both at one particular time and across time. Whether Levi-Strauss was studying the structure of myths or the structure of villages, he looked for recurring, common elements that transcended the differences within and among cultures.

Structuralists followed Saussure in preferring to think about the overriding langue, or narratives. Structuralists also followed Saussure's lead in believing that sign systems must be understood in terms of binary oppositions proposition later disputed by post structuralist Jacques Derrida. In analyzing myths and texts to find basic structures, structuralists found that opposite terms modulate until they are finally resolved or reconciled by some intermesh that the war between God and the rebellious angels becomes a rift between god and sinful, fallen man, a rift that is healed by the Son of God, the mediating third term. Although structuralism was largely a European phenomenon in its origin and development, it was influenced by American thinkers as well. Noam Chomsky, for instance, who powerfully influenced structuralism through works such as *Reflections of Language* (1975), identified and distinguished between "surface structures" and "deep structures" in language and linguistic literatures, including text.

Deconstruction involves the close reading of texts in order to demonstrate that any given text has irreconcilably contradictory meanings, rather than being a unified, logical whole. As J. hillis Miller, the preeminent American deconstructor has explained in an essay entitled *Stevens Rock and Criticism As Cure* (1976), "Deconstruction is not a dismantling of the structure of a text, but a demonstration that it has already dismantled itself. Its apparently solid ground s no rock but thin air."

Deconstruction was both created and has been profoundly influenced by the French philosopher on language Jacques Derrida. Derrida, who coined the term deconstruction, argued that in western culture, people tend to think and express their thoughts in terms of binary oppositions. Something is white but not black, masculine and therefore not feminine, a cause rather than an effect. Other common and mutually exclusive pairs include beginning and speech. Derrida suggests these oppositions are hierarchies in miniature, containing one term that western culture views as positive of superior and another considered negative or inferior, even if only slightly so. Through deconstruction, Derrida aims to erase the boundary between binary oppositions—and to do so in such a way that the hierarchy implied by the oppositions is thrown into question.

Although its ultimate aim may be to criticize western logic, deconstruction arose as a response to structuralism and formalism. Structuralists believed that all elements of human culture, including literature, may be understood as parts of a system of signs. Serrida did not believe that structuralists could explain the laws governing human signification and thus provide the key to understanding the form and meaning of everything from an African village to Greek myth to literary text. He also rejected the structuralist belief that texts have identifiable centers of meaning—a belief structuralists shared with formalists.

Formalist critics, such as the new critics, assume that a work of literature is a freestanding, self-contained object whose meaning can be found in the complex network of relations between its parts. Deconstructors, by contrast, see works in terms of their undecidability. They rejected the formalist view that a work of literary art is demonstrably unified from beginning to end, in one certain way, or that it is organized around a single center that ultimately can be identified. As a result, deconstructors see texts as more radically homogeneous than do formalists. Formalists ultimately make sense of the ambiguities they find in a given text, arguing that every ambiguity serves a definite, meaningful, and demonstrable literary function. Undesirability, by contrasts never reduced, let along mastered. Though a deconstructive reading can reveal the incompatible possibilities generated by the text, it is impossible for the reader to decide among them.

8.3 The Underchanging Sociology in America and the West Europe

Thooretical perspectives in sociology are usually examined in terms of "classical" and "contemporary" periods, which might usefully be thought of as meaning nineteenth and twentieth century. The classical thinkers of the nineteenth century were all Europeans who established the basis and defined the interests of the discipline by making certain kinds of assumptions, and asking certain kinds of questions, about the nature of human nature and society. Contemporary theoretical perspectives, most of which are American, American, have to a great degree expanded and elaborated upon the work of the classical thinkers. Structural functionalism can be viewed largely as an outgrowth and elaboration of Durkheim's ideas, conflict theory as rooted in Marx, and symbolic interaction as stemming from Weber. Exchange theory has elements of both Marx and Weber. We will describe the major elements of each so as to expose the three basic assumptions that constitute a theoretical potion.

8.3.1 Structural Functionalism

Structural Functionalism theory, often called functionalism, has tended to dominate the explanatory reasoning of sociology for the past fifty years. It is the logical extension of Durkheim's thinking. Just as Durkheim saw individuals as action out the necessary requirements for collective survival, so the functionalists see people as fulfilling the requirements that the society has for its own perpetuation. Functionalism's views on the nature of human nature, the nature of society, and the way it works can be found in its conception of the relation between the individual and the society and its concepts of social system and function.

1. The Individual and Society

Functional theorists see people responding to the requirements of their societies. They find their place within the social order and tend to stay in that place. People can change, but they do it in the manner prescribed by the society in which they live. Thus to the functionalists, Society is the active agent in history, and human beings are basically passive responders. To a large degree, individuals are "overwhelmed" by the pressures their societies placed them to conform to societal expectations, and they reflect such pressures most of the time. If they assert their own wills to act differently, even the individuality of the act is likely to conform to societal definitions of what is possible and permitted. American social protestors, for example, are far more likely to burn property than themselves, although Buddhist monks Vietnam a few years ago took the opposite course.

2. The Concept of Social System

One of the crucial concepts of functionalism is that society is a system. System is defined by three characteristics: balance, boundaries, and interrelationships. First, a system is balance, or tends to be balanced. Any destabilizing forces present tend to be subject to the inertia of other parts of system. This "balance model" is an important element in functionalist thought and may be likened to a simple physical process. If one pushes down one end of a playground teeter-totter, the other end must rise, but its weight will resist the push. Or, for another example, pressing on one side of a rubber balloon results in a bulge outward elsewhere, which reduces itself as soon as the initial pressure is released a bulge outward elsewhere, which reduces itself as soon as the initial pressures released. The balloon thus destabilizes; it regains its "balance" or former state.

Second, a system has boundaries. You can describe the items are in the system and those that are outside it. Part of keeping the system balanced has to do with maintaining or slowly altering the boundaries of that system.

Third, all the parts or elements in a system are related to each other. That is, if one element in the system changes, all other parts of the system will also have to change their state in response. Each part is interrelated with and dependent on every other part.

The functional notion of system is clearly based on what is called the organic model in social science. This means the idea or conception of society is "like" a living organism or, at least, having some similarities to an organism. Although it is easy to carry such parallels too far—and they are often misleading—it probably does clarify the idea of system to use such language. Thus society, like the human organism, is composed of elements and subsystems, like the digestive and respiratory subsystems of the body, that are each balanced, boundaries, and internally interrelated. Each element in turn is related to the others as a whole, performing functions for the others and the body as a whole.

3. The Concept of Function

The way society works, in the functionalists' perspective, can be seen in the concept of function within a system. All parts of every system are either functional so dysfunctional. Most parts are functional; they perform a positive service by helping to maintain the system or its balanced state. Dysfunctional elements are either useless or have negative effects. The human heart, for example, is clearly functional for the body and all of the subsystems within it. But a heart defect is dysfunctional; its performance or existence not only does not contribute, it detracts or even endangers.

Functionalists also draw a distinction between latent and manifest functions, because the social utilities that that things have are not always apparent. An element's manifest function is overt and obvious, that purpose or end for which it is explicitly intended. Its latent function, if any, is the social purpose served "unconsciously", unknown and unintended by those who perform the act in question.

The functionalists view human nature as plastic, readily modeled by the society into any shape useful to the society. The nature of society is similar to that of an organism; it is a system of action and interaction among its members that is balanced, boundaries, and interrelated. The mechanism through which society works is the cooperation or coordination created by systemic interdependence.

8.3.2 Conflict Theory

Conflict theory: the idea that conflict is at the base of all social arrangements is the pure model for conflict theory. At the present time, however, there are no pure conflict theorists. In the history of sociology, there have been only two or three people who have taken conflict as the basis for their thinking about human societal life. The two most influential modern conflict theorists are Ralf Dahrendorf and Lewis Coser. Their work has helped redirect the attention of sociologists to the nature and functions of conflict in modern life. Paradoxically, these two thinkers have focused on the integrative nature of conflict. They raise the question of how conflict holds society together, but do not assume it is the basis of social life. The conflict perspective's assumptions about human nature, the nature of society, and how it works are found in its views on power and authority, the role of associations, and the role of conflict in society.

Power and authority: power is a crucial concept for conflict theorists. Power is defined as the probability that an actor can carry out his will despite resistance. Authority is also crucial. Authority is the probability that a command will be obeyed. Authority is legitimate power, and is always associated with social roles. Legitimate power is assumed to be a common and necessary feature of social life, and therefore needs to study. By people must either be in dominating positions or be dominated by others, or at minimum, that direction and leadership are necessary in social affairs. The nature of most human being is to follow; only a few lead.

The role of conflict: in society the basic mechanism that makes society work is social conflict. By social conflict sociologists normally mean a struggle over values and claims to scarce resources—that is, status, power, and things. Conflict takes the form of attempting to neutralize, injure, or eliminate rivals. It is usually seen as a conscious and personal social process, taking place between organized groups.

Some of the outcomes of social conflict are described by Coser's theory, and have been expressed in a series of formal and abstract propositions as follows:

1. The more unlimited the goals of the opposing parties in a conflict, the more prolonged the conflict will be. This is true because when goals are global, or relatively unlimited, each participant will feel more threatened. It is harder to secure "unconditional surrender" from an enemy than a negotiated armistice.

2. The more that people think total attainment of goals will involve a cost greater than that required for victory, the less prolonged the conflict will be. The reason for this

is that when a victory is at hand, the temptation to "settle for" what one has won appears overwhelming when compared with the cost of further sacrifices for ends that may not be attainable.

3. The more intense the conflict, the more clear-cut will be the boundaries of the respective parties. The reason is that under the pressure of severe conflict, "fence straddling" will not be permitted; the "with us or against us" mentality will take over. There will also be strong efforts to draw away from and distinguish oneself from the enemy, as when the teaching of German was forbidden in some American schools during the First World War.

4. The more intense the conflict, the greater the solidarity within conflicting groups. This is in part 5 a function of the "with us or against us" mentality and in part a result of the ideological simplification that occurs under pressure; fine points and qualifications become obscure. As people withdraw from and identification with the enemy, they draw more closely together and identify more closely with each other, seeing themselves as "all in the same boat" and therefore sharing common interests.

For the conflict theorists, the nature of society is usually some kind of balance of forces between opposed or conflicting groups or associations. Human nature is largely passive in that most people are followers, dominated by a few. But because rewards and resources are scarce, the effect is to make human nature competitive. The mechanism that keeps society going is conflict between organized groups over the rewards available within the social system. Because it is rarely possible for one to dominate another permanently, a kind of dynamic stability is created by the continuing contest.

8.3.3 Symbolic Interaction

Symbolic Interaction: symbolic interaction theory was introduced to American sociology through the lectures of George Herbert Mead at the University of Chicago in the 1930s. Symbolic interactions are usually regarded as a micro theory designed to explain socialization. Some integrationists do treat it as a total theory of society, however. What it looks like in this regard is sketched below. The theoretical assumptions implicit in interactions are found in its views of symbols and meaning, expectations and behavior, and roles and interaction.

1. Symbols and Meaning

Mead begins his reasoning with the assumption that human beings, like other animals, are incessantly active. They constantly make gestures—movements or sounds—

that are reacted to by others. But only human beings quickly turn gestures into symbols, sounds or acts that come to stand for something else, to have a meaning. Symbols become significant when they have the same meaning for the person receiving them as they do for the person making them. Meaning, thus, is shared and social. It is learned through interaction with others. Being human means possessing the capacity for thought, which is a phenomenon. People are thus entirely social beings, and their very humanity is the product of symbolic social interaction with others. Human nature is entirely social.

2. Expectations and Behavior

Society is the total sum of the interactions its members have with one another. It is composed of groups within which people relate to one another and the relationships between such groups. Behavior within groups and intergroup relations are ordered, or structured, by expectations created by both significant and generalized others. Through interaction, people learn to reflect on their own behavior, and come to have certain expectations about it and the behavior of others. That is, they observe behavior and learn to expect that similar patterns will occur as new saturations are created. They also learn that others have similar expectations for themselves. The patterns of relations between people and their groups constitute the structure of society. The nature of society is that it is a collection of reciprocal expectations and expectation—fulfilling behavior.

3. Roles and Interaction

Society works because human beings are capable of symbol—using behavior, as a consequence of the possession of language. The most important product of this fact is self-consciousness. The human infant becomes self-conscious as a result of exposure to language. As his own language skills develop, the child learns first the meanings of words and the attitudes associate with them by those who use the words, and later the expectations these people have for his behavior. In time, he comes to have similar expectations for others. Sets of these expectations that are associated with the behavior of particular other persons are called roles, and roles are functions or reflections of group membership. Thus through his interaction with "Mommy" and "Daddy", the child learns both how he may expect them to behave and how they expect him to behave. Mommy and Daddy, in turn, behave the way they do because they are action gout a social role; a "part" in a "play" called" the family".

The generalized "parts" that people learn to play exist in the culture of any given society at a particular time and define "how one ought to act" in particular roles. These are called role expectations and also include how one behaves toward members of other groups and what the relations between groups should be or how they should take place. For example, in growing up in a family the child will learn not only how he or she is expected to act toward other family, members, but also how the family and its members relate to other groups such as the church, the government, and so forth. Mommy and Daddy may gamble as they prepare their tax forms but they acknowledge that they ought to pay taxes, and the child learns that aspect of the relation of the citizen to the state.

Summary: in the interactions view, human beings are active and communicative. Society is an extremely complex network of actions and interactions between individuals, all of them organized and "powered", or motivated, by group membership, with its resulting roles and role expectations from the time of birth and because the interdependency of individuals makes them rely on each other for necessary services and rewards. Further, the internalization of the requirements of various roles motivates the person to wish to fulfill them; thus society works through cooperation in fulfilling expectations. Punishment or withdrawal of rewards for inadequate role performance provides additional motivation.

8.3.4 Exchange Theory

Exchange theory: another modern view of social reality is exchange theory. This is neither so well developed nor so widespread as the other theories we have discussed, but it is becoming more popular among sociologists. Because it is based on only a few works by two or three individuals, it is not yet a fully elaborated theory, and so is only briefly summarized here.

1. The Nature of Human Nature

People act rationally. Each person sets goals and finds the most appropriate means within the society to achieve those goals. Since goals are sought in the presence of and from others, those others must be taken into consideration, because they will often influence, or even control, one's access to goals. This situation produces the basic exchange relationship. Behavior in this sense becomes social. Behavior often takes the form of exchange because social and psychological resources are in short supply and must often be obtained from others. Thus we exchange money for goods, labor for money, submission to legal or bureaucratic authority for employment or safety, emotional "strokes" for reciprocal reinforcement of support from others, and so forth.

2. The Nature of Society

Reality is to be found in the individual, and not in the abstract entity called society. The sum of the individuals and exchanges adds up to and is equivalent to society. From time to time, these exchanges may result in complex organizations. Exchange theorists tend to concentrate their research on complex organizations.

The way society works the process of exchange is a process of accommodation, a sharing of values and meanings. According to this view, people must get what they can from theirs in given relationships by giving the others what they require. People are able to reward and punish each other, actually or potentially, and to accommodate themselves to the social situations they find themselves in by exchange of goods, services, and psychological rewards.

Summary: for exchange theorists, people are rational and dependent on others to achieve their goals. Society is merely an exchange network. Society works through the exchange process, the mechanism of accommodation.

To sum up, sociology is the study of social life, in particular its orderliness or regularity. It is also a particular way of thinking about social reality or, more precisely, a set such ways of thinking, all of which use a common set of ideas and categories. Along with economics, political science, anthropology, and psychology, sociology is one of the social sciences.

Sociology has conventionally understood itself as standing within the scientific tradition, and although there is now some disagreement about this, most of its practitioners would still put it there. Science may be understood most broadly as a framework, or model, for a particular kind of analysis and as a method. This model and method are applicable in many subject areas, but to be called a science, a discipline must also demonstrate the four characteristics of the scientific method: ①intersubjective reliability, ②objectivity, ③quantifiablility, and④theoretical orientation. Science, then, is a particular way of knowing certain kinds of things, those that can be observed and quantitatively expressed. To the degree that sociology follows into the scientific tradition, it, too, is a way of knowing such thing, and to some degree it meets the four criteria enumerated above. It does have a subject matter, social order and change, that is largely its own. It uses the scientific method to some degree, although not all sociologists agree that this is possible in the study of social live. It has a body of theories, some of which are quantifiable to some degree.

All sociological theories are based on assumptions concerning①the nature of human nature,②the nature of society,and③the way society works. In general,the differences between the classical and contemporary views of social reality flow out of divergences in these assumptions.

Contemporary sociological perspectives are, in significant part, extensions and elaborations of classical views. There are four major "schools", or positions in today's sociology:①structural functionalism,②conflict theory,③symbolic interactionism, and ④exchange theory.

Any of them provides a reasonable explanation of the way the social world works, but each calls our attention to different aspects of it, emphasizing some things and ignoring others. That is the purpose of theory.

8.4 The Western Economics after Keyes

Optimism during the 1930s was generally the property of those writers who were prepared to advocate a violent change in the social order, most notably men and women sympathetic to the doctrines of communism and the achievements of Soviet Russia. An exception to this rule was the British economist John Maynard Keynes(1889—1946), who argued that capitalism, could be made to work if governments would play a part in its management, and whose theories helped shape the economic policies of the New Deal. Keynes had served as an economic adviser to the British government during the 1919 treaty-making at Paris. He was disgusted with the harsh terms imposed upon the Germans, recognizing that they would serve only to keep alive the hatreds and uncertainties that breed war. Keynes believed that capitalism with its inner faults corrected could provide a just and efficient economy. Capitalism, though, would require a thorough rethinking. First, Keynes abandoned the sacred cow of balanced budgets. He did not advocate continuous deficit financing. He would have the government deliberately operate in the red whenever private investment was too sacred cow of balanced budgets. He did not advocate continuous deficit finacing. He would have the government deliberately operate in the red whenever private investment was too scanty to provide or the economic needs of the country. When depression gave way to recovery, private financing could take place of deficit spending for most purposes. He favored the accumulation and investment of large amounts of venture capital. Finally, Keynes recommended monetary control as a means of promoting prosperity and full employment. He would establish what is commonly called a "managed currency", regulating its value by a process of contraction or expansion in accordance with the needs of the economy. Prosperity would thus be assured in terms of the condition of the home market, and no nation would be tempted to "beggar its neighbor" in the foolish pursuit of a favorable balance of trade.

8.4.1 Samuelson and His Neoclassical Synthesis

Within a few years, the General Theory had transformed macroeconomics. Not everybody was converted, and few agreed with it all. But most discussions became organized around it.

By the early 1950s, a large consensus had emerged, based on an integration of many of Keynes's ideas and the ideas of earlier economists. This consensus was called the neoclassical synthesis. To quote from Paul Samuelson in the 1955 edition of his textbook, *Economics*, and the first modern Economics textbook:

In recent years, 90 percent of American economists have stopped being "Keynesian economists" or "anti-Keynesian economists." Instead, they have worked toward a synthesis of whatever is valuable in older economics and in modern theories of income determination. The result might be called neo-classical economics and is accepted, in its broad outlines', by all but about five percent of extreme left-wing and right-wing writers.

The neoclassical synthesis was to remain the dominant view for another 20 years. Progress was astonishing, and the period from the early 1940s to the early 1970s can be called the golden age of macroeconomics.

8.4.2 New Cambridge School

One of the most prominent economists of the century, Joan Robinson incarnated the "Cambridge School" in most of its guises in the 20th century : as a cutting-edge Marshallian before and after 1936; as one of the earliest and most ardent Keynesians and finally as one of the leaders of the Neo-Ricardian and Post Keynesian schools. Robinson's contributions to economics are far too numerous to elucidate fairly. Unlike most economists, she was not a "one idea" person, but rather made many fundamental contributions to very different areas of economics.

During the 1930s, Joan Robinson taught Cambridge, published three books and numerous articles, participated in John Maynard Keynes's "circus" took up activities for the British Labor Party and still found time to give birth to two daughters. She became a full lecturer in 1937.

However, Joan Robinson promised trouble from the start. In her famous 1933 book, she introduced the theory of imperfect competition to economics following this up with an explanatory article (1934). E. H. Chamberlin, who independently discovered a similar theory, itched for a fight, but never got one. Robinson was quick to move on beyond her theory of imperfect competition—in spite of the fact that its success was given in modern textbooks.

The cause of her sudden turnaround was J. M. Keynes'General Theory. As a member of Keynes's "Circus" at Cambridge during the writing of that treaties. Robinson produced early faithful expositions of Keynes's theory (1936, 1937).

Prompted by Kalecki, Robinson soon set out to tackle the work of Karl Marx. Although not exactly entranced by the labor theory of value, Robinson's 1942 Essay on Marxian Economics proved ground-breaking, fresh, insightful, and critical and, above all, was among the first studies to take Marx seriously as an economist. It effectively helps draw Marxian economics from its moribund and half-chewed existence in political debate.

In the 1940s and 1950s, her activities continued apace. During the war, she had worked on various economic committees for both the Labor Party and for government. She also made several official trips to the Soviet Union, China and Ceylon. She became a reader at Cambridge in 1949. In a famous incident, she declined an invitation from Raggnar Frisch in the early 1950s to become vice-president of the Econometric Society because, in her explanation, she could not be part of the editorial committee of a journal she couldn't read.

In 1956, Robinson published her magnum opus, *The Accumulation of Capital*, which sought to extend Keynes's theory to account for long-run issues of growth and capital accumulation. This was followed up by a more lucid exposition of growth theory (1962), whereupon the concept of a variety of "golden age" growth paths were laid out. Her work on growth paralleled and complemented that of fellow Cantabrigian, Nicholas Kaldor. Together, they developed what became known as "Cambridge Growth Theory".

Her work on capital had been initiated with an investigation of the problem as arising from capital aggregation (1954), which was followed up with the exposition of the "Ruth Cohen Curiosum" in her *The Accumulation of Capital* (1956). Drawing upon Sraffa (1960) and Robinson. The Neo-Ricardian "classical revival" began with a storm—the Cambridge Capital Controversy, in which she led the Cambridge assault on the American Neo Keynesians.

Towards the end of her life, Robinson's work concentrated mostly on methodological problems in economics and trying to revive the original message of Keynes's General Theory. Her many popular writings brought her an even greater prominence with a wider public. She was invited to address the American Economic Association in 1971, wherein she gave one of her most provocative deliveries. An attempt to bring the Cambridge approach to a wider audience culminated in the publication of a rather unique "principles" textbook with John Eatwell in 1973, but it failed to make a substantial headway.

Robinson was also intensely interested in problems in underdeveloped and developing countries—a natural outgrowth of her work on growth—and made substantial contributions in that direction as well.

Joan Robinson never won a Nobel Prize in Economics. Some people believe that this was due to her gender; a female has never won a Nobel Prize in Economics. Other people believe that she never won this coveted prize due to her eclectic study of economics. However despite the fact that she didn't win this important prize, Joan Robinson's works are still being studied while many Nobel Prize winners' works have faded away.

8.4.3 Friedman and Monetary Policy

The Keynesian Revolution soon stirred a counterrevolution by modern monetarists, who recognize some holes in classical theory but reject any need for massive government intervention to stabilize an economy. Their counterattack, led by Milton Friedman, began with are formation of the demand for money.

Milton Friedman is among the most publicly visible of modern economists. He was won respect of both his followers and those economists who disagree strongly with his views. Few significant honors in economics have not come Friedman's way. He was president of the American Economic Association in 1967 received the Nobel Prize in economics. Looking very much like everyone's "favorite uncle", Friedman often disarms his adversaries with a wink and a gentle smile, but those who have argued with him find him a formidable debater. He is able to express complicated ideas in simple terms understandable by those untrained in formal economic theory. This makes him popular with the media and keeps Friedman in touch with a wide audience.

Friedman has been a vital force in attacking the orthodoxy of the "new" (Keynesian) economics. He has done this in a way that combines his argumentative talents with solid empirical research and a desire not merely to tear down existing economics theory but to restructure it. Friedman's most notable research has involved monetary theory, but, as with all master economists, his thoughts have touched many areas of economics. In the monetary field, Friedman has reconstructed the quantity theory of money, reemphasized the importance and significance of monetary policy, questioned the Keynesian interpretation of the Great Depression and developed his own prescriptions for preventing future economic catastrophe.

Friedman has also made major contributions in such are as risk and insurance and has developed a theory of consumption based on wealth, as opposed to the Keynesian view that consumption depends only on current income.

Along the way, he has attempted to testate the classical liberal philosophy of Adam smith in terms pertinent to the modern era. Reedman has offered many ideas about replacing the influence of government with market solutions. For example, he argues that government could eliminate public schools and give the parents of students' vouchers so that all children could attend private schools tailored to their individual needs. He also argue that cash grants to poor people make more sense because these grants would leave more choices in the hands of the poor as well as require fewer tax dollars.

Friedman's restatement of the quantity theory of money is important because it made the theory statistically testable, something the old theory was not. His restatement is essentially a theory of the demand for money whereas the original version was a theory of the price level. Friedman's analyses of the statistical evidence indicate that the demand for money is stable over the long run and conclude that large changes in the supply of money cause undesirable fluctuations in employment and in the price level. His disenchantment with fiscal policy is due in large measure to the fact that government deficits are most often financed by inflationary expansions of the supply of money and credit. Finally, Friedman has been critical of the performance of the Federal Reserve System because he sees the FED as either following the wrong policy or yielding to political pressure rather than sound economic logic.

8.4.4 Supply-side Economics

The force of international competition by 1980 resulted in locally devastating closing of old heavy-industrial plants in the traditional production centers of the East and Midwest. The growth of business in the Sun Belt was underway, adding to the woes of rising industrial unemployment. In the 1980, the huge Chrysler Corporation threatened to go belly-up and joined the ranks of other major firms seeking federal aid to avoid bankruptcy. The other auto firms also reported huge losses that year.

From such a sea of troubles, the conventional policy prescriptions seemed to offer no way out. The argument for larger deficits to reduce unemployment was no longer heard. The deficits were already huge, and both unemployment and prices were rising. James Buchanan and Richard Wagner, in *Democracy In Deficit*, underlined the unspoken problem with the conventional, Keynesian, fiscal policy tradition. In one basic sense, it really was depression economics. It assumed that the economy would rise to the bait of money stimulus and expand real output and employment. However, the huge increases in deficit-financed money demand raised prices more than output, even with unemployed capacity and unemployed workers.

The policy of the 1946 *Employment Act* now seemed a dead issue altogether. As Buchanan and Wagner argued, it had been a piece of sheer pretense form the beginning;

This act pledges the government to do something it cannot possibly do, at least so long as our underlying fiscal and monetary institutions are themselves the primary source of instability.

And, said Buchanan and Wagner, if these institutions were stable, there would be no need for the *Employment Act*.

The old-time liberal Democratic ideal, with such long roots in American history, was stated eloquently by Senator George Mcgovern in 1980 in his address to Americans for Employment Action. He argued, acceding to *The New York Times*, that government was the only "humane" institution in American society. In 1980, he was retired by his constituents, as were other leading liberal Democrats.

Jimmy Carter had been served by economic advice from a profession that did not fully understand his problems. He experienced essentially the same frustration that Herbert Hoover had faced in 1930—1932. In Hoover's case, prices were stumbling and unemployment rose. In Carter's case, prices were soaring and unemployment rose. Economic orthodoxy did not understand the early 1930s, and it did not understand the late 1970s either.

The conservative Republicans came back with Ronald Reagan in 1981. Once again, they pledged to stop the inflation, to reduce government "interference" in economic life, and to adopt policies that would revitalize the American economy. They spoke of capitalism, free markets, and Reagan even used the word entrepreneur in his inaugural speech. They came also with a piece of baggage, supply-side economics, last seen during the prosperous days of fine-tuning along the New Frontier. They would, through big, general tax cuts, induce the entrepreneurial classes to give up ; the tax-avoidance life and return to productive work. They would hopefully take the unemployed and the chronic welfare cases to work with them. The tax cut of 1964 had been in part supported by these same arguments, as Herbert Stein pointed out. It was a gamble in 1981, just as it had been in 1964, and it was based on three assumptions:

1. The 1981 tax cut assumed that potential profit from new investment could be made more remunerative for individuals and corporations than was tax avoidance and diversification of investment into real estate, commodities speculation, and whatever.

2. The tax cut assumed that since the growth of expenditures would have to be curtailed if gigantic new deficits were to be avoided, Congress would cooperate.

3. It assumed that the American voter would agree with congressional support for a policy of slower growth of government and curtailment of regulation.

All three assumptionswere questionable, given the source of the American welfare state.

As 1981 progressed, the Federal Reserve System, under the leadership of Chairman Paul Volcker, made a determined, independent effort to crush the inflation rate with high positive interest rates, while the Reagan administration wondered aloud if taxes had been cut too much. By spring of 1982, there was a deepening recession in the land, with unemployment above 9 percent. The rate of inflation had fallen, but interest rate were still high, and the markets for housing and durable goods were flat. In addition, projections of federal revenues showed budget deficits in excess of 100 dollars billion coming down the track. Even administration supporters in Congress were backing away from supply-side economics. The financial markets anticipated the forthcoming strain of funding the huge debt increases, interest remained high, and stock-market values were melting down once more. The cries from members of Congress to reduce the budget deficit by raising tax rates again were hardly the blueprint for a Keynesian solution to unemployment. Once again, as in the carter administration, the feeling of mindless policy drift was in the air.

By the fall of 1982, the rate of inflation was down, interest rates were falling, and stitch and bond prices were rising. But the rate of unemployment temporarily exceeded 10 percent of the labor force, private investment had not gone up in response to the supply-side tax cuts, and the 1982 recession lingered.

By the end of 1982, real GNP was down slightly from the annual rate of the 1981, but unemployment was on average nearly 10 percent. The rate of inflation had been cut in half to below 4 percent per annum for the first time in years. In terms of unemployment alone the recession was the worst since the 1930s, but by other measures it was relatively mild. The policy mystery of stagflation had not been solved.

The recovery and expansion of 1983—1988 then occurred in the presence of huge deficits in the Federal budget, a strictly orthodox Keynesian prescription, and a powerful rise in private investment. The latter represented to a large extent the administration's changes in tax policies designed to encourage private investment. The tax cuts of 1981—1982 weren't those advocated by the 1980 supply-siders, but were strung out over three years, which dampened their impact. Not surprisingly the rate of private savings did not increase significantly, and the country was sported the predicted "crowding out" effects of the giant increases in federal debt by foreign investors seeking both safety and high interest rates. Billions of dollars of foreign investment poured in. Both the unprecedented federal deficit and the huge balance to payments deficits were "financed" by foreign investors. The unemployment rate sand back to about 7.5 percent in 1984—1985, the economy continued to generate net increases in total employment, and real wages began to rise again along with real disposable income. By the end of 1988, the unemployment rate dipped to about 5 percent as the expansion continued.

One extraordinary outcome was the U. S. dollar, freely floating on the foreign exchanges. Instead of collapsing under the weight of its own excess supply, the dollar rose to astounding strength in 1984—1985 as foreign investors poured billions of their own savings into the U. S. A., driving the dollar up against all currencies in the foreign exchange markets. Once worth 20.5 percent of a British pound, by the spring of 1985 the dollar had soared to about 95 percent of a pound. The dollar then caved in and declined to the rage of 1080 dollars to the pound in 1988. The huge excess supply of dollars generated by our balance of payments deficits finally made its impact felt in the foreign exchanges. Devalued dollar was inflationary inside the USA. as import prices soared, but our exports, now correspondingly cheaper, soared.

Supporters of "reaganomics" naturally credited these favorable economic singularities in the whirlwind to "the success of the President's policies". Opponents warned of the dangerous economic threat implied. What if, in the next recession, USA interest rates should fall back enough to inspire a mass withdrawal of these hundreds of billions of foreign investment? A recession could be converted into a catastrophic depression. Meanwhile the deficits all continued: the federal government could not reduce its spending. President Reagan resisted proposed tax increases, and the deficits mounted.

At the end of 1985, Congress passed the gram—Rudman Bill, an extraordinary piece of legislation designed automatically to cut spending in the interests of deficit reduction. By 19898, the bill was give part of the credit, a along with the increase in revenues in lowering the deficit. Import quotas remained in steel and autos despite the Present's much-declaimed admiration of free trade.

8.4.5 New Institutional Economies

In summarizing the chronological tree of institutional economists, Allen Crunchy wrote: Although there has been some overlapping of generations of institutionalists, one can discern three well-defined periods in the development fo institutional economic thought. The first period is associated with The orste in Veblen's work, which was done in the years 1890—1925. The second period includes institutionalists such as Westley C. Mitchell, John R. Commons, and John M. Clark who came later after Veblen and worked during the years 1925—1939. The third or current period is that of the present-day institutionalists such as John K Calbraith, Clarence E. Ayre, and Gunnar Myrdal whose contributions to institutional economics have been made primarily since 1939.

What, then, are the elements which ally them in the same camp? We may summarize them under the following four headings:

1. The emphasis of the open-system character of production and consumption, thus a broader view of the scope of economics;

2. An interest in the evolutionary course along which the industrial economics are moving. With emphasis on the dynamic process of technological change and circular cumulative causation;

3. Awareness of a growing need for guidance that can be supplied only through some

form of overall social management of planning.

For the purpose of illustrating modern institutionalism in the above sense, we may draw upon the examples of John K. Galbraith, William K. Kapp, and Gunnar Myrdal. All three economists echoed the warning that conventional mainstream economics was no longer able to meet the requirements for an effective tool of analysis for the problems with which modern society is confronted. Myrdal spoke, in the American Economic Association meeting of December 1971, that "economic science is in a serious crisis, in my view very much more" revolutionary for our research approaches than was the Keynesian revolution three decades ago. Galbraith referred to the situation as the "disconcerting obsolescence in the profession of economics", which was due to the fact that "economics" becomes progressively more inadequate as a basis for social judgment and as a guide to public policy.

Galbraith was of the opinion that "Veblen was not a constructive figure; no alternative economics system and no penetrating reforms are associated with his name. As Arthur Schlesinger, Jr. wrote, "What is salient from the viewpoint of political economy is the skill with which Galbraith bought institutionalism to bear on public policy. Galbraith was especially qualified to unite institutionalism with dynamic equilibrium analysis; to marry, as to speak, Veblen and Keynes. The result was an institutionalist model that could deliver policy choices.

Of the four characteristic strands of institutionalism mentioned earlier, Galbraith shares all of them, though in differing fullness. Before he launched upon his famed trilogy, he proposed the concept of "countervailing power" in his analysis of American capitalism—the concept which clearly goes beyond the closed-system character of neoclassical economics. The concept of "independence effect" is also an example of the open-system character of consumption where the consumers' sovereignty is circumscribed by the aggressive policies of suppliers.

In addition, on the role which technology plays in the evolutionary process of modern economies, Galbraith mad a telling point that "the enemy of the market is not ideology but the engineer", and he developed the theme of the imperatives of technology under six headings, as follows:

First, an increasing span of time separates the beginning from the completion of any task... the more thoroughgoing the application of technology—in common or at least frequent language, the more sophisticated the production process—the farther back the application of knowledge will be carried. The longer, accordingly, will be the time between the initiation and completion of the task.

Second, there is an increase in the capital that is committed to production aside from that occasioned by increased output. The increased time, and therewith the increased investment in goods in process costs money. So does the knowledge with is applied to the various elements of the task.

Third, with increasing technology the commitment of time ad money tends to be made ever more inflexibly to the performance of a particular task. That task must be precisely defined before it is divided and subdivided into its component parts.

Fourth, technology requires specialized manpower. This will be evident. Organized knowledge can be brought to bear, nor surprisingly, only by those who possess it.

Fifth, the inevitable counterpart of specialization is organization. This is what brings the work of specialists to a coherent result... so complex, indeed, will be the job of organizing specialists.

Sixth, from the time and capital that must be committed, the inflexibility of this commitment, the needs of large organization and the problems of market performance under conditions of advanced technology, comes the necessity for planning.

Thus we are led to the third characteristic strand of institutionalism, i. e., the problem of planning, not only as an inevitable concomitant of technological progress for modern business firms onthe forefront but also for the economy as a whole. On this latter point, another typical Galbraithian terminology came into vogue, i. e., "social imbalance." According to his own words, "the line which divides our area of wealth form our area of poverty is roughly that which divides privately produced and marketed goods and services form publicly rendered services. Our Wealth in the first is not only in startling contrast with the them eagerness of the latter but our wealth in privately produced good is, to a marked degree, the cause of crisis in the supply of public services. For we have failed to see the importance, indeed the urgent need, of maintaining a balance between the two."

Thus we have the undeniable condition of "social imbalance", recognition of which comes from Galbraith's institutinalist inference that the market mechanism by itself does not "deliver the goods", so to speak, with the normative criterion of social goals and objectives demands. This, incidentally, is the fourth strand of institutional economics mentioned earlier. Galbraith's concern with this aspect led him to *The Nature of Mass Poverty*, in which he developed the theme of "the equilibrium of poverty evoking an explanatory tool of circular causation—a methodology common with Myrdal."

It may be appropriate to conclude institutionalism by quoting a paragraph form Galbraith's latest book as representing the well-nigh common opinion shared by institutional economists today:

The separation of economics from politics and political motivation is a sterile thing. It is also a cover for the reality of economic power and motivation. And it is a prime source of misjudgment an error in economic policy. No volume on the history of economics can conclude without the hope that the subject will be reunited with politics to form again the larger discipline of political economy.

8.5 The Modernist Literature and Art in the Post World War Ⅱ

Literature since 1956 showed the impact of the two world wars. Writers and artists never quite recovered from the shock and destruction of the global nightmares. The feeling of uncertainty found in the early 20th century literature now developed into a protest against traditional culture. All the literary developments to be discussed in this section, such as "Angry Young Men" in England, "Beat Generation" in the U. S. A. "Nouveau Roman" in France, etc. , seem to share the belief that the world is absurd and life meaningless. All of them may be labeled as counter-cultural developments.

8.5.1 The Existence Literature

Existentialism is a philosophy that became a self-conscious movement in the 20th century. Its basic concern is human existence. It is an inquiry into the conditions of man with relation to the problems created by an extreme crisis in historical and intellectual contexts. It advocates human freedom in the face of established ideas and institutions.

A key concept of Existentialism is that man is nothing but what he makes of himself. Existence is believed to proceed and decide essence. As an individual and active existence, each man must have the freedom of choice, and create his own existence. A man becomes a man only when he thinks his own thoughts, lives is own life and keeps his individuality.

Little wonder that the most influential expression of western thought and sensibility in the early post-war years was Existentialism: the thought of Kierkegaard, Heidegger, Jaspers, Husserl, above all Jean Paul Sartre—the Parisian philosopher who had resisted the Germans, measured from the heart of war and occupation the key questions of moral responsibility, whose vision of anguish, forlornness and despair in *Being and Nothingness* (1943) express a philosophical spirit based as much on the contemporary historical situation as on the collapse of the Enlightenment traditions of humanism and reason. In Sartre's famous novel of alienation and contingency, *La Nausee*, begun as early as 1931, though not published till 1938, Antoine Roquentie lives in a world divided between swooning abundance and nonexistence, unable to realize himself as essence, he seeks a philosophical discovery. As his Murdoch writing brilliantly about the book as she started her own first novel *Under the Net-observers*, it is an intensely philosophical novel of bad faith, about a man with no proper human attachment. It opens the way to Sartre's crucial occupation trilogy *Les Chemins de la Liberte* (1945—1949), translated as *The Roads to Freedom* (1947—1950), which takes its hero from a condition of "nothingness" to the moment when, gun I his hand, ideas become actions, existence essence, and he can assert "Freedom is exile, and I am condemned to be free". Camus too published a wartime novel *L'Etrager*, set in Oran, Algeria, about an aimless acute gratuity: the anti-hero Meurault commits a pointless murder to test the limits of his being and his capacity for sensation.

8.5.2 The Absurd Drama

"The Theatre of the Absurd" is a term referring to the works of some European, particularly French, playwrights of the 1950s and 1960s and The word "absurd" originated from the works of Camus, who saw human situation as "absurd." In their plays, these playwrights attempted to convey the idea that human existence is purposeless, meaningless, and that in this world man feels constantly bewildered, troubled and threatened.

The employed many techniques used by the popular theatre such as: mime, acrobatics and conjuring. Their language is very often dislocated, with plenty of jargon, cliches and repetitions. The structures of their plays are often by the idea they wish to convey. For instance, they used a pattern of images instead of a series of events to convey the idea of irrationality of events.

These plays often appear to be ridiculous and comic. But in fact, they are full of philosophical implications and suggestions.

Samuel Beckett was born is Dublin of Jewish parents. He was educated at Portora Royal School and trinity College in Dublin. Upon his graduation in 1927, he went to teach English at a French university in Paris, where he met James Joyce and became closely associated with him and his circle—an experience which was to prove significant in his own writing. In 1930, he returned to Trinity College as a lecturer in French, but gave it up after a year's teaching. He went again to the continent, wandering about for some years, then settled down in Pairs.

During the Second World War, Becket became actively involved in the French Resistance Movement, fighting against the Nazi Germany, though Ireland kept a neutral position in the war. The arrest of some of his close fellow fighters in the Movement in 1942 obliged him to move away to a remote part of the country. He returned to Paris after the war.

Beckett began his literary career in his early twenties, while teaching English in Paris. He wrote poems, stories, novels, plays, and critical essays. He published two volumes of poetry: *Who Roscope* (1930) and *Echo's Bones* (1935), a collection of short stories entitled *More Pricks Than Kicks* (1934), and *A Critique of Proust* in 1931. Beckett wrote the play *Waiting for Godot*, which, it's successful production in Paris in 1953 and in London in 1955, made Beckett a famous writer. Beckett was awarded the Nobel Prize for literature in 1969, and he died in December, 1989.

Samuel Beckett is one of the great controversial writers of the contemporary time. Some critics regard him as the most original writers after the Second World War; others find his work unintelligible. However, with his modern plays, he has established himself as the representative of the Theatre of the Absurd.

Under the influence of Jean Paul Sartre, Becket accepts Existentialism, a philosophy which is concerned with personal "commitment" of the unique existing individual in the "human situation". From this philosophy, Beckett has developed a very pessimistic view towards life and human society. Human thought, says Beckett, can reveal nothing to men in the final analysis. All ultimate truth is forever beyond the understanding of the human mind, and, therefore, truth does not, in effect, exist. And he regards human existence as a very brief, unimportant event in an indifferent universe, "a flash of light between the darkness fo the womb ad of the tomb". Actually, Becket is the prophet of negation and sterility. He holds up no hope to humanity in an alien and decaying world. His vision to man's entire life is a torment, a hell, an incomprehensible nullity enveloped by colorful patterns which, in essence, are composed of absurd and futile activities. Artistically, Becket has come under the strong influence of James Joyce. His works, which parody the unsympathetic world and man's wretched lot, derive obviously from Joyce. If Joyce is concerned with portraying the richness and variety of life. Beckett is preoccupied with rendering the human impotence and nihilistic vacuum of life.

Beckett is an atheist, and his atheism springs form the scares left from a Christian belief once deeply felt. With rich religious images and symbols, Becket presents in his works strong Christian nihilism, which shows his bitter rejection and blasphemy against his early beliefs. A typical example of this kind is the famous line about God from his play, *End Game*, "the dirty dog, he doesn't even exist!" which best reflects his grudge against God.

8.5.3 Black Humor

Black Humor is a term derived from Black Comedy. Its origin can be traced back to Shakespeare's time. But now the term is usually used to refer to some western, especially American Post-World War Ⅱ writers. Black Humor is a kind of despair humor. It is the laughter at tragic things. In this meaningless world, according to black Humorists, man's fate is decided by incomprehensible powers. We can't do anything about it; therefore we may as well laugh.

Joseph Heller, American writer, is the author of the best-selling novel *Catch*-22 (1961), which has been considered the major work of black Humor. *Catch*-22 is, according to the novel, an army regulation designed to trap the pilots of the air Force into flying more missions. It says an officer can only be sent away from war when he is mad. But if he says he is mad, the doctor will say no madman will admit he is mad. Therefore he has to fly more missions. This book is a bitter attack on the dehumanizing military institutions in the U. S. A.

8.5.4 New Novel

The New Novel or Nouveau Roman refers to a movement in French literature that flourished in the mid-fifties and early sixties which called into question the traditional modes of literary realism. It is seen by some commentators as standing mid-way between modernism and postmodernism. Associated with the works of Marguerite Duras, Alain Robbe-Grillet, Michel Butor, Caude Simon, Phillipe Sollers, and Nathalie Sarraute, the new novel is characterized by an austere narrative tone which often eschews metaphor and simile in favor of precise physical descriptions, a heightened sense of ambiguity with regards to point of view, radical disjunctions of time and space, and self-reflexive commentary on the processes of literary composition.

In *Pour un Nouveau Roman* (1963), Robbe-Grillet argues that the traditional novel, with its dependence on an omniscient narrator, and adherence to the unities of time and place, creates an illusion of order and significance which is inconsistent with the radically discontinuous and aleatory nature of modern experience. The task of the new novel, as he presents it, is to foster change by dispensing with any technique which imposes a particular interpretation on events, or which organizes events such a way as to endow them with a determinate meaning. The ambiguities of the new novel saturate the reader as the site of meaning and, as a model of what Barthes call the writerly text, invite re-reader as the sit of meaning and, as a model of what Barthes call the writerly text, invite re-reading and reinterpretation.

Chapter 9 The Customs of International Communication

Communication—our ability to shore our ideas and feelings—is the basis of all human contact. Whether we live in a city in Canada, a village in India, a commune in Israel, or the jungles of Brazil, we all participate in the same activity when we communicate. Also, some writer says, "To be human is to be in communication in some human culture, and to be in some human culture is to see and know the world—to communicate—in a way which daily recreates that particular couture."

But the sufficient condition of that which constitutes human reality is the way in which a people construct and maintain that reality in communication.

The development of technology, science and economics provide people opportunities to communicate with people from oil around the world. When you do business with a foreigner, what should you do to be successful? When you study in a foreign country, what should you do to develop a good relationship with your classmates? How to behave in a formal dinner party in different countries? To do these successfully we need much knowledge of the cultures and customs of the world. Emily Post, the philosopher, offers a way of living: "Manners are made up of trivialities of deportment which can be easily learned if one does not happen to know them; manner is personality—the outward manifestation of one's innate character and attitude toward life."

Most authorities agreed that the Orient was the seat of early culture and that manners are oriental in their origin. This may be true, but it did not take long for manners to spread everywhere. Although we find early sprouting of culture and of cultivated manners in China, Persia and Japan, it was not until later, in Spain, France, and other European countries, that etiquette took any serious form.

The origin of the Golden Rule as we interpret it, and which is, after all, the true basis of all etiquette, is accredited to Confucius, the sage of China. That is, we tend to associate etiquette exclusively with a stiff code of cold ceremonial forms and courtesies that would be accepted as correct and proper. Admittedly, there is an element of truth in that view, particularly when exercising customs and protocols unfamiliar to us today. Ye etiquette extends beyond that narrow range of unfamiliar usage to encompass the forms ad manners of social intercourse that make our social dealings more comfortable and relapsed because they train us and prepare us in what we should say and do in almost any given situation. When we understand etiquette, we then are able to conduct ourselves with suitable poise and confidence.

Etiquette provides a codified method of dealing with social situations. Social rules were based on restraint, or the ability to control one's tongue and actions. They were also based on sentimentality, and the traditional rules of women being domestic goddesses, children being miniature adults, and men being the strength and staff that led the domestic sphere.

Social etiquette varied according to class distinction and the geographic area in which a person lived, too, etiquette was affected by whether activities were scheduled during the day or after dusk, and if activities involved both genders. Etiquette manuals were not restricted to the subject matter of manners exclusively. Some also served as guides to choosing the proper or appropriate colors of women and men in their dress, recommendations for personal care or hygiene, recipes for shampoos, skin creams, hair pomades, and breath fresheners. They sometimes extended so far as to give household cleaning tips, laundry care advice, and suggestions as to how to clean kid gloves, train children and servants and manage a household. Such manuals would prove invaluable to ladies whose households were devoid of a male presence to conduct the family business.

Manuals of etiquette became relatively popular as America developed a better understanding of its place in the world, and a greater and more popular consciousness of the manner in which Americans were perceived in England and Europe.

Every area of life is in the process of changing. Progress is being made in so many areas of life. Yet with each step forward, society was disrupted. Change—even the best of changes—is unsetting to most, and the rate of progress on a multitude of fronts was dizzying to many. The progress in which so many took pride also left them adrift in many ways, not knowing the right things to do any more.

Today, etiquette has become the reflection and manifestation of a country's politics, economy, and culture in people's social contact. And it includes the principal and moral that people should obey in daily life.

9.1 Introduction to Etiquette

Out of the past we have come. Into it we are constantly returning. Meanwhile, it is of the utmost importance to our lives. It contains the roots of all we are. It contains the records of ruins of all the experiments that has made during a quarter and a half million years in the art of living in this world.

"Etiquette," says Mrs. Lydig Hoyt, "really means civilization life as we live it today as distinguished from what it was in days of primitive." It is just a thread drawn through the many—colored fabric of civilization. And it is an important thread, of course, since it helps hold the fabric together; but by no means the only thread.

9.1.1 Definition of Etiquette

We have many words about etiquette in English. For example. Courtesy which means courteous behavior, good manners; protocol which means system of rules governing formal occasion, e. g., meetings, between governments, diplomats, etc.

There are many conflicting opinions about the correct origin of the word "etiquette."

What does it mean? Where does it come from?

Some authorities believe the word etiquette drives from the Greek Stichos which means order, rand. Others claim it a French origin. Etiquettes, or tickets, became popular in France and were fastened upon the outside of parcels and documents, to indicate their contents. And alter we find etiquettes distributed among the people who are to be presented at court. The purpose is obvious. These etiquettes, being printed rules on what to do and what not to do were intended to keep people from making blunders before the royal personages.

Webster defines it as "the forms, manners, and ceremonies established by convention as acceptable or required in social relations, in a profession, or in official life."

And in *Oxford English Dictionary*, we can find the following definition: the prescribed ceremonial of a court; the formalities required by usage of diplomatic intercourse; the order of procedure established by custom in the army or navy; the conventional rules of personal behavior observed in the intercourse of polite society, etc.

Etiquette, if regarded simply as ceremonial, is just another word for pride or caste. But if regarded as custom, habit, as the accepted mode of life, it becomes—as it actually is—a fundamental factor in the evolution and development of man. And by "custom" we do not mean the custom of the moment—the fashion of the which of popular fancy. Since the very dawn of life man has had habit forced upon him by various external influences—the conditions under which he lived, the forces with which he had to contend, the instincts which he blindly obeyed. Thus did the mode of life induce special habits?

These habits passed into custom; custom passed sometimes into ceremonial, sometimes into religion, frequently into law. Custom, then, as we interpret it, means the habits of life as observed by mankind throughout its existence—the things we do, and say, and feel without stopping to think about them.

Few of the ceremonial customs of courtesy which we observe today have originated in recent times. Most of them are vestiges of the past; they have grown out of the slow evolution of social life.

Etiquettes are covered in every aspect of our life. "Just try to imagine what our life would be like without etiquette!" Pursues some people. "It would mean, for instance, more difficulty in boarding trolleys and subways, in driving automobiles. We'd all still be eating with our hands only and goodness knows what other things we would be doing!"

9.1.2 Contents of Etiquette

With the development of social civilization, etiquette in our country has abandoned many old outdated customs and put forth many new ideas. The contents are more perfects, more reasonable and more colorful.

1. Etiquette

Etiquette is the rules of conduct, action, or practice binding on members of a profession in the irrelations with one another. Etiquette is the component of the outside part of civilization. It reflects the contents of certain moral principles, shows respect to the self and others. In modern society, both the form and the contents of etiquette show the equality between people. The modern etiquette includes etiquette about greeting, introduction, salutation, meeting, kissing, dating, dining, banquet, telephone, talking, etc. Modern world is a multicultural world. People in different countries, differ races, has formed their own customs and etiquette.

2. Courtesy

Courtesy refers to the polite behavior and speech manners people behave in the social association. It includes good speech manners and written language, attitude and polite behaviors. It is the easiest and most direct way to show a person's moral quality.

And it is the basic request of modern civilization. In modern society, one should be kind to others and behave oneself in every occasion.

3. Appearance

Appearance refers to the exterior. It includes facial appearance, costumes, and manners. It reflects a person's spirit state. Decency appearance is a respect both to the others and to oneself. It reflects self-esteem and self-respect.

4. Ceremony

Ceremony is a formal act or set of acts performed as prescribed by ritual or custom. To show respect or remember something or somebody, we often hold ceremonies in social intercourses. The most common ceremonies are the ceremony of marriage, burial, valediction, opening and closing, welcoming, signature, congratulation, etc.

5. Customs are folk etiquette

It is a special form of etiquette. Customs developed along with the history. It is common in people's everyday life. Every country, every people, every region, even every village will have some special customs.

9.1.3 Characteristics of Etiquette

Etiquette is formed in the process of the deposition of culture and social contact. So every nation has their own etiquette standard which creates with the spirit of their nation. Because of this it formed the cultural differences between different nations, as languages are the carrier of the human culture. These differences must reflect in the language of different nations. Some in the following, we will discuss the characteristics of etiquette.

1. Civilization

Etiquette is the crystallization of human civilization, constituting the most important part of the modern civilization. People set out to pursue civilization the day they set feet on the earth. The invention of language signifies great improvement of human civilization. In the civilized societies, people respect others as well as respect themselves. People help each other and treat people with great warmth and politeness. in a word, etiquette is the synthetical embodiment of the overt civilization and the overt civilization of people.

2. Changeability

The etiquette has no permanent mode. With the progression of time, the etiquette undergoes great change. In other words, every kind of etiquette has its own process of formation, evolvement and development. Etiquette covers a wide area, ranging from the custom to the religion, from the behavior to the standardization, from the clothes and ornaments to the appearance. It's very flexible to a apply the etiquette to real life. Generally, in informal occasion, people don't have to conform with the stipulated norms. While in formal occasions, it's indispensable to comply with the etiquette.

3. Divergence

Each culture or region has its own etiquette. Since each nation has its specific history, national culture, religious belief, customs and the trend of the time, there are differences in its etiquette. What's more, the same etiquette many signify entirely different meaning. For example, "nodding" means "yes" in many countries, while in many other countries, it indicates "no".

9.1.4 Principles of Etiquette

Etiquette has some principles. People employ them to behave properly when communicating with others. The following are the principles.

1. Tolerance of others

When people make use of the rite in the social intercourse, they must be strict with themselves, what's more important, they should tolerate others. Being tolerant is to be generous and large-minded instead of being fastidious and critical. Tolerance embodies a kind of mind, a conciousness of accommodation and an ability to control.

2. Respecting people

People should respect others instead of failing to show due respect to others. When in social association, people should respect others and can't hurt personal dignity of others. Humiliation the personality of the other party is the worst thing for people to do.

Respecting people is to respect oneself. And we should protect the organization's image as well as the personal image.

3. Principle of obedience

In the social intercourse, each participant must be aware of self and obey the rite voluntarily, with the rite regulation the participant's words, actions and bearing in the activity. The principle of obedience is a basic request that puts forward to the behavior corpus which is also the basic embodiment of the personality. Only by complying with the rite norms can people gain other's respect so as to attain the expected result in the social activity.

4. Principle of following the customs

Because of the dissimilarity of the state, the nation, the race, the cultural background. We must insist on adopting the customs of the native, in accordance with the majority of persons' habitual way of doing things. Never to be too self-conceited and show no respect to others.

Following the customs means that everyone should respect the customs and habits mutually and also respect each other's taboos. Without paying attention to taboos, people will get obstacles and troubles during the social activity.

5. Equality

Equality is the core of all rites. It means respecting the partner, treating mutually with politeness, giving the same treatment to every counterpart.

The rite came into being with the foundation of equality. It is an expression of treating each other equally and mutually, the core question is to respect and satisfy the partner's needs.

9.1.5 Functions of Etiquette

Etiquette to society is what costume is to the individual. Without costume men would go in shameful nudity which would surely lead to the corruption of morals; and without etiquette society would be in a pitiable state and the necessary intercourse between its members would be interfered with by needless offences and troubles.

If society were a train, the etiquette would be the rails along which only the train could rumble forth; if society were a state coach, the etiquette would be the wheels and axis on which only the coach could roll forward.

The lack of proprieties would make the most intimate friends turn to be the must decided enemies and the friendly or allied countries declare war against each other. We can find many examples in the history of mankind.

Therefore I advise you to stand on ceremony before anyone else and to take pains not to do anything against etiquette lest you give offences or make enemies. Etiquette has many social functions.

1. Regulation

Etiquette has the function of regulating the social interaction. On the one hand, it regulates and constraints the relationship between people; on the other one hand, some ceremonies and polite behaviors can dissolve misunderstandings and create new relationship models.

2. Restraint

As behavioral norms the rites have strong constraint on people's social behavior. As soon as the rites are formulated and carried out, they become customs and behavioral regulation. Every person, living in some environment governed by certain protocols and customs, will be confined with those protocols, consciously or subconsciously. He who doesn't comply with the customs will be restrained with social moral and public opinion. When it is proper, the society will resort to the law.

3. Respect

The function of respect shows respect and gratitude. It means the esteem toward the other party, while the other also returns with politeness at the same time. Courtesy demands reciprocity. Interacting with rites expresses high respect of each other.

9.2 General Rules of Communicating With Foreigners

9.2.1 Stick up for One's Image

"You never get a second chance to make a first impression" is unjust as true today as it was originally. You cannot redo your first impression or take it back. Each time you meet someone, remember that the first impression you communicate is a lasting one. You will want to take whatever steps are needed to make the memory favorable.

Many things affect first impression. The way you greet other people influences whether or not your relationships will be strong ones. People also notice your dress habits. Because these reveal your status and confidence. So, it is important to be properly attired, neat, ad clean for every occasion. People will notice your movements. Maintain an erect posture, cheery facial expressions, and relaxed movements. Analyze any nonverbal clues about your demeanor. People will use these to derive their first impressions.

First impressions are enhanced by good listening habits and eye contact, which show your interest. Symbolic gestures, such as a wave or smile, suggest friendliness. Speaking of others positively or standing up to greet a visitor, will help make a favorable impression. Poor first impression can be corrected with time ad thought, but you do not need to start off on the wrong foot. If you took a positive approach, you communicate a positive first impression.

Some people once said: "It is not enough just to be able to do the job, chief executives and top managers need the finesse that puts them at ease in any company. They require a certain amount of polish, which means being familiar with the social graces. A good sense of dress and knowledge of how to use their voices are also essential tools. "Public image brings confidence and style to those who want to succeed.

9.2.2 Neither Humble nor Arrogant; To Show neither Inferiority nor Superiority

Neither humble nor arrogant is a basic principle of the etiquette that concerns foreign affairs. Its main requests are: when participate in international association, each person has to be aware that in the eyes of the foreigners, one is representing one's own nation, own race, or representing one's own corporation. Therefore, his or her words and actions should be in proper form. One should neither show humble nor show unbridled and overbearing behavior. We should not be a lickspittle or megalomania.

This is an important matter that concerns the nationhood and selfhood. Cordial and independent are equal important, we can't be partial to anyone. Comrade Jian Zeming once pointed out that the personnel who concern foreign affairs must have the ability to judge the direction in the situation of the changing situation. Hold on one's position in the complex conflicts. And they should be loyal to the motherland under all circumstances, supporting the national interest and dignity. These concrete requests should become the behavior standards of the people who do things that concern foreign affairs.

9.2.3 Seek Common Points while Reserving Difference

Seeking common points is to obey international convention, obtain a consensus, so it will be easy to communicate and can avoid misunderstanding. Reserving difference is to notice characteristics, to understand the etiquette and customs of the communicator and respect the special etiquette and customs.

We need to consider two problems. First, how should we treat the differences between others and us? Second, in international association, which etiquette is the best?

We should recognize the differences between China and other countries. We only need to understand the differences rather than judge them. In international association, there are three methods to follow.

1. Regard oneself as the principle. That's to say, to adopt one's native etiquette.

2. Consider the others. While reserving one's own etiquette, adopts some other's etiquette properly.

3. Seek common points while reserving difference. It's the most viable way of communication with foreigners. It not only shows respect to the partner's etiquette, but

also follows the international communication convention.

9.2.4 When in Rome, Do as Romans Do

There was once such a story happened. Xiao Wang, a young Chinese student went to the U. S. to travel with a friend. One day they were lost and it seemed they would never find their way back to the hotel. Suddenly an elderly lady came near them. Excited and trying to be polite, Xiao Wang approached her and asked, "Excuse me, how old are you?" This polite opening remark in Chinese culture made the lady stare at him in surprise, because age is a taboo in western cultures. Seeing the embarrassment, his friend asked, "Beautiful weather isn't it?" Of course the lady said "Yes" and happily told them the way to their hotel.

The lesson that can be drawn from the above example is obvious. Whether we know the local customs will play a crucial role in our relationship with others. More importantly, doing everything as the locals do will help us make more friends and avoid troubles.

What people observe and how they interpret what they see are influenced partly by culture and partly by personal biases. When one is living in another country, the ability to observe as objectively as possible can help one understand a culture.

Living in a second culture can be like riding on a roller coaster. Sometimes foreign visitors are elated; sometimes they are depressed. A foreign visitor usually has high expectations and is eager to become familiar with a new culture.

Of course, not everything is easy during a long stay in a second culture. International travelers may have difficulties understanding the adjustment problems that beset them. Many people do not recognize that the problems, feelings, and mood changes that are related to living in a second culture are not unique. It is common for international visitors or immigrants to vacillate between loving and hating a new country. The newness and strangeness of a foreign culture are bound to affect a traveler's emotions.

When visiting a foreign land, follow the customs of those who live in it. It can also mean that when you are in a an unfamiliar situation, you should follow the lead of these who know the ropes. There is a proverb: "When in Rome, do as the Romans do." That's to say: "Don't set your own rules when you are someone's guest." The proverb has been traced back to the 1530 *Commonplace Book* and it is first cited in the United States in *Voyages of Radisson* (1885). The proverb is often attributed to Saint Ambrose

(c,340—397.)

There is no denying that we should do as the Romans do when I Rome. This is an accumulated experience we inherit from our forefathers, and now it is still widely applied to our daily life.

9.2.5 Keep One's Promise

Punctuality means different things to people in different cultures. Students in Brazil, for example, commonly arrive 30 ~ 60 minutes later than the starting time for a tow-hour class, but they continue asking questions and begin leaving 15 ~ 30 minutes after the scheduled class time has ended. This approach is more casual than on U. S. campuses, where classes normally start and end within five to ten minutes of scheduled times Business appointments begin at the time named, as do those with doctors, dentists, college professors, advisors, administrators, and counselors. Americans are considered quite time conscious.

When to arrive for classes, appointments, and other campus events is based on traditions viewed differently from what you may be used to at home. Being 15 minutes late to lunch date or sports activity will probably not be taken too seriously by a friend or colleague. However, in your U. S. college courses, being punctual for classes, tests and on assignments may help you a great deal.

When you have a hotel reservation, it is a good idea to ask: "By what time do I have to arrive?" If you arrive later than the specified time, the hotel personnel may cancel your reservation unless you call ahead of time to tell them that you'll be late. If you have to cancel your reservation, call in advance to notify the hotel.

People who keep appointments are considered dependable. If people are late to job interviews, appointments, or class, they are often viewed as unreliable and irresponsible. In the business world, "time is money" and companies may fine their executive for tardiness to business meetings. Of course, it is not always possible to be punctual. Social and business etiquette also provides rules for late arrivals. Calling on the telephone if one is going to be more than a few minutes late for scheduled appointments is considered polite and is often expected. Keeping a date or a friend waiting beyond ten to twenty minutes is considered rude. On the other hand, arriving thirty minutes late to some parties is acceptable.

Respecting deadlines is also important in academic and professional circles. It is expected that deadlines for class assignments or business reports will be met. Students who hand in assignments late may be surprised to find that the professor will lower their grades or even refuse to grade their work. Whether it is a question of arriving on time or of meeting a deadline, people are culturally conditioned to regulate time.

9.2.6 Warmth at a Proper Degree

In China, we always say "You must be very tired to show our consideration when somebody comes back from a far place." While the westerners do it in a different way. They will say, "How is your trip? It must be very interesting." These sentences all express psychological aspect. Concerning the old people is the virtue of human race. But different cultures have different styles. In China, people will say "You are old, please sit down!" and they will offer their seat to an old man. But this is regarded as taboo in many other countries.

"Warmth in a proper degree" is one of the principles that concern foreign affairs. It has the meaning that when contact with foreigners, one should show great enthusiasm and be friendly. But more importantly, one should have a proper degree of warmth, or things will go contrary to one's wishes.

Don't show too much care to others. Chinese like to show concern to other's health, family, kids, and marriage, while people in many countries don't want others to interfere these. They think these are their own business or privacy. They do not want to tell about them. Don't criticize others too directly and seriously. Try to criticize others in a more acceptable way. Finally, pay attention to use space in communication process. According to Hall, informal space directly affects the way we communicate with others. Hall classified American cultural interpersonal distances into eight categories of interaction: ①Very close-activities include soft whispering and discussing top secrets. The distance is between 3 and 6 inches. ②Close-activities include audible whispering and talking in a very confidential way. The distance is between 8 and 12 inches. ③Near-activities include soft talking indoors and talking in full voice outdoors. The distance is between 12 ~ 20 inches. ④ Neutral-activities include talking in a soft voice and at low volume and discussing personal matters. The distance is between 20 ~ 36 inches. ⑤Neutral-activities include talking in full voice and discussing nonpersonal matters. The distance is between 4.5 and 5 feet. ⑥Public distance-activities include talking in full voice somewhat too loudly and discussing public matter for others to hear. The distance is between 5.5 and 8 feet. ⑦Across the room-activities include talking in a loud voice and talking to a group. The distance is between 8 and 12 feet. ⑧Stretching the limits of distance-activities include those requiring a distance of 20 to 24 feet indoors and up to 100 feet outdoors.

The use of informal space varies cross culturally. For example, while North Americans feel most comfortable an arm's length apart in interactions, Latin Americans tend to keep a much closer distance, and the Japanese and Chinese prefer to keep somewhat greater distance. These differences often cause misunderstanding in intercultural communication. So it is important for us to know the use of space when communication with foreigners.

9.2.7 Don't Be too Modest

Compliments and response to compliment is to praise the addressee's virtues, ability, behavior, appearance, clothing, personality and belongs.

Western and Chinese culture are at polar opposites about compliment. A western hostess, if she is complimented for her cooking skill, is likely to say, "Oh, I am so glad that you liked it. I cook it especially for you." They will say"随便做几个菜,不好吃。" If translate this into English "I just made some dishes casually and they are not very tasty." perhaps the foreigner will think why you invite me to you family and have the untasty food. You aren't respecting me.

The English-speaking people are more active to praise others and to be praised than Chinese people. For example, the Americans are "straight forwardness", the Chinese take pride in "modesty". That modesty has left many a Chinese hungry at an American's table, for Chinese politeness calls for three refusals before one accepts an offer and the Americans hosts take "no" to mean "no", whether it is the first, second or third time. The Chinese people regard modesty as a most valuable virtue, so they seldom agree to the compliment on their own.

9.2.8 Not Proper to Be the First

The so-called "not proper to be the first" principle is also called the principle of "not to be the first" by some persons. It tells people how to do and what to do when they are in the association concerning foreign affairs, if facing some situations hard to cope with, or in a shilly-shally situation, not to know how to behave properly. Probably, the wisest way of doing is not eager to take any action as far as possible; particularly you should not be eager to take any presumptuous behavior. That's to say, if possible, don't take any action first, then quietly observe other people around you to see how they behave, and take a consistent action.

The "not proper to be the first" principle has two meanings. On one hand, when facing hard situations, it requests people not to take any action in case bring shame. On the other hand, it requests people to take proper action when they have to by observing others first, then take into mimicry, or to keep consistent on the activity with the majority of the present.

9.2.9 Respect One's Privacy

The basis of western society is the individual. Each individual is allowed to act as he pleases according to his own free will. Because each person expects his own rights to be recognized, he respects other people's rights. As a natural consequence, Westerners, especially English speaking people, dislike to ask about personal matters. They think it is their own business, but no concern of others.

9.3 Everyday Etiquette

9.3.1 Dressing Etiquette

From corporate meetings to weddings, knowing how to dress appropriately can be quite a challenge. We understand the phrases "Casual Friday", and "Dress Code in Effect" however, when it comes to choosing an outfit for a special occasion not qualified by the above list, there are many variables to take into consideration when choosing the perfect outfit. You must take ownership of the challenge by using the clues you are given on the invitation, by the hostess, or by the nature of the event.

Clue Number One: the words on the invitation. "It is not acceptable to put appropriate attire instructions on the invitation to the ceremony"; however, sometimes a hostess will go against this advice and indicate a dress code on her invitation. Deciphering the notation at the bottom of the invitation takes some thought. "Black Tie" literally refers to the dress for the males in attendance. "Cocktail", for example, calls for "an elegant-looking dress in any color, but not formal gowns." "White Tie" affairs "are the most formal of all functions." A woman should wear a long, formal dress, while her male companion should be in "Full Dress", which means a black tailcoat, black pants. And a shirt, tie and vest which are all white.

Clue Number Two: note the time of year, time of day, and location indicated on the invitation. A bachel or out door wedding location means that you must also take the elements into consideration. A "brunch" reception or "afternoon tea" calls for an outfit that is quite different from a "cocktail reception." Women should wear their hair "done" every day, so it is not necessary to get it "done" for a special occasion, noting that "the only time is arranged differently is for riding."

And there are some more tips for ladies' clothing. Women were not to leave their homes in a state of anything but preparedness. It was unseemly for a woman to leave home and put her hat on in the street, for instance. A woman was likewise considered ill-bred if she were to draw her gloves on outside of the home. It was looked upon as tantamount to dressing in the street.

Ladies were not to show their ankles except in an unusual circumstance of some description. A lady was considered vulgar indeed if she lifted both sides of her skirts, even when making her way up or down a staircase or stepping up onto or down form a curb. Should a situation arise requiring the lifting of the skirts—especially both sides of her skirts—it would only be acceptable if she was crossing a muddy spot, for example and even then it was only acceptable for the time needed to cross that muddy spot. As a practical matter, though, ladies whose skirt hems were three to four inches above the ground should find that some part of their ankles were exposed, and that was not deemed scandalous.

Casual clothing is appropriate when not attending a work related meeting. Building a casual wardrobe using classic lines and colors will give you a look that is stylish and professional even when you are relaxed. Clothing, whether formal or casual, should be clean and neat in appearance.

9.3.2 Table Manners

Ages before man felt the need of indigestion remedies, he ate his food solitary and furtive in some corner, hoping he would not be espied by any stronger and hungrier fellow. It was a long, long time before the habits of eating in common was acquired; and it is obvious that the practice could not have been taken up with safety until the individuals of the race know enough about one another and about the food resources to be sure that there was food sufficient for all. When eating in common became the vogue, table manners made their appearance and they have been waging an uphill struggle ever since.

—Richard Duffx

Eating habits, or manners, have been molded by a million external influences through the ages of human existence. The development of eating habits has kept pace with man's own development.

As surely as a compass point the direction a floundering ship must take, the eating habits of a people point to the direction those people have trod in the path of civilization.

Richard Duffx once relates an interesting anecdote of the World War Ⅱ which we want to quote here:

In the midst of the war, some French soldiers and some non-French of the Allied Forces were receiving their rations in a village back of the lines. The non-French of the Allied Forces were receiving their rations in a village back of the lines. The non-French fighters belonged to an army that supplied rations plentifully. They grabbed their allotments and stood about while hastily eating, uninterrupted by conversation of their concern. The French soldiers took their very meager portions of food, improvised a kind of table on the top of a flat rock, and having laid out the rations, including the small quantity of wine that formed part of the repast, sat down in comfort and began their meal amid a chatter of talk. One of the non-French soldiers, all of whom had finished their large supply of food before the French the little bit of grub they give you to eat? The French replied: "Well, we are making war for civilization, are we not? Very well, we are. Therefore, we eat in a civilized way."

The "civilized way" seems to be on tables, out of dishes, and with knives and forks instead of fingers.

Here this part may help avoid conspicuous and embarrassing blunders.

About forks and knives, the knives and spoons are placed at the right, in the order in which they are to be used. The proper number of forks is placed to the left. Not more than three folks should ever appear on the table at one place. This custom originated a century ago when the introduction of many new dishes threatened to swamp the table with forks. Etiquette writers then helped to establish the rule that no more than three forks appear on the table at one place and that other forks be brought in as needed.

The first rule to be remembered is that the knife is never used for any purpose other than cutting food. It is unforgivable to use a knife to convey food to the mouth.

Don't cut large pieces of food, such as steak or chops, into small pieces all at one time. Cut only one or two bites as you eat. Some people find it difficult to cut meat. That is because they don't use their knives close to the fork. When you have finished eating something. Put the knife and the fork diagonally on the further side of your plate. Don't place them leaning on the plate. Always place the knife with the sharp edge in.

The knife is held in the right hand and the fork in the left. When the desired morsel of food is cut, the knife is laid aside temporarily and the fork is shifted to the right hand. But in most European countries the fork remains in the left hand and food is so conveyed to the mouth. The foods eaten with the fork are meats, vegetables, fish, salads, oysters and clams, lobster, ices, frozen puddings, and melons. Hearts of lettuce and lettuce leaves are folded up with the fork and conveyed to the mouth. If the leaves are too large to be folded conveniently, they may be cut with the blunt edge of the fork—never with a knife. It is still a custom today, when a course is completed, to place one's knife and fork on the plate to indicate that one has had sufficient.

Place your napkin on your lap, completely unfolded if it is a small lunch eon napkin; or in half diagonally, across your lap point at your knees, if it is a large dinner napkin. Never tuck the napkin into any part of your clothing or remove it during the meal, unless you are called upon to stand for a toast. In that case, fold your napkin neatly and place it to the left of your plate before standing, and do not forget to return it to your lap when retaking your seat. After a toast is the only time a lady would remove her napkin from the table herself and replace it on her lap. Typically, you want to put your napkin on your lap soon after sitting down at the table. The napkin remains on your lap throughout the meal and should you need to, and after each course without fail, it should be used to gently blot your mouth.

Never wipe your silverware with your napkin. If you should drop a utensil, or one is not absolutely clean, call a waiter or server to assist you and have it replaced. If you need to leave the table during the meal, fold your napkin twice and place it on the seat of your chair.

The host will signal the end of the meal by placing his or her napkin on the table. Once the meal is over, you too should place your napkin neatly folded on the table to the left of your plate.

When passing the food, always pass to the right. It is OK to pass to your immediate left if you are the closest to the item requested. Always pass the salt and pepper together. Ask the person nearest to what you want "to please pass the item after they have used it themselves."

After each course you should lightly dab your mouth with your napkin and wipe the corners of your mouth, using your right hand to lift a corner only of the napkin to your face to do so. Never push your plate away from you when you are finished eating, or move it aside. Leave your plate where it is and it will be collected by your waiter. Never try to help your waiter, or attempt to hand him or her a plate that you have finished with, merely lean to one side.

The most common way to inform the waiter that you are finished with a course of the meal is to lay your fork and knife together across your plate. Place your knife and fork side by side, with the sharp side of the knife blade facing inward and the fork, fines up, to the left of the knife with both of the handles nearest to you. Make sure that they are placed so that they touch each other and that they will not slide off the plate as it is removed.

Once you have used a piece of silverware, never place it back on the table. Do not leave a used spoon in a cup either; place it on the saucer. You also leave a soup spoon in a soup plate when you have finished eating, bowl facing upwards and with the handle again nearest to you. Any unused silverware is simply left on the table as it was originally laid.

Don't make noises with your mouth. A polite person always closes their mouth while eating. This is why taking only small portions into your mouth are a sensible way to eat in the company of others. People make mouth noises because they eat without closing their mouths. When you drink your soup, don't sip it, but swallow it all in one mouth.

Don't talk with your mouth full. If someone talks to you, wait until your mouth is empty before answering. Although it is of course possible to talk with a small piece of food in your mouth, only do so in answer to a question and only if you really have to. If someone talks to you while your mouth is full, polite manners is to point to your closed mouth to indicate your inability to reply at the moment, and when you finish what you are eating, reopen the conversation before taking more food into your mouth.

If food gets between your teeth while you are eating, and you are not able to remove it with your tongue, ask the waiter to bring you a toothpick, then lower your face until you are looking into your lap and cover your mouth with your free hand to use the toothpick. Eat what you dislodge never wipe it on your napkin and never do this unless you absolutely have to.

It is better to accept a little of each course on one's plate and eat a bit of it although one does not particularly care for it, than to refuse it entirely.

The old pressing hospitality of the French bourgeois which seemed to spread everywhere that the hostess heaped food upon the guest's plate, assumed that the guest was too timid to ask for it himself. This was a form of vanity, of course, induced by the selfish desire to see one's good things appreciated. Some hostesses carried this custom to such extremes that the guest was obliged to turn his plate upside down. Of course this pressing hospitality is gone and rarely nowadays. And pay attention, when you are the host of a party, don't urge someone to "have another helping", this can be seen as an unpleasant insinuation that the guest has eaten too much. It is best to phrase each offer of food as if the dish has just been brought out for the first time.

In the East guests not only were feasted but they were expected to carry away with them the food they were unable to consume. Among some eastern peoples, if the guests did not carry away food with them it was regarded as a reflection upon the host's generosity. Among the Westerners, the hostess sometimes insists upon the favored guest carrying away a piece of the birthday cake; the country hostess frequently prevails upon her city guest to take away a jar of home-made preserves, some maple syrup, or some other city rarity.

When eating, the conversation on the table is very important. The Egyptian host felt it his duty to keep the conversation interesting and animated, and the guests felt it their duty to respond.

But on the contrary, most early peoples ate in silence, and there are even today certain peoples who never talk while at their meals. The Japanese, Chinese, and other Orientals eat in silence. The Maoris, Hindus rarely talk when eating. The Arabs of Syria mutter a Bismillah before eating, then take their meals in absolute silence. The Buddhist priests say "to eat and talk at the same time is sin", while in some western countries, it is customary to bar all intellectual conversation at the dinner table and "engage in simple, pleasant, light talk that everyone can enjoy".

9.3.3 Living Etiquette

There are some manners of living at home with the family members. In the present day of rush and hurry, there is little time for one to stay at home. To the over-busy or gaily fashionable, "home" might as well be a railroad station, and members of a family are passengers who see each other only for a few hurried minutes before taking trains in opposite directions. The days are gone when the family sat in the evening around the fire, or a "table with a lamp", when it was customary to read aloud or to talk. Few people "talk well" in these days; fewer read aloud, and fewer still endure listening to any book literally word by word.

Any numbers of busy men scarcely know their children at all, and have not even stopped to realize that they seldom or never talk to them, never exert themselves to be sympathetic with them, or in the slightest degree to influence them.

Just as no chain is stronger than its weakest link, no manners can be expected to stand a strain beyond their daily test at home.

Those who are used to losing their temper in the bosom of their family will sooner or later lose it in public. Families which exert neither courtesy nor charm when alone, can no more deceive other people into believing that either attribute belongs to them than they could hope to make painted faces look like "real" complexions.

A mother should exact precisely the same behavior at home and every day, that she would like her children to display in public, and she herself, if she expects them to take good manners seriously, must show the same manners to them alone that she shows to "company".

A really charming woman exerts her charm nowhere more than upon her husband and children, and a noble nature through daily life though unconscious example is of course the greatest influence for good that there is in the world. No preacher, no matter how saint-like his precept or golden his voice, can equal the home influence of admirable parents.

It is not merely in such matters as getting up when their mother or other older relatives enter a room, answering civilly and having good table manners, but in forming habits of admirable living and thinking that a parent's example makes.

If children see temper uncontrolled, hear gossip, uncharitableness and suspicion of neighbors, whiteness arrogant sharp-dealing or lax honor, their own characters can scarcely escape perversion. In the same way others cannot easily fail to be thoroughbred who have never seen or heard their parents do or say an ignoble thing.

No child will ever accept a maxim that is preached but not followed by the preacher. It is a waste of breath for the father to order his sons to keep their temper, to behave like gentlemen, or to be good sportsmen, if he does or is himself none of these things.

9.3.4 Walking Etiquette

A gentleman, whether walking with two ladies or one, takes the curbside of the pavement. He should never sandwich himself between them.

A young man walking with a young woman should be careful that his manner in no way draws attention to her or to himself. Too devoted a manner is always conspicuous, and so is loud talking. Under no circumstances should he take her arm, or grasp her by or above the elbow, and shove her here and there, unless, of course, to save her from being run over! He should not walk along hitting things with his stick. The small boy's delight in drawing a stick along a picket fence should be curbed in the nursery! And it is scarcely necessary to add that no gentleman walks along the street chewing gum or, If he is walking with a lady, puffing a cigar or cigarette.

All people in the streets, or anywhere in public, should be careful not to talk too loud. They should especially avoid pronouncing people's names, or making personal remarks that may attract passing attention or give a clue to themselves.

One should never call out a name in public, unless it is absolutely unavoidable. A young girl who was separated from her friends in a baseball crowd had the presence of mind to put her hat on her parasol and lift It above the people surrounding her so that her friends might find her.

Do not attract attention to yourself in public. This is one of the fundamental rules of good breeding. Shun conspicuous manners, conspicuous clothes, a loud voice, staring at people, knocking into them, talking across anyone—in a word do not attract attention to yourself. Do not expose your private affairs, feelings or innermost thoughts in public. You are knocking down the walls of your house when you do.

To an old lady or to an invalid a gentleman offers his arm if either of them wants his support. Otherwise a lady no longer leans upon a gentleman in the daytime, unless to cross a very crowded thoroughfare or to be helped over a rough piece of road, or under other impeding circumstances. In accompanying a lady anywhere at night, whether down the steps of a house, or from one building to another, or when walking a distance, a gentleman always offers his arm. The reason is that in her thin high-heeled slippers, and when it is too dark to see her foothold clearly, she is likely to trip.

Under any of these circumstances when he proffers his assistance, he might say: "Don't you think you had better take my arm to a lady in taking her in at a formal dinner, or taking her into supper at a ball, or when he is an usher at a wedding. Even in walking across a ballroom, except at a public ball in the grand march, it is the present fashion for the younger generation to walk side by side, never arm in arm. This, however, is merely an instance where etiquette and the custom of the moment differ. Old-fashioned gentlemen still offer their arm, and it is, and long will be, in accordance with etiquette to do so. But etiquette does not permit a gentleman to take a lady's arm!"

9.3.5 Visiting Etiquette

As with every other are of social intercourse, the etiquette surrounding visits to others' homes has an extensive code. Since occasions for us to pay visits to others' homes while re-enacting are highly limited, a very brief overview will suffice.

Every culture has certain conventions as to how a visit should proceed. In other words, there is a number of broad guideline that both the visitor and the host should normally keep within. Of course the nature of the relationship between the people concerned will very much affect the situation. If the people are very close friends, there is considerable freedom to do as you want. But if the people are just acquaintances or ordinary friends, there is a stronger expectation on both sides that the normal conventions will be kept to. It will be assumed here that the visits concern people who are just acquaintances or ordinary friends.

Before going to visit people, the first thing you have to do is to arrange the visit. The most common ways are:

To telephone him/her to ask when it would be convenient to do so;

To ask him/her when you see him/her;

To write a letter to tell him/her the day and the time when you will go to visit him /her;

To go directly to his/her home without telling him/her in advance.

The tacit assumption for the vast majority of visits is that a lady would be making the call on another lady. Visits of ceremony must be necessarily short and not made before the hour of lunchtime. Half an hour is sufficient time. These visits may not always be made necessary y businessmen, as they may not have time. These visits are such as to talk someone for dinner the night before. Young married ladies may visit their acquaintances alone, but they may not appear the public places unattended, either by their husbands or elder ladies. In any event, a married lady never class on a gentleman unless professionally or officially, and then it would be with the knowledge of her husband.

It should be observed that the rules regarding visiting are primarily aimed at the ladies since married men are supposed to have too much business to attend to make ceremonial calls. For that reason, it is customary for wives to take their husband's cards, and to leave one of their own and one of their husband's. If your acquaintance or friend is not at home, leave a card. In visiting your intimate friends, some ceremony may be dispensed with and visits with these people will make mere ceremony unnecessary.

Ladies are urged to bear in mind that when they do make a call, the call is to the wife and not to the husband, except on matters of business.

For men making visits, the rules began with ensuring propriety for ladies present in the home when the man of the house might be absent. Upon a gentleman's arrival, if Miss Harrison is discovered to be home, but Mrs. Harrison is not at home, the gentleman should leave a card and depart. Young ladies do not receive calls from gentlemen unless they are very intimately acquainted with them. Gentlemen are permitted to call on married ladies at their home, but never without the knowledge and full permission of the husband.

Older ladies are often thoughtless and say to a young man: "Bring your fiancée to see me!" His answer should be: "Indeed, I'd love to any time you telephone her." or, "I know she'd love to come if you'd ask her." If the lady stupidly persists in casually saying, "Do bring her", he must smile and say lightly: "But I can't bring her without an invitation from you." Or, he merely evades the issue, and does not bring her.

It is normally polite to arrive at the time decided upon, if they have arranged the visit in advance. And it is still better to arrive as near as possible to the arranged time.

When you get to the house where you expect to visit, ring the bell, stand near the entrance and wait for someone to open the door. When you are asked to come in, walk right in without hesitation but be sure to see to it that your shoes are clean so that you may not bring mud into the house.

Men never wear hats indoors. A gentleman never leaves his hat on in a room, even if alone, unless there is no place for him to put his hat. Always carry your hat in your hand, and do not look for a table or chair to put it on. Hold onto your hat gracefully.

But women usually keep them on until later. Men should always take them off, even if the visit is only a brief one. This is because it is considered very impolite in the west for men to wear hats indoors.

After entering the home, it is then normal for the visitors to take off their coats or outer jackets. This is a very common practice in the west because it is warmer inside the home than outside. If the visitors do not take off their coats and yet stay for a long time inside the home, it is thought that they may easily catch cold when they go outside. In fact, not taking off their coats indicates that they only plan to stay a few minutes. When the host offers to take your coat, hand it over, saying "Thank you".

A lady should neither remove her shawl nor bonnet, even if politely asked, unless they are in the presence of a particularly special friend, and then only with the help of the lady of the house. When a lady enters a room where there may be a gentleman, she is requested to sit on the sofa by a gentleman. In the event that several ladies arrive, due respect is paid to age and rank and they must be seated in the most honorable places, one of which is close to or beside the fire, should there be one; or close to an open window in the heat of summer when a breeze may be hoped for.

As a lady is sitting down, she should never lift her skirts up onto the seat of her chair when sitting down. Instead, she should wait for assistance when sitting down at a table or on a small light chair. When seated, ladies should never sit with their legs crossed, or at least not crossed in the fashion of a man. She may cross her legs at the ankles if that is necessary for comfort, or as a matter of habit.

A visiting gentleman does not wait to be invited to sit down, but takes a seat at once easily. He should not take a principal place in the room, however, or sit at a distance from the lady of the house that will make it awkward or inconvenient for her to converse with him.

Gentlemen, if seated, stand up when a lady enters a room. Should you be in a large room where you are seated while others are seated or stand or mill about, at the point that a lady enters your circle of associates, you must likewise stand up. When all are seated and a lady rises up from her seat, a gentleman stands up. Offer a lady your seat if no others are available. Assist a lady with her chair when she sits down or stands up, and most especially when at a table or when the chairs are large and heavy.

In China it seems to be normal for the host to serve the visitors with something to drink as soon as they have arrived and sat down. But in the west this is not normally the case. The host usually offers a drink rather than gives one, and this offer may not be given right after the guests arrival. If the visitors are expected to stay for a while, they may chat together for half an hour or so before the host offers them a drink. On the other hand, if the weather is hot, and the visitor seems to be thirsty, the host will normally offer them a drink immediately. But in English the phrase "a drink" often means an alcoholic drink. So the offer "Would you like a drink?" frequently refers to an alcoholic drink, especially if it is given just before dinner. So if any kind of soft drink is meant, the host usually uses the phrase "something to drink" rather than "a drink".

If the visitors accept the host's offer of a drink, then the host will usually place it on the table next to them. Unlike in China, it is usual for the visitors to stand up and takes the drink from the host. In the west, the host usually waits the cup is almost empty, and then asks if they would like another cup.

Formal visits usually last for about half anhour, a little longer when tea or coffee is served, but should not be longer than an hour. In any case, don't wear out your welcome.

9.4 Etiquette of Welcoming

9.4.1 Greeting Etiquette

The correct formal greeting is: "How do you do?" If Mrs. Younger is presented to Mrs, worldly, Mrs. Worldly says "How do you do?" If the Ambassador of France is presented to her, she says "How do you do?" Mrs. Younger and the Ambassador likewise say "How do you do?" or merely bow.

There are a few expressions possible under other circumstances and upon other occasions. If you have, through friends in common, long heard of a certain lady, or gentleman, and you know that she, or he, also has heard much of you, you may say when you are introduced to her : "I am very glad to meet you." or "I am delighted to meet you at last." Do not use the expression "Pleased to meet you." then or on any occasion. And you must not say you are delighted unless you have reason to be sure that she also is delighted to meet you.

To one who has volunteered to help you in charitable work for instance, you would say: "It is very good of you to help us" or "To join us".

In business a gentleman says: "Very glad to meet you" or "Delighted to meet you".

Or, if in his own office: "Very glad to see you!"

Informal greetings are almost as limited as formal, but not quite; for besides saying "How do you do?" you can say "Good morning" and on occasions "How are you?" or "Good evening".

On very informal occasions, it is the present fashion to greet an intimate friend with "Hello!" This seemingly vulgar salutation is made acceptable by the tone in which it is said. But remember that the "Hello" is spoken, not called out, and never used except between intimate friends who call each other by the first name.

There are only two forms of farewell: "Good-by" and "Good night". Never interlard your conversation with foreign words or phrases when you can possibly translate them into English; and the occasions when our mother tongue will not serve are extremely rare.

Very often in place of the over-worn "How do you do", perhaps more often than not, people skip the words of actual greeting and plunge instead into conversation: "Why, Mary! When did you get back?" or "What is the news with you?" or "What have you been doing lately?" The weather, too, fills in with equal faithfulness. "Isn't it a heavenly day?" or "Horrid weather, isn't it?" It would seem that the variability of the weather was purposely devised to furnish mankind with unfailing material for conversation. In bidding good-by to a new acquaintance with whom you have been talking, you shake hands and say: "Good-by. I am very glad to have met you." To one who has been especially interesting, or who is somewhat of a personage you say: "It has been a great pleasure to meet you." The other answers: "Thank you."

Gentlemen always shake hands when they are introduced to each other. Ladies rarely do so with gentlemen who are introduced to them; but they usually shake hands with other ladies, if they are standing near together. All people who know each other, unless merely passing by, shake hands when they meet.

A gentleman on the street never shakes hands with a lady without first removing his right glove. But at the opera, or at a ball, or if he is usher at a wedding, he keeps his glove on. When a gentleman stops to speak to a lady of his acquaintance in the street, he takes his hat off with his left hand, leaving his right free to shake hands, or he takes his hat off with his left hand, leaving his right free to shake hands, or he takes it off with his right and transfers it to his left. If he has a stick, he puts his stick in his left had, takes off his hat with his right, transfers his hat also to his left hand, and gives her his right. A gentleman always rises when a lady comes into a room. When a lady goes to a gentleman's office on business he should stand up to receive her, offer her a chair, and not sit down until after she is seated. When she rises to leave, he must get up instantly and stand until she has left the office.

The standing bow, made by a gentleman when he rises at a diner to say a few words, in response to applause, or across a drawing-room at a formal dinner when he bows to a lady or an elderly gentleman, is usually the outcome of the bow taught little boys at dancing school. The instinct of clicking heels together ad making a quick bend over form the hips and neck, as though the human body and two hinges, a big one at the hip and a slight one at the neck, and was quite rigid in between, remains in a modified form through life. The man who as a child came habitually into his mother's drawing room when there was "company", generally makes a charming bow when grown, which is wholly lacking in self-consciousness. There is no apparent "heel-clicking" but a camera would show that the motion is there. Under formal circumstances a lady is supposed to bow to a gentleman first;but people who know each other well bow spontaneously without observing this etiquette.

In meeting the same person many times within an hour or so,one does not continue to bow after the second or at most third meeting. After that one either looks away or merely smiles. Unless one has a good memory for people,it is always better to bow to someone whose face is familiar than to run the greater risk of ignoring an acquaintance.

9.4.2 Meeting Etiquette

The life of every person is made up of a series of meetings and greetings. When meeting people both your nonverbal and verbal behavior help to define your social skills. Using effective handshakes,good eye contact,and making the proper introductions show proper etiquette. Whether you are making the initial contact with a client or a colleague, you want to get off on the right foot. Doing so will make the first encounter and subsequent ones go smoothly and easily. Getting off on the wrong foot can make for a difficult recovery. Save your energy for later and use these simple strategies for a successful start.

1. Stand up when you meet someone

This allows you to engage the person on an equal level-eye to eye. By remaining seated,you send a message that you don't think the other person is important enough to warrant the effort it takes to stand. If you find yourself in a position where you can't stand up,offer an apology and an explanation. You might say something like, "Please excuse me for not getting up. I can't seem to get around the foliage."

2. Smile

Your facial expressions say more than your words. Look as if you are pleased to meet the other person regardless of what is on your mind. Put a smile on your face for the person standing before you.

3. Make eye contact

Looking at the people you meet says you are focused and interested in them. If you are staring off somewhere else,you may appear to be looking for someone more to your liking to come along. Eye contact is another critical factor when meeting people. Eye contact increases trust. It shows confidence and good interpersonal skills. Eye contact also shows respect for the person in a business situation when you meet people in the west world.

4. Introduce yourself immediately

As soon as you approach people you don't know or are approached by them, say who you are. Don't stand around as if someone else is in charge of introductions.

5. Include a statement about who you are when necessary

It is not always enough to say, "Hello, I'm Mary Jones". Give more information. "Hello, I'm Mary Jones. I work for XYZ corporation."

6. Offer a firm handshake

Extend your hand as you give your greeting. The person who puts a hand out first comes across as confident and at ease. Make sure that this physical part of your greeting is professional. Don't offer bone-crushing grips or wimpy limp-wristed shakes. If you are confused about men and women shaking hands, don't be. There once was a time when women didn't shake hands with men. We are past that. Everyone in business shakes hands with everyone else. Handshakes are vital in social situations. Develop a comfortable handshake and keep it consistent. Handshakes should not be too hard, or too soft. Make a solid connection of the web skin between the thumb and forefinger. The host or person with the most authority usually initiates the handshake.

7. Learn how to make smooth introductions

In business you always introduce less important people to more important people. The way to do this is to say the name of the more important person first, followed by the words "I'd like to introduce..." and then give the other person's name. Be sure to add something about each person so they will known why they are being introduced and will have some information with which to start a conversation.

8. Know who the more important person is

The client or the business prospect is more important than your boss. Just hope your boss agrees.

9. Pay attention to names when you meet people

It is all too common to be thinking about what you are going to say next and not focus on the other person. If you concentrate and repeats the name as soon as you hear it, you stand a better chance of remembering it later.

10. Greeting

Use first names of people whom you have just met only after they give you permission.

Not everyone wants to be addressed informally on the initial encounter. It is better to err on the side of formality than to offend the other person right off the bat.

Your goal within the first few minutes of meeting other people is to make them feel comfortable and to put them at ease so they will want to communicate with you. When you are confident of the rules for those critical initial encounters, you will have a solid start for long-term profitable relationships.

9.4.3 Conversation Etiquette

What part does language play in modern social life? And how does it affect us, who are a part of that social life?

It was Aristotle, standing beneath the porch of the Lyceum, who first taught the world that words bind souls together, that language can illumine like some magic torch the simplest and most unobtrusive environment.

Manners in conversation that we appreciate in others today are not vastly different from the fundamental conversational manners of the antebellum and war periods. Saying "please" without fail is a common courtesy, even when dealing with those employed by us or those who are socially inferior to us. Please always say "please" when you make a request, no matter how trivial or important the request is. By the same token, say "thank you" without fail.

A pleasant tone of voice and a melodious voice is far more pleasing to the ear than a harsh voice, or the words of one who speaks in a monotone. Speak clearly and plainly, and employ of the uneducated and socially deficient. Those who speak rather loudly tend to be regarded as ignorant or hard of hearing. A loud tone of voice in conversation is to be avoided, as well as the "horse laugh." Both are considered vulgar in the extreme. As one mid-Victorian wrote of loud talk and horse laughs, "... if practiced, strangers may think that you are a retired politician, who had acquired the practice in barroom harangues."

Should your request be granted—whether the nature of the request is as a personal favor or an impersonal transaction—always look the other person in the eye, offering them a pleasing smile, and sincerely tell them "Thank you." If the depth of your thanks is greater than simple common courtesy, there is no harm in dressing up your expression of gratitude with "Thank you so much." or "Thank you kindly"; or even "I appreciate it." Even should your request be denied, proper form requires that you respond graciously with "thank you anyway." When the request is rudely or harshly denied, that is precisely the moment in which you should employ your best "turn-the-other-cheek" manner.

At the same time, speaking in a whisper, particularly for the purpose of excluding others from a conversation or a confidential aside, is exceptionally rude. If there are matters which must be communicated privately, there is almost always a better time and place to do so than while in the company of more than just the two who are communicating privately.

Matters of precedence in conversation still seem to concern the writers on etiquette, "A gentleman waits until the lady has spoken to him," says one writer. "Always let your hostess lead the conversation." says another.

In China, speech is standardized by age. In the past, no well-bred Chinese will introduce into the conversation a subject, no matter how important, upon which his senior has not touched.

A simple custom is observed among the Armenians. A young Armenian woman would be horrified at the idea of addressing a woman older than herself unless first spoken to.

It seems to us that the best way to obtain conversational ease is to develop first a complete unself-consciousness. This is not as difficult as it may sound or seem. Anyone can, with a little patience and perseverance, develop the kind of poise and self-possession that opens all social doors.

It is said of the famous Hawthorne that he was so shy-conscious that he ran out of the house whenever he saw visitors approaching, to avoid having conversation with them. His wife, who was also timid and retiring by nature, was left to entertain the guests as best she could. Instead of trying to overcome his self-consciousness, Hawthorne sought and found of forgetfulness in his books. His wife, on the other hand, was forced to overcome her natural timidity and soon amazed herself by the marvelous poise she developed.

Courtesy is the very foundation of all good conversation. If you want to be considered a good conversationalist, let your proverb be "Talk well, but not too much". Listen politely, talk agreeably, avoid interrupting and express your ideas clearly and simply. Above all, be careful not to give too strong an expression of your likes and dislikes.

We heartily approve of the dictionary habit. A good command of the language gives one a great social advantage. And an excellent way to gain that command is to add one new and useful word each day to one's vocabulary.

As to matter of slang, which seems to bother most writers, we endorse its use at the risk of inviting criticism. Slang can be colorful and expressive without being discourteous. It is part of the American language and as such must be recognized and accepted. Just one word of caution: use it discriminately and in moderation. Avoid the use of slang terms and phrases in polite company. Those terms belong to bar rooms and other low places. To be truly colorful and expressive, the word of slang must be like the uncut diamond in a velvet jewel case—an unpolished word in a setting of beautiful language. In the same vein, by all means should you avoid the vulgar habit of joking at the expense of women?

There are those with whom we are exceedingly familiar. It is still appropriate to call them by their proper name when in a public gathering. An engaged or married man should always call his fiancee's or wife's mother, or his own mother, "Mama" or "Mother" or "Mrs. ＿＿＿＿＿＿". No matter what the gentleman's age may be, it is never appropriate for him to call his mother, prospective mother-in-law, or mother-in-law by her first name. It is considered impolite for a lady to address another lady or a gentleman by first name when in public.

Tend to positive words and comments, all of which are so much more delightful to hear and so much more uplifting than pettiness, criticisms of others, and sarcasms. Refrain from discussing truths which, true though they may be hurtful to another. You need not tell all the truth in a conversation, but let all you tell be the truth.

Personal or private matters should never be discussed on the street or in public gatherings, and certainly should never be discussed between members of the opposing sexes. By the same token, speaking in whispers or hushed tones in public places is extremely rude, as it smacks of exclusivity and meanness.

Topics of conversation that were met with wide approbation by the etiquette experts of the day included the weather, travel, books, daces and balls, bonnets, and metaphysics.

All of those topics were deemed appropriate for personal and general improvement, and were, by and large, not apt to result in disputes or arguments.

Many men lose sight of the fact that the object of conversations to entertain and amuse, and that for society is to be agreeable, it should not be made an arena for dispute. The art of conversation lies in making others feel that they are the center of your attention, a position most find highly flattering. Initiating conversation with others relies on four basic concepts which, if followed strictly, cannot but render a good result. Namely, to compliment others; ask after others; tend to positive words and comments; and smile.

Always ask-never tell. There is only one proper way to make a request, and that is in the form of a question, not a directive. "Would you please help me with this package?" is almost certain to be well received and render a favorable response. "Pick up that end of this package and carry it for me." has a demanding, surly sound, and is much less apt to be heard agreeably and result n giving you the aid you request.

9.4.4 Entertainment Etiquette

In modern life, hospitable entertainment divides itself into two kinds. There are the formal entertainments on occasions of moment; and the jolly informal entertainments that go the round of the social clock.

Formal entertainments include the large dinner, the ceremonious luncheon in honor of a visiting guest, the elaborate garden party, the musical, and the costume ball.

Informal entertainments include the simple dinner, the simple luncheon and afternoon tea, the card party, the simple dace, the supper, the Christmas, New Year, or birthday party. The bachelor dinner and the shower tea are invariably informal in nature. Wedding anniversaries are usually celebrated in an informal manner, but the dinner which celebrates the gold wedding anniversary is always formal.

The Greeks and Romans were fond of dinner giving. They were surprisingly advanced, and they had elaborate table appointments. Guests were entertained with wrestling, races, feats of strength and daring.

Entertainment or amusement of some sort appears to have followed eating even in the earliest times. Greeks, Romans, Egyptians, all had dancing, games, or entertainments after dining.

The whim of the moment is to gather about the bridge tables as soon as dinner is concluded, hostesses deliberately invite guests upon their qualifications as bridge players. Sometimes dancing follows the formal dinner; sometimes a musical. Frequently the guests gather in the drawing room for conversation. At large formal dinners, professional are sometimes brought in to entertain with dancing or singing.

The little dinner, or the simple, informal dinner, is quite a delightful social function. It has less of the dignity and elaborateness of the formal dinner, but more of a jolly, informal joyousness. It follows in the wake of Christmas and thanksgiving. It conjures in one's mid pictures of turkey and stuffed potatoes and all good things to eat. And somehow, such impressive appointments as silver candlesticks and finger bowls fade into nothingness!

The afternoon tea, in the sense of cup of tea and a muffin at five o'clock, is unquestionably an English institution. And we interpret it in the sense of social entertainment.

People also play games like bridge or golf as entertainment. Remember that there are fixed rules for the playing of every game—and for proper conduct in every sport. The details of these rules must be studied in the "books of the game", learned from instructors, or acquire by experience. A small boy perhaps learns to fish or swim by himself, but he is taught by his father of a guide—at all events, some one—how and how not to hold a gun, cast a fly, or ride a horse. But apart from the technique of each sport, or the rules of each game, the etiquette or more correctly, the basic principles of good sportsmanship, are the same.

In no sport or game can any favoritism or evasion of rules be allowed. Sport is based upon impersonal and indiscrimination fairness to everyone alike or it is not "sport."

And to be a good sportsman, one must be a stoic and never show rancor in defeat, or triumph in victory, or irritation, no matter what annoyance is encountered. One who cannot help sulking, or explaining, or protesting when the loser, or exulting when the winner, has no right to take part in games and contests.

If you would be thought to play the game, meaning if you aspire to be a true sportsman, you must follow the rules of sportsmanship the world over.

Never lose your temper.

Play for the sake of playing rather than to win.

Never stop in the middle of a tennis or golf match and complain of lame ankle, especially if you are losing. Unless it is literally impossible for you to go on, you must stick it out.

If you are a novice, don't ask a expert to play with you, especially as your partner. If he should ask you in spite of your shortcomings, maintain the humility proper to a beginner.

If you are a woman, don't ape the ways and clothing of men. If you are a man, don't take advantage of your superior strength to set a pace beyond the endurance of a woman opponent.

And always give the opponent the benefit of the doubt! Nothing is more important to your standing as a sportsman, though it costs you the particular point in question.

A true sportsman is always a cheerful loser, a quiet winner, with a very frank appreciation of the admirable traits in others, which he seeks to emulate, and his own shortcomings, which he tries to improve.

9.4.5 Gifting Right

To master the gifting right method requires a new way of thinking. When you put it into action, your gift selections will give both you and the recipients satisfaction ad pleasure.

Every gift sends a message whether you intend it to do so or not. The message doesn't necessarily have anything to do with the cost of the gift. It primarily has to do with how appropriate the gift is. And this is accomplished by matching the gift with a person's interests, desires and lifestyle. If you remember this fundamental principle, you will already be well on your way to gifting right every time.

There are four categories that all gifts fall into: practical gifts, decorative gifts, durable gifts, and emotional gifts. Of course, some gifts may fall into more than one of the four categories listed above; and, you may select more than one gift for a very special person. So that you give him or her something from each of the four categories. By choosing a gift purpose immediately your search will be more focused. By reviewing your chosen purpose after you have decided on a gift in relation to all your gift categories, you can ensure that its final selection and presentation is complete. You will be "completing" your gift message.

First you decide under what underlying messages you want to send to the gift through the gift. Next, you must decide which of the four basic categories or kids of gifts you wish to give. Understanding and selecting gifts from these choices will not only keep you close to the gift message, but will cut your gift selection time in half.

We do not make gifts to people we dislike, as a rule. And we feel always a little more friendly toward the person who was made a gift to us.

Gift making is reciprocal. In New Guinea the natives exchange slight gifts with visitors as a sign of friendship. In certain sections of New Guinea, even today, visitors are expected to return trifles of some sort to the natives who present them with gifts, if they wish to be secure from harm during their stay.

Travelers, coming in contact with strange peoples, habitually propitiate them by gifts. Two results are achieved. Gratification caused by the worth of the thing given tends to beget a friendly mood in the person approached; and there is a tacit expression of the donor's desire to please, which has a like effect. It is from the last of these that gift-making as a ceremony proceeds.

However, we can be reasonable certain that gift-making between the sexes begins when love begins.

One of the quickest and simplest ways to win a person's favor is to present him, or her, with a gift. There is a feeling of gratification. An attitude of friendliness is created.

Gift-giving customs vary greatly from country to country. What is considered appropriate in France may been tirely inappropriate in Japan. How do you know that you are not making a cultural "faux pas" when giving a gift to your top international client?

You are not alone. U. S. Presidents and executives from large high visibility corporations have encountered embarrassment when giving gifts to their foreign counterparts. To help you make sensible gift giving decisions, please view the following list of tips on international gift-giving.

Here are some tips for you to give a proper gift in some countries.

For Brazilians, giving a gift is not necessary during a first meeting. Instead, offer to buy lunch or dinner and use this opportunity to learn more about the recipient's tastes. This way, when the appropriate time comes to present a gift, you will be able to make more of an informed choice.

Do not give anything that is obviously expensive. Your generosity will cause embarrassment or be misinterpreted as a bribe. Small electronic items, tapes and CDs of popular singer. Entertainers, inexpensive cameras and name-brand pens are good choice.

Avoid giving items in black or purple, since these are the colors of mourning. Moreover, handkerchiefs are also associated with funerals. Gifts of knives, scissors, or letter openers are interpreted as the severing of a close bond. Avoid practical gifts, since they may be perceived as too personal. For example, do not give items such as wallets, key chains, ties, sunglasses, jeweler, and perfume.

For British, small gifts such as a pen or a book would be suitable tokens of genuine gratitude and flowers or wine/champagne suffice to thank colleagues for their services. Do not, however, appear patronizing or unduly forward.

If you are invited to a British home, it is standard practice to bring wine, flowers and/or chocolates for your hosts. Do not feel offended if the host does not open your gift of quite simply that he or she has probably already chilled the white wine and opened the red that are appropriate for that meal. Champagne, though, is never unwelcome and can always be put quickly in the dinner.

Bibliography

[1] BRITON C, CHRISTOPHER J B, WOLFF R L, et al. A history of civilization [M]. Englewood Cliffs: Prentice-Hall, 1960.

[2] ROBERT E L, MEACHAM S, BURNS E M. Western civilizations [M]. New York: W. W. NORTON & COMPANY, 1984.

[3] 吴岳添. 法国小说发展史[M]. 杭州:浙江大学出版社,2004.

[4] MATTEWS R T, PLATT D. The western humanities[M]. California: Mountain View, 2001.

[5] MORGAN L H. House and house-life of the american aborigines[M]. New York: Kessinger Publishing, 2007.

[6] RADCLIFFE A R. The andaman islanders[M]. New York:Free Press, 1948.

[7] RASMUSSEN K. People of the polar north[M]. New York:Lippincott, 1980.

[8] STAVRIANS L. A global history [M]. Beijing: Peking University Press, 2004.

[9] PROVINE J H. Cooperative ricefield cultivatin among the siang dyaks of central borneo[J]. In American Anthropologist, 1937,39(1):80 –91.

[10]朱维之. 希伯来文化[M]. 上海:上海社会科学院出版社,2004.

[11] BEATTY J L, JOHNSON O A, REISBORD J. Heritage of western civilization: anceit civilization and the emergence of the west [M]. Beijing:Peking University Press, 2004.

[12] ARTHUR C. The encyclopedia of ancient civilizations [M]. London: The Rainbird Publishing Group Limited,1980.

[13] EURIPIDES. The Trojan women of Euripides [M]. New York: Oxford University Press,1995.

[14] BENJAMIN F. Greek science[M]. Baltimore: Penguin Books, 1961.

[15] 张伯香. 英国文学教程[M]. 武汉:武汉大学出版社,2006.

[16] MCNEILL W H. A world history [M]. New York: Oxford University Press, 1971.

[17] NAGLE D B, Pearson. The ancient world: a social and cultural history[M]. Englewood Cliffs: Prentice -Hall, 1979.

[18] MARVIN P. Western civilization: sources, images, and interpretations[M].

New York: McGraw-Hill,1995.
[19] ERDMANN C. The origin of the idea of the crusade [M]. Princeton: Princeton University Press, 1997.
[20] DENYS H. Europe the fourteenth and fifteenth centuries [M]. New York: Holt, Rinehart, 1966.
[21] HOLISTER C W, JUDITH B. Medieval europe [M]. Boston: McGraw-Hall, 1998.
[22] JOHN P M, BENNETT D H, Patricia B E. A history of world societies [M]. Boston: Houghton Mifflin, 1996.
[23] EDWARD P. Europe and the middle ages [M]. Englewood Cliffs: Prentice-Hall, 1989.
[24] STEVEN R. A history of the crusades [M]. Cambridge: Cambridge University Press, 1955.
[25] STEVEN R. Byzantine civilization [M]. London: A. and C. Black, 1933.
[26] 王佐良. 欧洲文化入门 [M]. 北京:外语教学与研究出版社,2004.
[27] ALISTER E, MCGRATH. Reformation thought: an introduction [M]. Oxford: Oxford University Press, 1988.
[28] BURNS M, EDWARD ,LERNER E. Western civilization [M]. New York, London: W. W. NORTON &COMPANY, 1984.
[29] CUNNINGHAM S, LAWRENCE ,REICH J J. Culture and values, a survey of the western humanities, alternate volume [M]. Florida: Saunders College Publishing, 1990.
[30] BURKHOLDER J P ,GROUT D J, PALISCA C V . A history of western music [M]. London: W. W. Norton &Company, 1988.
[31] WILLIS F R. Western civilization, an urban perspective: from the seventeenth century to the contemporary [M]. Lexington: D. C. Heath and Company, 1981.
[32] 高福进. 西方文化史论[M]. 上海:上海交通大学出版社,2001.
[33] 王立新. 西方文化简史[M]. 郑州:河南人民出版社,2005.
[34] BYRNS R T, STONE G W. Economics (fourth edition) [M]. London: Scott, Foresman and Company, 1989.
[35] WANG Z L. European culture: an introduction [M]. Beijing: Foreign Language Teaching and Research Press, 1992.
[36] 罗静兰. 西方文化之路[M]. 武汉:湖北教育出版社,1990.
[37] BLANCHARD O. Macroeconomics [M]. 北京:北京大学出版社,2001.

[38] MALCOLM B. The modern british novel 1878—2001 [M]. Beijing: Beijing Foreign Language Teaching,2005.

[39] BARNETT N. Selected writings and interviews [M]. California :Berkeley and Los Angeles University of California Press, 1992.

[40] Herbert R. Dictionary of art and artists [M]. London: Thames and Hudson Ltd, 1985.